ACTS OF ATTENTION
The Poems of D. H. Lawrence

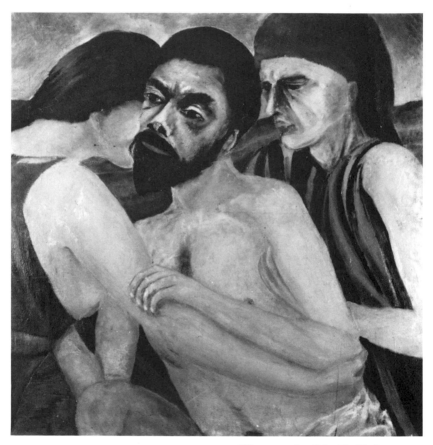

"Resurrection" by D. H. Lawrence

And so I cross into another world
shyly and in homage linger for an invitation
from this unknown that I would trespass on.
        "New Heaven and Earth"

(Reproduced by courtesy of the Humanities Research Center, University of Texas, and by permission of Laurence Pollinger, Limited, and the Estate of the late Mrs. Frieda Lawrence)

ACTS OF ATTENTION
The Poems of D. H. Lawrence

SANDRA M. GILBERT

CORNELL UNIVERSITY PRESS

ITHACA AND LONDON

821
L432G

First published 1972 by Cornell University Press.
Published in the United Kingdom by Cornell University Press Ltd.,
2-4 Brook Street, London W1Y 1AA.

International Standard Book Number 0-8014-0731-1
Library of Congress Catalog Card Number 72-4386

Printed in the United States of America by Vail-Ballou Press, Inc.

*Librarians: Library of Congress cataloging information
appears on the last page of the book.*

Yankee 10.95/8.77

AUG 23 1973

FOR ELLIOT

"The Genius of Poetry must work out its own salvation in a man: It cannot be matured by law and precept, but by sensation & watchfulness in itself. That which is creative must create itself—"

John Keats, letter to James Augustus Hessey,
Friday, 9 October 1818

Preface

"Never trust the artist, trust the tale" is perhaps the most often quoted of Lawrence's critical adages, and justifiably so, for it is a striking anticipation of all that the New Critics tried to say a generation later. The work of art, they tell us, must always have primacy: we are interested in *Hamlet* because it is *Hamlet* and not because Shakespeare wrote it; and if we are interested in Shakespeare at all, it is only because he wrote *Hamlet* and the other plays. Yet useful and reasonable a reminder as Lawrence's adage is, "Never trust the artist, trust the tale" has had some pernicious effects. Critics have occasionally taken it to mean that artists generally don't know what they're doing (or worse, what they've done), that there is an impassable intellectual gulf between the writer and his work, and that the "objective" critic is inherently superior to the subjective and ignorant artist, who merely sees himself through a glass darkly. Of course, this last is sometimes the case, though not as often as we are led to believe, and, I would argue, it was rarely the case with Lawrence himself.

That Lawrence knew what he was doing in poetry is one of my main premises in this book. His work in verse may have begun with "the hot blood's blindfold art," but as an artist he did not grope in darkness long. Though his vision of himself was at first only intermittently clear, finally it was precise and keen. In fact, despite a tradition of criticism which often implies that Lawrence disguised or repressed a series of crucial facts about himself, ranging from his feelings about his parents to his latent (or blatant) homosexuality, from his attitudes toward politics to the uses of his art, I believe that he saw himself more clearly than many of his readers have, and that he was as a rule one of the most perspicacious Lawrence critics of all. For this reason, I have drawn heavily on his own comments to illuminate many of the techniques and goals of his poetry.

These comments are taken from his fiction as well as from his letters and essays. Lawrence wrote ten novels and many short stories, so that to read his poetry as if it were produced in isolation from his fictional work would be to ignore one of the major and continuing forces that conditioned his ideas about verse. I have wanted not merely to give an account *of* Lawrence's poetry, but in some sense to account *for* it, to account for its successes and failures, for its function in his life as an artist and for its role in our own lives as readers and writers.

As part of my attempt to account for Lawrence's poetry, I have traced the development of his art in verse from its uncertain beginning to its strange and visionary conclusion. I hope I will not seem to be imposing a pattern of my own devising on this growth, for I believe that in Lawrence's poetic career, as in many others, there is implicit a pattern of discovery. Lawrence was sufficiently self-aware to learn—through mistakes, through luck, through self-examination—what he could and could not do in verse. His education of himself seems to me to be, as he would have said, "a thing to behold" almost as his best poems are things to behold, since to observe him educating himself educates us.

My further attempts to account for the poems are, in Lawrence's large sense of the word, efforts to "attend" to them. I have analyzed many (though not all) of the poems closely, and tried to relate them to Romantic traditions in which they are rooted. But that even more extensive notice could be given some of these works seems to me certain. For serious attention is what Lawrence's poetic acts of attention most of all deserve. They have had too little study in the years since they were written, and much of what they have had has been, as I try to show, of the wrong kind. At the least, then, I have sought to foster a newly appreciative attention to Lawrence's verse. More ambitiously, I have tried to define some of the ways in which what Keats called "the Genius of Poetry" worked out its impressive salvation in Lawrence.

In exploring Lawrence's poetry, I have been beneficiary of many acts of attention from friends, colleagues, and professional organizations, which should be noted here. This book was researched with the aid of a President's Fellowship from Columbia University and written with the assistance of a fellowship from the American Association of University Women. It is a pleasure to acknowledge the support and encouragement of both these organizations, and to acknowledge as well the assistance of the California State College, Hayward, Research Foundation, which more recently awarded me a grant for clerical help.

My deepest thanks, however, must go to individuals—to teachers, friends, students, and colleagues who have been helpful in so many ways that without their interest my own growth toward an understanding of Lawrence's poetry would have been much slower and more painful. I am especially grateful to Kenneth Koch, whose scrupulous readings of the manuscript in its early stages were extraordinarily useful; to William York Tindall and Robert Gorham Davis, whose comments were always helpful; to Harold Bloom, whose advice and encouragement were later crucial; to my colleagues George Cuomo, Jean Kennard, Robert J. Griffin, and Jerry Bryant, whose support furthered my work in subtler ways; and to many students whose attention helped me test my ideas and who offered illuminating thoughts of their own. Tom Marshall's recent book on Lawrence's poetry, the first full-length study in many years, appeared too late for me to make much use of it in my own work, but its existence was an encouragement to me, as was the existence of many other perceptive studies of Lawrence's thought and art, the chief of these being the magnificent and richly annotated edition of his complete poems produced by F. Warren Roberts and the late Vivian de Sola Pinto.

My debt of longest standing is to my husband, Elliot Gilbert, without whose faith nothing would have been possible. To him I owe a debt of gratitude that neither public nor private thanks can ever fully repay.

SANDRA M. GILBERT

Berkeley, California

Acknowledgments

Grove Press, Inc. From *Selected Poems* by H. D.; copyright ©
1957 by Norman Holmes Pearson; reprinted by permission of the
publishers.

Harcourt Brace Jovanovich, Inc., and Faber & Faber, Ltd. From
Collected Poems of T. S. Eliot; copyright © 1930, 1958, 1962, 1964
by T. S. Eliot; reprinted by permission of the publishers.

Harper & Row, Publishers, Inc., and Olwyn Hughes. From
"Daddy" in *Ariel* by Sylvia Plath (published in England by Faber
& Faber, Ltd.); copyright © 1963 by Ted Hughes; reprinted by
permission of the publishers and Olwyn Hughes.

The Hogarth Press, Ltd. From Rainer Maria Rilke, *New Poems*,
translated by J. B. Leishman; copyright 1964; reprinted by permis-
sion of St. John's College, Oxford, and the publishers.

Alfred A. Knopf, Inc., and Faber & Faber, Ltd. From *The Col-
lected Poems of Wallace Stevens;* copyright 1923, 1931, 1935, 1936,
1937, 1942, 1943, 1944, 1945, 1946, 1947, 1948, 1949, 1950, 1951,
1954 by Wallace Stevens; reprinted by permission of the publishers.

Alfred A. Knopf, Inc., and Laurence Pollinger, Ltd. From *The
Plumed Serpent* by D. H. Lawrence; copyright 1926, 1951 by Al-
fred A. Knopf, Inc.; reprinted by permission of the publishers and
Laurence Pollinger, Ltd.

The Macmillan Company. From *The Collected Poems of W. B.
Yeats;* copyright 1903, 1906, 1907, 1912, 1916, 1918, 1919, 1924,
1928, 1931, 1933, 1934, 1935, 1940, 1944, 1945, 1946, 1950 by the
Macmillan Company; copyright 1940 by Georgie Yeats; reprinted
by permission of the publishers.

W. W. Norton & Company, Inc., and The Hogarth Press, Ltd.

Contents

xiii

ACTS OF ATTENTION
The Poems of D. H. Lawrence

Introduction: The
Effort of Attention

> The essential quality of poetry is that it makes a new
> effort of attention, and 'discovers' a new world within
> the known world.
>
> D. H. Lawrence [1]

i

"In England people have got that loathsome superior knack
of refusing to consider me a poet at all," D. H. Lawrence
wrote to his friend A. W. McLeod in February, 1914. " 'Your
prose is so good,' say the kind fools, 'that we are obliged to
forgive you your poetry.' How I hate them." [2] Now, over half
a century later, though Lawrence's genius as a novelist is even
more widely recognized than it was in 1914, his poetry has
still received comparatively little attention. Somehow, the
prose has always stood in the way. For one thing, it *is* "so
good," and, for another, it more obviously falls into a clearly
defined and widely accepted tradition. Thus most commen-
tators treat the poetry as a merely interesting,[3] if not embar-

[1] Preface to Harry Crosby, *Chariot of the Sun, Phoenix* (I), ed. and
with an introduction by Edward D. McDonald (New York, 1936), p. 255.

[2] D. H. Lawrence, *The Collected Letters of D. H. Lawrence,* ed. Harry
Moore (New York, 1962), V. 1, p. 264. Reference to Lawrence's letters
throughout this book will be to the Moore edition, unless otherwise
noted.

[3] See H. M. Daleski, *The Forked Flame: A Study of D. H. Lawrence*
(Evanston, 1965): The poems are "facets of the experience recorded in
the novels," p. 19. Mark Spilka, *The Love Ethic of D. H. Lawrence*
(Indiana, 1966): The novels "stand at the peak of Lawrence's achieve-

1

rassing,[4] by-product of the novel-making process, and a number of those recent critics who, like Vivian de Sola Pinto, Karl Shapiro, A. Alvarez, and Richard Ellmann, have in fact dealt with the poetry for its own sake, nevertheless defend it on the grounds of sincerity rather than style, content rather than form, intensity rather than skill.[5] As a result, even these "defenders" seem inclined to conclude, with Herbert Read, that "Lawrence's best poems are hidden in his prose." [6]

Of course, almost all writers on Lawrence are solidly agreed that the man was a poet in prose. Lawrence, wrote Horace Gregory in 1933, was "a great English poet who wrote better prose and fewer poems than any of his predecessors in the Romantic tradition." [7] Lawrence is "a poet who happens to write in prose," said Graham Hough in 1957.[8] And even Professor

---

ment," p. 5. F. R. Leavis, *D. H. Lawrence: Novelist* (New York, 1956): "Lawrence's genius is distinctively that of a novelist," p. 5.

[4] For instance, Eliseo Vivas, who confesses in *D. H. Lawrence: The Failure and the Triumph of Art* (Evanston, 1960) that what Lawrence "took to be verse" is "embarrassing," and R. P. Blackmur, who declares in "D. H. Lawrence and Expressive Form," in *Form and Value in Modern Poetry* (Anchor ed., New York, 1957) that as a poet Lawrence "developed as little art as possible and left us the ruins of great intentions," p. 267.

[5] Cf., for example, Richard Ellmann, "Barbed Wire and Coming Through," in *The Achievement of D. H. Lawrence,* ed. Harry Moore and Frederick H. Hoffman (Oklahoma, 1953): "One moment he is all thumbs, and the next he tells us something which we ignore at our peril," p. 267. Also Karl Shapiro, "The Unemployed Magician," in *A D. H. Lawrence Miscellany,* ed. Harry Moore (Carbondale, 1959): "In his sincerity [Lawrence] broke through the facade of artistry," p. 382. Also Vivian de Sola Pinto, "D. H. Lawrence: Poet Without a Mask," in *The Complete Poems of D. H. Lawrence* (New York, 1964), and A. Alvarez, "D. H. Lawrence: The Single State of Man," in *Stewards of Excellence* (New York. 1958).

[6] Sir Herbert Read, letter to Edward Dahlberg in *Truth Is More Sacred,* an exchange of letters between Read and Dahlberg (New York, 1961), pp. 116–117.

[7] Horace Gregory, *Pilgrim of the Apocalypse: A Critical Study of D. H. Lawrence* (New York, 1957), p. 118.

[8] Graham Hough, *The Dark Sun: A Study of D. H. Lawrence* (New York, 1957), p. 191.

Pinto, co-editor of Viking's recent edition of the *Complete Poems*, joined in. "There can be no question," he declared, "that Lawrence's poetic genius finds its fullest expression in prose works like *The Rainbow, Women in Love, St. Mawr,* and *The Man Who Died.*" [9]

Yet Lawrence did, after all, begin his literary career as a poet, producing in his lifetime ten books of verse, so that one must wonder why, if, as Gregory suggests, he "believed, with Shelley, that the distinction between poetry and prose was a vulgar error," he wrote sometimes in prose (essays, fiction, dramas) and sometimes, and so often, in verse.[10] Lawrence's dual production certainly suggests that he himself must have made at least a pragmatic distinction between the two forms, a distinction which, if we can discover it, may not only illuminate his aesthetic theories but also aid in an appreciative understanding of his too often neglected poems in verse.

Even Shelley, though he declared that "the popular division into prose and verse is inadmissible in accurate philosophy," conceded some distinctions between prose and what we call poetry, asserting that "poetry in a more restricted sense expresses those arrangements of language and especially *metrical language* which are created by [the imagination]." [11] This seems to be an admission that while poetry may be written in prose or verse, it is more likely to be written in verse—or, to use the popular term, in "poetry." But if even Shelley was willing to concede so much, how much more acutely would a poet-novelist like Lawrence have felt the distinctions among the various forms in which he worked. And such distinctions would surely have had to be based on certain definitions of poetry and prose or prose fiction, definitions that, whether explicit or implicit, would automatically have acted as guidelines for the writer, according to which he might choose to work in one genre or another.

[9] Pinto, Introduction to *Complete Poems*, 1964 (*CP*), p. 5.
[10] Gregory, p. xx.
[11] Percy Bysshe Shelley, "A Defense of Poetry."

Most poet-novelists have, as a matter of fact, formulated such definitions, no doubt because their practical experience enabled or required them to do so. We find the mature Hardy, for instance, copying down in his notebook, under the heading "Prose and Poetry," the following passage from *TLS*. "It is certain that the poetic form, by music as well as brevity, has conveyed you out of yourself and made its whole effect more swiftly; and this may be a sign that poetry is made out of feelings not necessarily deeper than the feelings in prose, but more intensely concentrated." [12] Though Hardy may not have wholly agreed with this sentiment, the statement was obviously addressed to a problem on which he had spent some thought. Earlier in his life, for instance, he had speculated that

Perhaps I can express more fully in verse ideas and emotions which run counter to the inert crystalized opinion—hard as rock —which the vast body of men have vested interests in supporting. To cry out in a passionate poem . . . will cause them merely a shake of the head; but to put it in argumentative prose will make them sneer or foam . . . If Galileo had said in verse that the world moved, the Inquisition might have left him alone. [13]

Though Lawrence too had much to say about poetry and poetic theory, in letters, essays, and introductions, his most important attempt at a general definition of poetry occurs in the preface to Harry Crosby's *Chariot of the Sun*, which he wrote toward the end of his life. He began this essay by demolishing some of the vaguer, more conventional definitions of poetry. "Poetry [some people say] is a matter of words. Poetry is a stringing together of words into a ripple and jingle and a run of colours. Poetry is an interplay of images.

[12] Evelyn Hardy, ed., *Thomas Hardy's Notebooks* (London, 1955), p. 94.
[13] Quoted from Hardy's Notebooks (Oct. 17, 1896) in Florence Emily Hardy (and Thomas Hardy) *The Life of Thomas Hardy*, two vols. (London, 1928, 1930), pp. 284–285.

Poetry is the iridescent suggestion of an idea." Well, Lawrence concedes, "poetry is all these things, and still it is something else. Given all these ingredients, you have something very like poetry, something for which we might borrow the old romantic name of poesy. And poesy, like bric-a-brac, will forever be in fashion. But poetry is still another thing. . . . The essential quality of poetry," he asserts, introducing his crucial definition, "is that it makes a new effort of attention, and 'discovers' a new world within the known world." Poetry, in Lawrence's view, is visionary: "Man and the animals, and the flowers all live within a strange and forever surging chaos. The chaos which we have got used to we call a cosmos. The unspeakable inner chaos of which we are composed we call consciousness, and mind, and even civilization. But it is, ultimately, chaos, lit up by visions or not lit up by visions." [14] And those visions are poems.

Lawrence now elaborates this central idea that poems are visions or, as he later puts it, "acts of attention," in one of his characteristically witty extended metaphors. The poem, in which the poet speaks the chaos of the cosmos as well as "the unspeakable" chaos of himself, is not merely a vision. It is a vision that is in constant danger of hardening into a structure.

In his terror of chaos man begins by putting up an umbrella between himself and the everlasting whirl. Then he paints the under-side of his umbrella like a firmament. Then he parades around, lives and dies under his umbrella. Bequeathed to his descendents, the umbrella becomes a dome, a vault, and men at last begin to feel that something is wrong . . . Then comes a poet, enemy of convention, and makes a slit in the umbrella; and lo! the glimpse of chaos is a vision, a window to the sun. But after a while, getting used to the vision, and not liking the genuine draught from chaos, commonplace man daubs a simulacrum of the window that opens on to chaos, and patches the umbrella with the painted patch of the simulacrum. That is, he has got used to the vision; it

[14] All references are to the text of this preface in *Phoenix* (I).

is a part of his house-decoration. So that the umbrella at last looks like a glowing open firmament, of many aspects. But alas! it is all simulacrum, in innumerable patches. Homer and Keats, annotated and with glossary.

Here is a further distinction between poetry and what Lawrence calls "poesy." Not only is poesy characterized merely by "words," "images," and "iridescent suggestions," it is distinguished by secondhand visions that have hardened into painted and patched umbrellas. True poetry, on the other hand, is the vision itself, things as they are, without the paint or plaster that might more readily accommodate the chaos of reality to man's anxious desires. "The joy men had when Wordsworth, for example, made a slit and saw a primrose!" Lawrence exclaims. "Till then, men had only seen a primrose dimly, in the shadow of the umbrella. They saw it through Wordsworth in the full gleam of chaos. Since then, gradually, we have come to see primavera nothing but primrose. Which means we have patched over the slit."

Wordsworth—that is, the true poet—made a real effort of attention and saw the thing itself; poetasters—producers of poesy—accepted the secondhand vision, thereby debasing the original, and concentrated their attention on structure rather than on new sight (or *in*sight). Thus true poetry is a self-renewing visionary process in which form or structure is of only secondary importance, while poesy is simply a matter of patching the umbrella, a sort of empty formalism, for, as Lawrence notes, "the fear of chaos is in [the] parade of forms and techniques." But true poetry, finally, is fearless, and in a courageous way, *passive:* it is the pure act of attention, the casting away of the umbrella and standing "naked," as Lawrence puts it in one of his letters—"for the fire of Almighty God to go through [one]." [15]

[15] Letter to Ernest Collings, 24 February 1913, *Letters,* p. 189. At least one critic, Eliseo Vivas, has taken the Crosby preface to be a definition of poetry in the larger, Shelleyan sense, but Lawrence's use of the phrase "the stringing together of words into a ripple and jingle and a

This distinction between mere formalism and true creativity, which Lawrence makes to differentiate "poesy" from poetry, could, of course, equally well be used to distinguish bad novels from good novels. Elsewhere, however, Lawrence spoke of what he felt was the difference specifically between a good novelist and a good poet, indicating that he, at least, did not consider himself a poet among novelists, but rather a novelist among novelists and, by extension, a poet among poets. "Being a novelist," he wrote in "Why the Novel Matters," "I consider myself superior to the saint, the scientist, the philosopher, and the poet, who are all great masters of different bits of man alive, but never get the whole hog. The novel is the one bright book of life. Books are not life. They are only tremulations on the ether. But the novel as a tremulation can make the whole man alive tremble. Which is more than poetry, philosophy, science, or any other book-tremulation can do." [16]

But if the novelist is the "great master" of "the whole man alive," we might ask what "bit" the poet masters. Judging by the *Chariot of the Sun* preface, the answer would have to be the visionary "bit," almost the religious or metaphysical "bit." Another, more important, Lawrence passage seems to bear out this conclusion. All art, Lawrence declares in "Morality and the Novel," is based on relationships: "The business of art is to reveal the relation between man and his circumambient universe, at the living moment." Thus poetry, as he asserted in the Crosby preface, is an effort of attention, a perceptual process through which the poet relates himself to the cosmos. But the novel, rather than poetry, "is the highest example of subtle inter-relatedness that man has discovered. Everything is true in its own time, place and circumstance, and untrue out-

---

run of colours" and his qualifying remark that "Poetry is all these things, and still it is something else," suggest that though "vision" lifts poesy to poetry, the use of verse ("a ripple and a jingle") is for him, as for Shelley, the foundation of one distinction between poetry and prose.

[16] *Phoenix* (I), p. 535.

side of its own place, time, circumstance. If you try to nail anything down, in the novel, either it kills the novel or the novel gets up and walks away with the nail." [17]

The key word here is inter-relatedness, for, as Lawrence sees it, the novel is able to extend the central vision on which all art is based into a complex structure of perceptions and inter-relationships that becomes, finally, an art form more nearly complete than poetry or painting in its reflection of man and his "circumambient universe." The poet is more passive than the novelist; his whole being is concentrated in pure aware-ness of the thing in itself.[18] The novelist, on the other hand, because of the greater length and complexity of the form in which he works, must be—or so Lawrence's statements imply —active in a way that the poet is not, for the structure of relationships that he raises on the foundation of his primary perception of man in the universe requires him to manipulate his material more extensively. The poet begins and ends with vision; he is passive and humble and open to "the divine in natural objects," [19] a kind of monk of the imagination, as Keats suggested.[20] But the novelist begins with vision—with metaphysics, as it were—and through delicate, careful ma-nipulation of that vision he ends with morality and psychol-ogy too, with ethics as well as metaphysics. Therefore he is the master of "the whole man alive," though in achieving his mas-tery he may have sacrificed some of the pure and naive vision of the poet.

In a way, this implicit Lawrentian distinction between the

17 *Ibid.*, pp. 527, 528.
18 In this respect, poetry is rather like painting, which Lawrence saw as "a form of supremely delicate awareness or atonement—meaning at-oneness, the state of being at one with the object." "Making Pictures," *Phoenix II*, ed. and with an introduction by Warren Roberts and Harry T. Moore (New York, 1968), p. 605.
19 *Ibid.*, p. 604.
20 John Keats, letter to P. B. Shelley, August 16 [1820?]: "My Imagina-tion is a Monastry [sic] and I am its Monk."

8

poet and the novelist is not far different from the criterion underlying Hardy's notion that "poetry is made out of feelings not necessarily deeper than the feelings in prose, but more intensely concentrated." Intensity has always been one of the distinguishing characteristics of lyric poetry, and Lawrence would assign intensity of vision specifically to poetry just as he attributes "subtle inter-relatedness" to the novel, for the pure act of attention is an act of *intense* awareness, one which, precisely because of its intensity, doesn't admit the ironies of comparison and qualification that are necessary to achieve the complex inter-relatedness of the novel. "It seems to me," Lawrence wrote in 1913, in a letter to Henry Savage, "a purely lyric poet gives himself, right down to his sex, to his mood, utterly and abandonedly, whirls himself round like Stephens' philosopher till he spontaneously combusts into verse. He has nothing that goes on [no impulse, that is, to extend and elaborate his material as the novelist does], no passion, only a few intense moods, separate like odd stars, and when each has burned away, he must die." [21]

ii

Perhaps a major reason for the prolonged neglect of Lawrence's verse is that while his theory of the novel falls within a definable and acceptable tradition, his view of poetry was the exception rather than the rule in the earlier part of this century. He himself was well aware that as a poetic theorist he consistently opposed contemporary critical opinion and, to a lesser extent, prevailing poetic practice. For one thing, his view of a poem as a pure act of attention, an act of absolute surrender to the visionary image, was very much at odds with the emerging belief of critics—and of many influential poets—that the essential qualities of poetry are irony, ambiguity, and paradox.

The faith of the first half of the twentieth century, at least

[21] *Letters,* p. 251.

in England, America, and France, was in double vision.[22] In fact, Lawrence's definition of the novel as "the highest example of subtle inter-relatedness that man has discovered" would come close to Eliot's or Empson's definitions of poetry. Lawrence's definition of poetry, on the other hand, implies a kind of whole or single vision. While he never rejected irony, ambiguity, and paradox as literary techniques, he did not regard them as essential, especially not in poetry. For him, poetry, unlike the novel, did not involve elaborated relationships. On the contrary, he believed that its essence was single rather than double vision or, as he put it, "naiveté." For the act of attention was not only an act of intensity but, more important, an act of "the intrinsic naiveté without which no poetry can exist, not even the most sophisticated. This naiveté," he added in the Crosby preface, "is the opening of the soul to the sun of chaos . . . [and] in this act, and this alone, we truly *live:* in that innermost naive opening of the soul, like a flower, like an animal, like a colored snake, it does not matter, to the sun of chaotic livingness."

But Lawrence's advocacy of naiveté is more than a stand against the kind of double vision that was coming to seem to many poets and critics the essence of poetry. It becomes clear in the Crosby preface that he is directing his definition of poetry against what he considers false sophistication in verse. Such sophistication appears chiefly in a preoccupation with form rather than substance ("the fear of chaos is in their parade of forms and techniques"), in empty traditionalism, and in foolish "flippancy" or irony. In all cases it is in Lawrence's view a sign of the poet's failure to submit himself with almost religious humility to the single demonic vision that should be the wellspring of poetry. Thus the formalist's vision of "chaos" is obscured by his preoccupation with form; the tra-

---

[22] I do not mean "double vision" in Blake's hermeticist sense ("May God us keep/From single vision and Newton's sleep") but in the sense of qualified or ironic vision, a kind of vision whose nature I will explore in Part IV.

ditionalist substitutes a patch on the umbrella for the wild sky of reality; and the flippant ironist is self-consciously unable to surrender himself in the effort of attention. For this reason, we can see that Yeats's *maker's* idea of poetry—the formalist aesthetic the Irish poet had inherited from the English and French *fin de siècle*—would not appeal to Lawrence. And he would see *A Vision,* whose ghostly authors supposedly brought Yeats "metaphors for poetry," as just another especially grotesque umbrella for fending off the "surging chaos" of the cosmos. Nor would he find Eliot's emphasis on tradition in the least preferable. In rejecting patched umbrellas "under which men bleach and go dissatisfied," he is patently rejecting the American writer's belief that every poet must take his place within the complex tradition of western poetry.

Lawrence's poet of naiveté, then, consciously choosing the path of visionary awareness, must be "sufficiently sophisticated to wring the neck of sophistication." He must be anti-formal and anti-traditional, as well as anti-ironic, not out of ignorance or literary incapacity—two faults of which Lawrence himself has often been accused—but because he deliberately chooses to go beyond or beneath technique to the naiveté at the heart of the artistic impulse. "Thought, I love thought," wrote Lawrence in one of his *Pansies,* perhaps replying to those critics who accused him of anti-intellectualism, but "not the jiggling and twisting of already existent ideas./I despise that self-important game." "Thought"—and we may take poetry to be one of the highest forms of thought—should not be "a trick or an exercise or a set of dodges." It is, rather, "the welling up of unknown life into consciousness." Thus the effort of attention is finally not crassly anti-intellectual or boorishly irrational, but a sophisticated striving for innocence; and to be a poet, to be able to *attend,* is to be in a state of grace.

Such a poetic, though it contradicts much early twentieth-century aesthetic theory, is obviously Romantic in its origins, and Romantic in several ways. To begin with, Lawrence's advocacy of organic or anti-formal form can be traced back through Whitman and Ruskin to Coleridge. In repudiating the artifice of premeditated form, Lawrence recommends and, at his best, writes a kind of unpremeditated process poetry that discovers its form both in its content and in the process of its composition. In verse of this sort, as Coleridge put it, "such is the life, such the form." [23] Moreover, in advising that the poet yield himself to the visionary process of attention, Lawrence clearly participates in the anti-traditional tradition of originality, spontaneity, and sincerity that was first fully articulated by Wordsworth in his Preface to *Lyrical Ballads,* and Lawrence's sense that the poet must be skillfully passive, like his belief in sophisticated innocence, recalls Wordsworth's advocacy of "wise passiveness."

Finally, Lawrence's formulation of the doctrine of "wise passiveness," together with his central idea that the poem is a selfless act of pure attention, can usefully be compared to Keats's well known theory of "negative capability." For to be attentive to the "surging chaos" of the thing in itself, without requiring the protection of an aesthetic or metaphysical umbrella, is to be capable, as Keats put it, "of being in uncertainties, mysteries, doubts, without any irritable reaching after fact and reason." And to be a poet of pure attention is to believe in the "poetical Character" as Keats described it: "It is not itself—it has no self—it is everything and nothing—it has no character—it enjoys light and shade; it lives in gusto be it foul or fair, high or low, rich or poor, mean or elevated." [24] Such a poet, Keats wrote, "is continually filling some other Body," continually attending with such intensity to his subject that he in effect *becomes* his subject. Thus, Keats concluded, "what shocks the virtuous philosopher delights the camelion Poet," a statement that might reprove those critics who are shocked by what seems the lack of discipline and con-

[23] Samuel Taylor Coleridge, *Lectures on Shakespeare.*
[24] John Keats, letters to George and Thomas Keats, Sunday [21 December 1817], and to Richard Woodhouse, Tuesday 27 October 1818.

sistency (really, as Harold Bloom notes, the lack of orthodoxy) in a "camelion Poet" like Lawrence.[25]

As a poetic theorist, then, Lawrence is a Romantic in modern dress; and he expresses his visionary Romanticism metaphorically as well as directly. In his "Song of a Man Who Has Come Through," for instance, he makes use of the central Romantic metaphor for creativity, "the metaphor of the correspondent breeze." [26] Like Shelley in the "Ode to the West Wind," Coleridge in "Dejection: An Ode" or Wordsworth in *The Prelude,* he longs to "yield" himself and be "borrowed/ By the fine, fine wind that takes its course through the chaos of the world"; he longs, paradoxically, for the strength to be passive, to be "keen and hard like the sheer tip of a wedge/ Driven by invisible blows." Only so, in the Romantic tradition, can he "come at the wonder," at the visionary guardians of creative renewal within his own soul.

But even in his use of this Romantic metaphor Lawrence was violating what we might call the ordinary usage of modern English poetry, for to many of the British and American poets who were his contemporaries the wind had become a symbol of futility rather than of creative vitality. In "Gerontion," for instance, De Bailhache, Fresca and Mrs. Cammell, hollow denizens of a dying world, are "whirled/Beyond the circuit of the shuddering Bear/In fractured atoms." The wind, woven by "vacant shuttles," is a force of dissolution, Gerontion "an old man in a draughty house/Under a windy knob." And in the fifth section of *The Waste Land* the abandoned Chapel Perilous is "only the wind's home." While Lawrence praised the "surging chaos" of the creative breath, Eliot sought "the still point of the turning world."

Among Lawrence's contemporaries, only the German poet

[25] Harold Bloom, "Lawrence, Blackmur, Eliot and The Tortoise," in *A D. H. Lawrence Miscellany,* pp. 361–366.
[26] Cf. M. H. Abrams, "The Correspondent Breeze: A Romantic Metaphor," in *English Romantic Poets: Modern Essays in Criticism,* ed. M. H. Abrams (New York, 1960), pp. 37–54.

Rainer Maria Rilke seems to have made similar use of the Romantic technique of visionary attention. Certainly the "objective" poems in *Neue Gedichte,* whether or not Lawrence ever read them (and though we know that Rilke read and admired Lawrence, we do not know whether Lawrence was familiar with Rilke), are exactly what Lawrence meant by "acts of attention." Penetrated by the poet's mystical intelligence, the archaic torso of Apollo flashes its command—"You must change your life"—and the Spanish dancer flares into flame.[27] For all his contact with the ironic double vision and craftsman's passion of *fin-de-siècle* Paris, Rilke never lost his Romantic seriousness. His "You must change your life" is an unquestionable, passionate command, one to which he himself is wholly committed. He feels none of the irony and unease with which Prufrock—or Eliot himself—confronts "the overwhelming question." Moreover, though he worked with a skill and precision that Lawrence could never attain in strict forms, Rilke felt, with Lawrence, that his best poetry was "given" to him through demonic channels; like Lawrence and Keats, he felt that if a poem did not come "as naturally as the Leaves to a tree, it had better not come at all." [28]

[27] "Spanische Tanzerin" in *Neue Gedichte,* "Erster Teil," and "Archaischer Torso Apollos" in *Neue Gedichte,* "Anderer Teil." Although it is not known whether Lawrence ever read Rilke (it would seem likely that he did, considering his familiarity with German literature and his German family-by-marriage), a number of critics have commented on the similiarities between the two writers, among them Frank Wood, extensively, in an article on "Rilke and D. H. Lawrence," *Germanic Review,* XV (Oct. 1940), 212–23, and both Eudo C. Mason, in *Rilke's Apotheosis* (Oxford, 1938), and Eugene Goodheart, in *The Utopian Vision of D. H. Lawrence* (Chicago, 1963), in passing.

[28] John Keats, letter to John Taylor, 27 February [1818]. Though Rilke at one point longed to "work" steadily at his poems as Rodin "worked" at his sculpture, in his later years he increasingly felt his poems to be "given" to him by some mysterious force outside himself. (Cf. Introduction to *Sonnets to Orpheus,* trans. M. D. Herter Norton [New York, 1962], p. 7.)

But though Lawrence in theory may have been neo-Romantic in the way Rilke was, we must still wonder whether he actually put his theories into practice or whether, as Gregory and others suggest, he failed in his creative work to make a distinction between prose and poetry. That he can be accused of such a confusion of forms certainly suggests he had some trouble implementing his own beliefs. For this reason, one of the critic's tasks in approaching his poetry may be to distinguish those works in which, as Anais Nin puts it, "he was repeating ideas better expressed in his prose and belonging more properly to prose" from those "in which the true poet in him spoke naturally and spontaneously." [29]

In studying Lawrence's poetry we shall see that, like most poet-novelists, he went through phases of greater or lesser interest in the different forms in which he worked. When he was in what we might call a fictional phase, his poetry frequently suffered as much from a blurring of distinctions, a failure to bear in mind his own definition of lyric poetry, as from anything else. When his interest in writing novels waned temporarily, as it did around 1920, his poetry gained in intensity and distinction, as though all his creative energy had flowed for the time being into this other channel. In short, while many of his weaker poems do usurp prose ideas and consequently have formal as well as substantial problems, his best poems deal with matters which, according to his own definition, are the special province of poetry. At his best, then, Lawrence is not a poet in prose but a poet in "poetry," for in his best poems, to quote Pinto, he "said something . . . that he could never have said in prose." [30]

At every point, however, we must know what to look for in Lawrence's poetry at its best, at least if, as I believe, Lawrence

[29] Anais Nin, *D. H. Lawrence: An Unprofessional Study* (New York, 1964—first pub. Paris, 1932), p. 98.
[30] Pinto, Introduction, *CP*, p. 5.

at his best really wrote the sort of poetry he himself admired. "I am bored by coherent thought," he wrote to J. O. Meredith in 1915. "Its very coherence is a dead shell." [31] So we must not, to return to his literary contemporaries, expect many poems of the sustained intellectual power, the logical and formal coherence, of, say, "In Memory of Major Robert Gregory." Nor can we expect the ironic cross-referencing, the double and triple vision, as through many artfully placed mirrors, of a "Prufrock." What we *can* expect from Lawrence at his best, judging by his own theories of poetry, is excellence of another kind: the total, anti-ironic surrender to his subject of a Romantic poet in the tradition of Keats, Wordsworth, Coleridge, Whitman, and Rilke, a poet who is making an intense effort of attention.

[31] *Letters,* p. 375.

PART I

THE YOUNG MAN
VERSUS THE DEMON

Whither to go, how to become oneself? One was not oneself, one was merely a half-stated question. How to become oneself, how to know the question and answer of oneself, when one was merely an unfixed something-nothing, blowing about like the winds of heaven, undefined, unstated.

The Rainbow, Chapter XI

—1
Young Man and Demon

i

Lawrence was not, of course, born knowing how to "attend." As he himself remarked, it took twenty years of struggle to let his "real demon . . . say his say." [1] He was aware not only that "it needs the finest instinct imaginable, much finer than the skill of a craftsman," [2] to be—in the terms of the "Song of a Man Who Has Come Through"—a "good wellhead," but also that more than many other poets he had *become* a "good wellhead" through a difficult and sometimes halting process of self-development.

Lawrence would no doubt have been the first to admit that he had neither the early ease of Yeats nor the almost precocious technical sophistication of Eliot. Most of his early poems were clumsy and derivative, and the slowly growing power of attention appeared only in brief flashes in a poem here and there. It is hard, moreover, to point to any *annus mirabilis* for signs of a transformation from promising versifier to mature poet. The poems of Lawrence's early period, specifically those collected in "Rhyming Poems," were written for the most part between 1906 and 1912, but some, like "Reality of Peace, 1916," "Tommies in the Train," "On the March," "Rondeau of a Conscientious Objector," "Obsequial

[1] Lawrence, Preface to *Collected Poems* 1928 (hereafter referred to as *Poems*), *CP,* p. 28.
[2] Letter to Marsh, 18 August 1913, *Letters,* p. 221.

Ode" and "War-Baby," though they are in what we can iden-
tify as the early style, were composed as late as 1916—1918,
and published (in *Bay*) as late as 1919. Furthermore, many
of these early verses were not published in the order they were
written in, and in some cases scholars have not yet ascertained
—perhaps never will—exactly when the works *were* written.

Even where precise dating is possible, however, we do not
find a steady, orderly growth in poetic strength throughout
Lawrence's early period, but rather a seemingly chaotic
search for "self-achievement" in the course of which the
young poet often experimented simultaneously with a num-
ber of different styles and subjects, some of which worked and
some of which did not. Certain of the techniques that proved
moderately successful in the early poems had eventually to
be abandoned as Lawrence matured into a clearer understand-
ing of what he could do best. Thus, in the most admirable of
the "Rhyming Poems"—pieces like "Lightning," "Cherry
Robbers," and a few of the mother poems—there is a tautness,
a neatness of language, even a metrical precision, that the poet
would never again recapture. But the young writer was able
only intermittently to master such artifice, and ultimately,
perhaps because he could never wholly master it, he aban-
doned the formalist attempt altogether. By his middle twen-
ties he had begun to realize that his art lay in a rejection of
obvious artifice. Yet despite his increasing consciousness of
what he could and could not do, his poetic successes, until he
wrote *Birds, Beasts and Flowers,* were fitful, achieved amid
failures and false starts.

Much of the unevenness of Lawrence's earliest poetry may
be attributed to the fact that, more than the work of most
young writers, it was the product of a number of conflicting
forces and influences, or to employ a metaphor Lawrence him-
self suggested, a number of different selves. The poet's desire
to become *himself,* that drive toward "self-achievement" which
is one of the major themes in Lawrence's novels, involved the
mastery and integration of several distinct and contradictory

personae. "I remember perfectly," Lawrence writes in the preface to the *Collected Poems* of 1928,

the Sunday afternoon when I perpetrated [my] first two [poems]: 'To Guelder Roses' and 'To Campions'; in springtime, of course, and . . . in my twentieth year. Any young lady might have written them and been pleased with them; as I was pleased with them. But it was after that, when I was twenty, that my real demon would now and then get hold of me and shake more real poems out of me, making me weary. I never 'liked' my real poems as I liked 'To Guelder Roses,' . . . but that is because a young man is afraid of his demon and puts his hand over the demon's mouth sometimes and speaks for him. And the things the young man says are very rarely poetry.[3]

We have in Lawrence's earliest poems, then, to use the writer's own terms, two discordant poetic selves: the "young man" and the "demon." But who exactly were these selves, and what were the literary characteristics of each? At least partial answers to these questions can be inferred from Lawrence's own statements. For one thing, the "young man" is clearly rather conventional in his tastes and talents ("any young lady might have written them") and his conventionality, or his youth, makes him "uneasy" in the presence of his own genius or "demon." We may define as the "demon," on the other hand, the one who "shakes out" the "real poems," that creative self within the self ("not I, but the wind") that wells up into the poet's consciousness as if out of nowhere.

R. P. Blackmur would disagree with these conclusions. In his well known and controversial essay on "D. H. Lawrence and Expressive Form," this anti-Lawrentian declared that the young man was "just what Lawrence thought he was not, the poet as craftsman, and the demon was exactly that outburst of personal feeling which needed the discipline of craft to become a poem." [4] But we may legitimately wonder whether

[3] Preface to *Poems, op. cit.,* pp. 27–28.
[4] R. P. Blackmur, "D. H. Lawrence and Expressive Form," *Form and Value,* p. 255.

Blackmur is reading either Lawrence's preface to the poems or the poems themselves with critical "craft." Lawrence tells us, for example, that the young man was responsible for—he "perpetrated"—"Guelder Roses" and "Campions," but a glance at either of these works will reveal that neither is the work of the poet as craftsman; that both were produced, rather, by the poet as young lady. Yet both poems are sentimental effusions full of precisely the sort of "personal feeling" Blackmur identifies with the demon. The guelder roses, writes the nineteen-year-old Lawrence swooningly, are

> Such pearled zones of fair sterility
> Girdling with jewels the meanness of common things
> Preaching in sad-moving silence a heart-hungry purity
> In a day they are lost in the nothingness purity brings.

There is the germ here of an idea that was to become central in many of Lawrence's mature writings: purity is sterility, "nothingness," while the "life-loving fruit" (mentioned later), less lovely, less aristocratic, is immortal. But the young man, lost in foggy syntax and secondhand poetic diction, is unable to clarify his idea. He cannot attend to it; he is too busy keeping his hand over the demon's mouth.

In "Campions" the young man shows even less craftsman-like control of his medium.

> Love-fire is drifting, though the bugle is prim and demure,
> Love-light is glowing, though the guelder-rose is too chaste and
>   pure
> Ever to suffer Love's wild attack,
> For with the redness of laughter the battle is waging in the
>   Campion's rosy wrack.

Lawrence knew that craftsmanship is not to be identified with conventionality. Indeed, if either of these early poetic selves might be termed the poet as craftsman—and Lawrence perhaps properly preferred the word "skill" to "craft" in connection with poetry—it would have to be the demon. Lawrence's concept of skill involved the ability, first, to attend, and second, avoiding what he saw as the manipulations of conventional craft, to "get an emotion out in its own course, without altering it," to "blur no whisper, spoil no expression." But the conventional young man, with his derivative tricks and his sentimentality, continually blocked the doorways of attention. It was only the demon—or rather, the demon integrated into the whole man—who had the art to keep the doorways open, channels for the wind.

If the demon had to be integrated into the *whole* man, however, even the young man could not be expelled entirely, and a third self had to be dealt with. Lawrence was certainly more than a "miss-ish" youth—say, the Cyril of *The White Peacock* —who was occasionally possessed by an urgent demon of poetic attention. He had another very important self: the novelist, and we might well wonder what position the novelist occupied throughout this prolonged struggle between young man and demon. Judging from some of the ideas advanced earlier, the answer to this question would seem comparatively simple. If Lawrence wrote his best poems when he was least interested in writing fiction and most mindful of his own at first implicit and later explicit definition of poetry, then we might expect the novelist, like the young man, to have been from the beginning a force at odds with the writer's poetic demon.

A number of the early poems confirm this idea. In many of what Lawrence called his "fictionalized" poems, lyrics that really do seem like notes for the novels, "the poet Lawrence," in one critic's words, is "inside the novelist." [5] Yet the relationship among the writer's three selves is more complicated than it seems at first. For in the early poems, more than ever again, the interests and abilities that made Lawrence a novelist seem to have both impeded and impelled his development as a poet. "As with Hardy," writes John Jones, "the greater prose talent seeps through the poetry and makes it consider-

[5] Geoffrey Grigson, "The Poet in D. H. Lawrence," *The London Magazine,* May, 1958 (Vol. 5, No. 5), 69.

able beyond anything you can point to on the page." [6] Certainly almost as many of the early poems were helped by Lawrence's fiction-writing as were hindered by it, helped not in what Lawrence thought was the special province of fiction, complexity and inter-relatedness, but in what he conceived to be the special task of poetry, the effort of attention. Throughout many of the early poems, the writer's novelist-self seems to have been an important third party to the relationship between the young man and the demon, sometimes working alone, or with the young man, to muzzle the demon; sometimes overwhelming the voices of both; sometimes joining with the demon in the struggle against the young man; and sometimes, in many of the best poems, uniting with both in a fully integrated poetic personality. For though the demon who wrote Lawrence's "real poems" was in the poet's own view the crucial member of this trinity, each aspect of the writer, even the young man, had something to contribute.

[6] John Jones, "The Prose and the Poetry," *New Statesman*, LIV (July 6, 1957), 23–24.

—2
The Young Man

i

The young man had faults, of course, that outweighed his virtues. He was capable, for instance, of the most vulgar and un-Lawrentian optimistic humanism, even, to use a phrase at which the later Lawrence would shudder, of "brotherly love." As late as 1913 we find the poet—the young man apparently ascendant for a time—rather sententiously writing to Henry Savage that "I'm glad you've discovered Humanity: it is fearfully nice to feel it round one. If you read my poetry—especially the earlier rough stuff which was published in the *English Review* . . . you would see how much it has meant to me."[1] One of the poems to which Lawrence was referring here might well have been "Dreams Old and Nascent," the first Lawrence poem Ford accepted for his magazine. There are a number of different versions of this piece, but in none of them was the writer able to free the lines from the sentimentality and sententiousness of the original.[2]

Divided into two main sections and a number of subsections, that version dealt, first, with the power of the past ("Old"), of "the misty indefinite dreams that range/At the back of my life's horizon, where the dreams from the past lives crowd," and then with the power of the future ("Nascent"), of

[1] Letter to Henry Savage, 22 Dec. 1913, *Letters*, p. 256.
[2] Besides the version published in the *English Review,* there was a revision included in *Amores* (1916), and a second, more elaborate revision in the 1928 *Poems.*

the "great, mysterious One . . . swelling and shaping the dreams in the flesh." Swinburne was one of the young man's heroes as he was even of the older Lawrence ("the pure realization in him is something to reverence")[3] so the style is Swinburnian, with echoes, too, of Shelley, another favorite:

> Over the bygone, hushèd years
> Streaming back where the mist distils
> Into forgetfulness: soft sailing waters, where fears
> No longer shake: where the silk sail fills
> With the unfelt breeze that ebbs over the seas, when the
>   storm
> Of living has passed. . . .
> Drifts my boat, wistfully lapsing after
> The mists of receding tears, and the echo of laughter.

Interestingly, there is also a rather bad imitation of Whitman, already a third literary idol, in "Nascent."

> The great activity swelling, through the round flesh pulsing,
> Impelling, shaping the coming dream;
> Visible under the changing eyes,
> Under the mobile features.

But if the style was predominantly Swinburnian, the sentiment was positively Tennysonian.

> The gigantic flesh of the world
> Is swelling with widespread, labouring concentration
> Into one bud on the stalk of eternity,
> Rounded and swelling towards the fruit of a dream.

Swelling, in short, toward that "one, far-off divine event/To which the whole creation moves," or, as Yeats also put it in his optimistic youth, "the bell that calls us on; the sweet far thing."[4] Besides the Swinburnian style and the Tennysonian

---

[3] Letter to Barbara Low, *Letters*, p. 474. Though in one letter to Louie Burrows he called Swinburne "shallow." See James Boulton, ed., *Lawrence in Love* (Nottingham, 1968), p. 85.

[4] Alfred Lord Tennyson, "In Memoriam." W. B. Yeats, "The Rose of Battle."

sentiment, however, the emphasis on dreams, on "wistfulness, and strange/Recognitions and greetings of half-acquaint things," on mist and blurriness and "hollow yearning," lends a *fin-de-siècle* cast to the whole of this poem, recalling early Yeats and the Rhymers Club.

It is not surprising, however, that the young man wrote poems in the Swinburne-Tennyson-*fin-de-siècle* vein, for though, as Graham Hough amusingly puts it (referring to T. S. Eliot's strange view of Lawrence's education) "a rather hoity-toity concept of culture has been used to show that Lawrence had a hole-and-corner upbringing, and remained therefore an inspired barbarian," [5] the young writer was well grounded in poetry, up to and including the latest developments in London and Paris. Of course Lawrence's friends at home knew that he had "in 1904 . . . sat as a P. T. [Pupil Teacher] for the King's Scholarship Examination, and passed with great distinction, being first among the hundreds who sat in all England [and Wales]—a truly remarkable performance for a collier's son." [6] But it was with some surprise that Violet Hunt, who met the young poet when Ford Maddox Ford first put him on display in London, noted that

his manner was gentle, modest, and tender, in a way I did not associate with his upbringing. His father was a 'butty man,' of a certain rank among miners, [but] I found that he, his sisters and his sweetheart met every Saturday evening round the fire to read Verlaine and Baudelaire, while commissioned not to allow his mother's loaves to burn in the oven. He was more conversant with decadent poetry than I or the editor [Ford], and that is saying a great deal, in fact, I think he had studied it too deeply.[7]

Lawrence himself in some of his letters, as well as in his early novels and stories, vividly portrayed those cosy intellectual evenings round the hearth, where the modishly well

[5] Graham Hough, *The Dark Sun*, p. 18.
[6] J. E. Hobbs (Lawrence's old schoolmaster), in Edward Nehls, ed. *D. H. Lawrence: A Composite Biography*, Vol. 1 (Wisconsin, 1957), p. 43.
[7] Nehls, Vol. 1, p. 127.

versed young writer held forth, basking equally in the fire-glow and in the admiration of not one but several sweet-hearts. "We shall be out all day," he wrote to Blanche Jennings in July 1908, happily anticipating one of these holi-days, "returning to the Haggs . . . where, in the low parlour, I shall read Verlaine to the girls (in French—the nut brown eyes of Louie will laugh and scold me; the soft dark eyes of Emily will look at me pensive, doubtful—not quite sure what I mean)—and perhaps I'll read Whitman . . ." [8]

No doubt all occurred according to Lawrence's expecta-tions, for Jessie Chambers, too, confirms that "at this time the two great poetic lights in his firmament were Verlaine and Baudelaire." [9] But his early reading both in poetry and prose, as she reports it, was impressively wide, including not only Whitman's *Leaves of Grass* (already "one of his great books") but also Browning, another "great favourite," and other fairly standard nineteenth century authors, ranging from the Ro-mantics (especially Coleridge and Shelley) to the Pre-Rapha-elites, Hardy, and all the major novelists as well as Carlyle and Ruskin. "You're the only man I've ever met," said Ford, according to Jessie Chambers, "who really has read all those people." [10]

Small wonder, then, that many of Lawrence's early poems, even, for a while, his early poetics, were conventional and derivative. In a lecture delivered to a Croydon literary so-ciety in 1910, the apprentice writer spoke enthusiastically

[8] Letter to Blanche Jennings, 30 July 1908, *Letters*, p. 25. "Louie" was Louise Burrows, later Lawrence's fiancée for a time. "Emily" was Jessie Chambers, also the Emily of *The White Peacock* as well as the Miriam of *Sons and Lovers* and *CP*.

[9] "E. T." (Jessie Chambers Wood), *D. H. Lawrence: A Personal Rec-ord*, p. 121. In 1929, however, Lawrence told Glenn Hughes that he derived "nothing at all . . . from the French, whose verse he had always considered 'piffling, like lacy valentines' " (Hughes, *Imagism and the Imagists* [Stanford, 1931], p. 170).

[10] "E. T.," pp. 122, 115, 172. (See also p. 146 for an instance of how thoroughly the young Lawrence had assimilated the writings of "all those people.")

about the *fin-de-siècle* poetry of Rachel Annand Taylor, a fashionable poetess with whom he had entered into a languidly witty correspondence (". . . your slow soft burning like almost invisible alcohol, with a yellow tip of cynicism now and again makes me crackle like burning straw").[11] It was certainly the young man, rather than the demon, who praised Mrs. Taylor "for her orthodoxy in the matter of rhythms and meters: 'She allows herself none of the modern looseness,'" he declared.[12] But then the young man was responsible, according to Lawrence's preface, for most of that orthodoxy in the matter of rhythms and meters with which the demon was uneasy.

Because he did believe in orthodoxy, there were times when the young man proved himself capable of handling strict forms with a certain dexterity. "Twilight," for example, which first appeared in *New Poems* (1918) but may have been written considerably earlier, shows a control of the stanza form that Lawrence had not exhibited in, for instance, "Dreams Old and Nascent." The rhymes are simple and smooth; the truncated last line of each quatrain emphasizes the poem's subject, the waning of day and its activities. Yet even here there is some sign that the young man has been struggling against the demon: freshly observed lines like "darkness comes out of the earth" and "the night stock oozes scent" are obscured by the pretentiousness of "wanes the old palimpsest" or "all that the worldly day has meant/Wastes like a lie."

"Transformations," first published in *Love Poems and Others* (1913), starts out from an even more interesting point —an idea rather than just a few observations—but the young man befogs the demon's perception with greeting-card rhymes

[11] Letter to Rachel Annand Taylor, 16 October 1910, *Letters*, p. 66.

[12] Harry Moore, *The Life and Works of D. H. Lawrence* (New York, 1951), p. 81. At the same time, Lawrence was longing for a "touch of harshness" in Mrs. Taylor's book *Rose and Vine,* and complaining that some of her "verses seemed fingered by art into a grace the experience does not warrant." See *Letters*, pp. 67–68.

and pseudo-romantic images. His plan is to show how a sub-ject—"The Town," "The Earth," "Men"—is continually transformed by the vision of the perceiver, but we are soon treated to the jingliness of

> Tomorrow swimming in evening's vague, dim vapour
> Like a weeded city in shadow under the sea,
> Below the ocean of shimmering light you will be.

More surprising is the Whitmanesque section on "Men," which fails to achieve the precision of Whitman at his best, uses sec-ondhand imagery (men "stand alone in despair like a gutter-ing light" or "curl in sleep like kittens"), and declines into bombast at the end ("what are you, oh multiform?"). Though Whitman was to play an important part in the writer's forma-tion of a mature *vers libre* style, Lawrence was evidently not yet ready to learn the lessons of the master.

Perhaps for this reason, however, the young man wrote lit-tle Whitmanesque poetry. A number of his chief efforts were influenced by Victorian or Romantic poetry, and an even greater number by *fin-de-siècle* verse. Almost all the poems to Helen fall into this latter category. "Seeing I am a bowl of kisses," the poet admonishes his mistress in "The Appeal," you "should put your mouth to mine and drink of me . . . oh you, who are Night's bacchante,/How can you from my bowl of kisses shrink?" His tone is sly and seductive, reaching for a decadent elegance it doesn't quite achieve. Making simi-lar use of the bowl of kisses image,[13] "Mystery" attempts the same kind of witty, *Yellow Book* exoticism:

> Now I am all
> One bowl of kisses
> Such as the tall

[13] Lawrence's relationship with Helen Corke, apparently a woman like Helena of *The Trespasser,* whose passion "ended at the mouth," seems to have generated this kiss-obsession. One of the purplest passages in *The Trespasser* (a reworking of Helen Corke's own autobiographical novel) includes a vision of "the stars and the sea and the trees . . . all kissing."

Slim votaresses
Of Egypt filled
For divine excesses.

"Tease," which was apparently meant for Louie Burrows, shows Lawrence assimilating such influences more skillfully. Though the poem is derivative and slight, it is redeemed by a light-hearted, *fin-de-siècle* virtuosity. "I will give you all my keys," the poet tells his *inamorata*. "You shall be my chatelaine,/You shall enter as you please,/As you please shall go again." For once his orthodoxy in the matter of rhythms and meters is especially useful, and all the images he employs work smoothly together:

Over every single beauty
    You have had your little rapture;
You have slain, as was your duty,
    Every sin-mouse you could capture.

But it is in "Tarantella," an early soliloquy apparently meant to be spoken by "Night's bacchante," that the young man showed how much he could do, at his best, with the poetics he had inherited from the nineteenth century. The long Swinburnian lines of the poem move with a music Lawrence had to try to master before rejecting:

Sad as he sits on the white sea-stone
And the suave sea chuckles, and turns to the moon,
And the moon significant smiles to the cliffs and the boulders,
He sits like a shade by the flood alone.

Dancing like early Yeats, the first three lines of the second stanza foreshadow later, more Lawrentian dances:

What can I do but dance alone,
Dance to the sliding sea and the moon,
For the moon on my breast and the air on my limbs and the
    foam on my feet?

The Dionysian speaker's complaint ("surely this earnest man has none/Of the night in his soul") echoes *Yellow Book* mockery of the bourgeois, but it also begins to formulate Lawrentian ideas about darkness. And the longing in the last stanza for the supernatural, the "soulless," recalls Yeats' longing for the immortal realm of the Sidhe, but it is expressed with a passion which reminds us that the young man and the demon were, after all, two aspects of the same personality:

> I wish a wild sea-fellow would come down the glittering
> shingle,
> A soulless neckar, with winking seas in his eyes
> And falling waves in his arms, and the lost soul's kiss
> On his lips: I long to be soulless, I tingle
> To touch the sea in the last surprise
> Of fiery coldness, to be gone in a lost soul's bliss.

This vision of a "soulless neckar" almost seems to reflect Lawrence's own desire for the still unimaginable intensities of his demon, whose paradoxical perceptions ("fiery coldness," "lost soul's bliss") he had not yet experienced. For though "Tarantella" may not be a purely original and Lawrentian poem, it is clearly a work by a very talented young poet who was in the process of finding himself, as most poets must, in his forebears.

ii

There was more to the young man, though, than his background of copious reading and his *fin-de-siècle* proclivities. For one thing, as soon as literary London became aware that such influential figures as Ford and Pound and later Garnett thought him a "genius," Lawrence was exposed to many of the latest literary trends. Between 1911 and 1922 his work appeared in four issues of *Georgian Poetry,* perhaps the most prestigious publication of what was then the literary "establishment." And beginning in 1914 his poems were used in a number of Imagist collections, ranging from *Some Imagist Poets* (1914) to the *Imagist Anthology* of 1930. Not that any one was certain that the young man was either a Georgian or an Imagist. On the contrary, it is probably true that, as Glenn

Hughes was "told by one of the Imagists," Lawrence "was included in the anthologies for the simple reason that in 1914 he was looked upon as a writer . . . who would certainly achieve fame and would therefore shed glory on the whole Imagist [or Georgian] movement." [14]

Reading the bucolic warblings of the rather cosily domesticated Georgians, one is immediately struck by the force of some of the Lawrence verses as by an alien wind. The demon, certainly, was no Georgian. The slick wit, the polished optimism of Rupert Brooke and Harold Monro; the sometimes turgid dramatic experiments of Abercrombie and Bottomley; the pretty primitivism of Davies; the often stagey romanticism of de la Mare and Flecker—most of these traits were basically repugnant to Lawrence's demon. The young man, on the other hand, was susceptible to Georgian influence. Some of the athletic exuberance of the more conventional early poems must have originated in the anti-decadent Georgian mood that had taken hold of London in the years when the young schoolmaster from Nottingham was making his literary debut. "We are waking up after a night of oppressive dreams," Lawrence proclaimed in a review of *Georgian Poetry* 1911–1912. "The nihilists, the intellectual, hopeless people—Ibsen, Flaubert, Thomas Hardy—represent the dream we are waking from . . . Our lungs are full of new air, our eyes of morning . . . We have faith in the vastness of life's wealth." [15]

The exultant but soulful materialism of the first version of "The Wild Common," one of Lawrence's earliest poems, embodied this philosophy. "The warm clinging air,/Rich with the songs of seven larks singing at once," is that "new" and mildly invigorating air of Georgian England—the air of Grantchester, of Davies' meadows, of Thomas's and Blunden's farms. "Their poems are romantic," declared the young poet, "tinged with a love of the marvelous, a joy of natural things, as if the poet were a child for the first time on the seashore,

[14] Hughes, *Imagism*, p. 170.
[15] Lawrence, *Phoenix* (I), pp. 304–306.

33

finding treasures." [16] Yet even in this joyful air Lawrence's demon was present, trying to attend to more than the sunshine. He was trying, in fact, to make a Lawrentian point about substance—"how splendid it is to be substance, here!"—but the young man, like many of his Georgian counterparts, could not reject conventional formulations of the relationship between soul and body. The later Lawrence, knowing more about how to let the demon "say his say," deleted awkward references to "my soul like a passionate woman" and substituted a more vivid image of "my shadow . . . like a dog on a string." He admitted, though, presenting his revised versions of many of the early poems in the *Collected Poems* (1928), that he'd all along "been struggling to say something which it takes a man twenty years to be able to say." [17] Especially, he might have added, when he must free himself from uncongenial techniques.

But just as in his *fin-de-siècle* phase the young man had been capable of lyrics as skillful as "Tease" or "Tarantella," in his Georgian mood he could produce good verses, too. The two-stanza "Gipsy" is a moving and carefully controlled poem, though certainly Georgian in derivation, reminding us of the gypsy preoccupation among writers like Gibson, Hodgson and de la Mare. Gypsies, after all, are wild yet romantic, quaint and picturesque; they appeal to "a love of the marvelous." It was, then, the Georgian young man, who produced this taut little lyric with its ambiguous "Thou shalt shut doors on me." [18] Yet though the poem is moving and controlled, it

[16] Lawrence, *Phoenix* (I). In his unpublished Preface to *Poems* (*CP*, p. 850) Lawrence said he wrote "The Wild Common" when he was nineteen, instinctively anticipating the mood of the Georgians.

[17] Preface to *Poems, CP,* p. 28.

[18] Pinto and Roberts suggest in the revised (1971) edition of *CP* that "Gipsy" must have been based on a 1910 translation of an Arabic poem that Lawrence made from the German of Fritz Krenkow. (See *CP* 1971, p. 974.) In revising his original translation, Lawrence tightened and strengthened the poem considerably, transforming the "laborer" of his first draft into a gypsy, and adding the most dramatic line in the work: "Thou shalt shut doors on me."

34

lacks, finally, the sense of intensity, of dramatic conflict, that characterizes what Lawrence called his "real poems," the poems in which the demon was let loose. The demon's profounder view of gypsies would have to wait until Lawrence got around, in 1928, to *The Virgin and the Gypsy*. Meanwhile, the apprentice poet struggled with the intoxications of his time.

Imagism, the other literary germ to which he partly succumbed, left more important after-effects than Georgianism did. While the Georgians were essentially traditional in orientation,[19] the Imagists were decidedly modern; they rejected at least the recent English past in both style and sentiment, and their example must have played some part in shaking the young man loose from conventional verse forms. Indeed, though Lawrence was never "really" an Imagist, either in principle or practice (he lacked Pound's interest in literary dogma, and his lines never attained the chaste clarity of H. D.'s), and though he may have been included in the anthologies from mere expediency, he made some serious experiments with the Imagist approach to poetry.

The three short stanzas on the moon originally published in *Love Poems* (1913), for example, though they may not have been consciously Imagist in intention, are certainly Imagist in mood. In "Aware," the moon "rising out of the ruddy haze,/Divesting herself of her golden shift" becomes "a woman I did not know/I loved"—a sentimental image when we compare it with T. E. Hulme's "red-faced farmer," but Imagist in its concentration on the associations radiating from a single object. And in "A Pang of Reminiscence" adolescent melodrama is filtered through an Imagist image of a "wistful and candid" moon that, "trembling blue in her pallor," holds "a tear which I had hoped that even hell held not again in store."

---

[19] Moore suggests that the Georgian movement derived "mainly from nineteenth century poetry," (Moore, p. 59), but Georgian verse has many of the qualities of mid-eighteenth century landscape poetry as well.

35

"A White Blossom" escapes some of the youthful flaws of the first two poems. Here Lawrence's vision of how "a tiny moon as small and white as a single jasmine flower/Leans all alone above my window" almost reminds us of Pound's "In a Station of the Metro." Unlike Pound, however, Lawrence still cannot resist the impulse to rhyme ("on night's wintry bower") and, more important, he cannot resist his novelistic tendency to transform every lyrical perception into a dramatic situation. "She shines, the first white love of my youth, passionless and in vain," he adds, and where the other two poems had ended with generalized sentiment or melodrama, this one immediately evokes the whole Jessie Chambers-Miriam-Emily situation, reflected in the light of the virgin goddess.

But then Lawrence was for the most part incapable of the cool "objectivity" for which the Imagists were striving. The two-poem sequence entitled "Baby Movements," for instance, one of his most successful early works, is Imagistic in its loosened rhymes and rhythms, its frequent use of repetition instead of rhyme.[20] In fact, the first verse in the sequence is a perfect little Imagist poem. "I wait for the baby to wander hither to me," Lawrence writes

> Like a wind-shadow wandering over the water,
> So she may stand on my knee
> With her two bare feet in my hands
> Cool as syringa buds
> Cool and firm and silken as pink young peony flowers.

The restraint in the ebb and flow of the lines, the unsentimental portrait of the baby with her feet "cool as syringa buds," and even the precise observation of "cool" for the baby's grass-cooled feet, when "soft" or "pink" or "white" would have come more easily to mind, recall H. D.'s

---

[20] Surprisingly, Lawrence changed this poem considerably in *Poems* 1928, tightening up the stanza structure and *adding* rhymes. Whatever the revised version may have gained in symmetry, it lost much of the grace of the original.

> Whirl up, sea—
> Whirl your pointed pines.
> Splash your great pines
> On our rocks.

But though "Trailing Clouds," the second poem of the sequence, also uses Imagistic repetitions and analogies,

> She who has always seemed so light
>   Sways on my arm like sorrowful, storm-heavy boughs,
> Even her floating hair sinks like storm-bruised young leaves,

these mannerisms now have a special Lawrentian intensity that seems to penetrate the subject in a new way. It is as though the demon had suddenly forced the young man to attend. Every detail is right:

> As a drenched, drowned bee
> Hangs numb and heavy from the bending flower,
>   So clings to me,
> My baby, her brown hair brushed with wet tears
>   And laid laughterless on her cheek,

and every detail seems to reinforce a central idea more interesting than the usual Imagistic noting of similarities:

> My sleeping baby hangs upon my life
>   As a silent bee at the end of a shower
>   Draws down the burdened flower.

These lines contain the two main points of the poem: first, that the baby is overwhelmed by the almost impersonal enormity of her emotion as a bee is half-drowned in the enormity of a shower, for which it is not, after all, responsible; and second, that this weak, helpless creature is utterly dependent on the speaker: "My sleeping baby hangs upon my life."

But these two perceptions, which generate the attentive power of the poem, are a novelist's insights. It is to the novelist that the dramatic *situation* of the baby—her weakness, her helplessness before her own emotion—is of most importance, of much greater importance, certainly, than the "winsomeness" of the baby's feet was to the young man. This poem, then, which perhaps began as a derivative, Imagistic verse, marks a point where Lawrence the novelist intervened in the relationship between the young man and the demon. Directing the young man's attention away from himself and his second-hand poetics, the novelist enabled the demon to "shake out" a "real poem," a poem that is an act of attention rather than a pact with convention.

—3
The Novelist

i

Not all the poems in which the novelist intervened are as successful as "Trailing Clouds." As I suggested earlier, the interests of Lawrence the novelist often differed so markedly from those of the writer's poetic demon, that he, too, with his interest in complexities of "inter-relatedness," blocked the doorways of poetic attention. The famous dialect poems, for instance, which Ezra Pound (and later Louis Untermeyer) considered Lawrence's finest work in verse, pay comparatively little *poetic* attention to their subjects.[1] Perhaps what intrigued Pound about them was their skillful conversion of natural speech-rhythms into a fairly regular metric, a technical achievement that points the way to Lawrence's later accomplishments with organic rhythm and free verse. Or perhaps Pound was simply impressed by Lawrence's skill in handling the traditional form of the dialect ballad. But though both "Violets" (first published in 1916) and "Whether or Not" (first published in 1913) are accomplished dialect ballads, they lack the intensity that the ballad form can sometimes impart to a subject through use of the supernatural, straightforward narration of extraordinary events, incremental repetition, condensation and other devices. Consequently both works

---

[1] "When he writes low-life narrative . . . there is no English poet under forty who can get within shot of him," declared Pound in the July 1913 issue of *Poetry*. (Cf. also Untermeyer, *Modern British Poetry* [New York, 1950], p. 285.)

seem more like versified sketches for short stories than like completed acts of attention.

"Violets" does attend closely to the behavior of the strange, sobbing girl by the graveside:

> Tha should ha' seed her slive up when we'd gone,
>   Tha should ha' seed her kneel an' look in
> At th' sloppy wet grave—an' 'er little neck shone
>   That white, an' 'er shook that much.

But the moral dispute between the sisters seems actually to dissipate some of the poem's dramatic intensity, rather than enriching it with further detail:

> Yi, an' 'im that young,
>   Snapped sudden out of all
> His wickedness, among
>   Pals worse n'r ony name you could call.
> Let be that; there's some o' th' bad as we
>   Like better nor all your good, an' e' was one.

Such complexities of "subtle interrelatedness" are precisely the material Lawrence treated best in prose fiction.

But if the preoccupations of the novelist interfere somewhat in "Violets," they are almost continuously present throughout both versions of the much longer and more complicated sequence of dialect verses called "Whether or Not." The case of the frustrated constable who, roused by his daisy-pure sweetheart, seeks relief in the arms of his landlady—"a widow of forty-five,/A tough old otchel wi' long/Witch teeth"—fascinated Lawrence. He dealt with a similar triangle in a play (*The Daughter-in-Law*) and in a story ("Fanny and Annie"), as well as in this really very comical and skillfully versified cycle of dialect poems.

Because it *is* so comical, we can hardly say that "Whether or Not" isn't a successful poem. It is full of amusing, almost vaudevillean asides on the part of Lizzie, who tells much of the story—for example,

Now sithee theer at th' railroad crossing
Warmin' his-sèn at the stool o' fire
Under the tank as fills the ingines
If there isn't my dearly-beloved liar!

My constable wi' 'is buttoned breast
As stout as the truth, my sirs!—an' 'is face
As bold as a robin! It's much he cares
For this nice old shame and disgrace.

But the complicated moral issues raised by the virginal be-
havior of a girl who keeps herself "shut like a daisy bud,/
Clean an' new an' nice," but sends her young man home
nightly "a'most bustin' mad o' mysèn/An' walkin' in agony"
to the dubious mercies of his landlady with her "clawkin'
tiger's eyes," though they make a clever poem, might more
profitably have been dealt with in prose right from the start.

There is a whole dimension of the story, after all, that the
poem cannot reach. The dramatic, moral conflict between the
"good" virginal girl and the "wicked" sensual landlady, with
all its ironies and reversals, is easily conveyed. But the pro-
founder feelings of the landlady, hinted at in Lizzie's smug
"I'll rear thy childt if 'er'll yield it to me,/An' then wi' that
twenty pound we gi'e 'er I s'd think 'er wunna be/So very
much worser off than 'er wor before," require the sort of ex-
tended analysis that only prose fiction will allow. In the later
version, Lawrence deleted the "happy ending" to which Ed-
ward Garnett had objected and, in adding an important
speech for the disgusted constable, he tried to clarify the
moral questions obscured by the dramatic swiftness and comi-
cal exaggerations of the first version, as well as by its smug,
virtue-triumphant ending. Unfortunately, however, he suc-
ceeded only in turning poor Tim into a second-rate Mellors,
without the latter's passion or conviction.

So I s'll go an' leave yer,
Both on yer.

I don't like yer, Liz, I want ter
        Get away from yer.

An' I really like 'er neither,
        Even though I've 'ad
More from 'er than from you; but either
        Of yer's too much for this lad. . . .

What bit o' cunt I had wi' er
        's all I got out of it.
An' 's not good enough, it isn't
        For a permanent fit.

We are left in the end with the feeling that, though both ver-
sions of "Whether or Not" display a rich, Burnsian humor,[2]
and perhaps prepared Lawrence to make use of natural
speech-rhythms in his later poetry, neither advanced the
writer very far in the direction his demon wanted to take, the
direction of attention and concentration, rather than super-
ficial complication.

ii

A number of Lawrence's other fictionalized poems bear out
the contention that "if as a novelist [Lawrence] often writes
like a poet, as a poet he far too often writes like a novelist." [3]
"A Man Who Died," for instance, first published in 1914 but
almost certainly written much earlier, seems like a versified
monologue meant to be spoken by the heroine of "Odour of
Chrysanthemums" or *The Widowing of Mrs. Holroyd.* Yet be-
cause it doesn't have the cumulative dramatic pressures of the
story or play behind it, it lacks the power of either. Though
it contains good lines—the widow's vision of her dead hus-
band as a "stern" and "cold man" lying "relentless hard"
while she washes him "with weeping water," her vision of him
as a "masquerader" with "bowels of steel,"—there is too much

[2] Lawrence once began a novel on the life of Robert Burns. See *Let-
ters,* p. 167, and Nehls, pp. 184–195 for an early draft.
[3] Conrad Aiken, *Scepticisms* (New York, 1919), p. 99.

that is banal in "A Man Who Died" ("You were many men in one;/But never this, this null/This never-warm!") or merely awkward ("Can you never discard/Your curt pride's ban?"). It is as though Lawrence's demon momentarily showed himself here but could not break through the dramatic situation that interested the novelist. What started out to be a work of the order of Rilke's "Leichen-Wäsche" really did become a "byproduct" of one of the early stories. Only in "Odour of Chrysanthemums" itself did Lawrence's perception of death approach the magnitude of Rilke's climactic "Und einer ohne Namen/Lag bar und reinlich da und gab Gesetze,"[4] a line produced by an effort of attention that was so far, for the most part, beyond the young English poet-novelist.

Quite a few of Lawrence's fictionalized poems succeed, however, in their own way. If they do not represent his most attentive work as a poet, they are nevertheless often neat, skilled and ironic in a Hardyesque fashion. Hardy was one of the apprentice writer's favorite authors, and his influence is particularly strong in many of these early works. The apparently strained though often deliberately awkward versification that characterizes so much of Hardy's poetry—versification that seems to arise from a conflict between the poet's desire for what Blackmur calls "objective form" and the novelist's impulse to speak plainly—is everywhere apparent in the "Rhyming Poems." The sense, too, of an enduring landscape, "where the instinctive life heaves up," perhaps came to Lawrence from Wordsworth through Hardy as well as through the more optimistic Georgians.[5]

But most of all a feeling for the poetic possibility of dramatic situations is what Lawrence learned from this late-Victorian predecessor, who was no doubt himself impelled toward such subjects by his talent for "fictionalizing." Cer-

[4] "Leichen-Wäsche" ("Corpse-Washing"), in *Der Neuen Gedichte: Anderer Teil,* first pub. Aug. 1908. "And one without a name/Lay bare and cleanly there and set down laws."
[5] See *Thomas Hardy, Phoenix* (I).

tainly the spirit of Hardy informs the dialect poems (though Tennyson and even Kipling may be influential also), and the Hardy of *Time's Laughingstocks* broods behind a number of the other fictional verses: Hough specifies "Lightning," "Reading a Letter" and "Two Wives," but many others could be mentioned. "A Winter's Tale," which seems almost a versified variation of the early story "A Modern Lover," is a good example.

Like most of Hardy's narrative and dramatic poems, Lawrence's "A Winter's Tale" presents a drastically condensed dramatic situation, and the poet has narrated the circumstances of the scene so as to make them seem most suspenseful. In stanza one, for instance, we are told only that the speaker has seen a girl's footsteps on the snowy hillside. We do not learn until the end of stanza two that the girl who is waiting for him (we assume the narrator is male) "at the hill's white verge" is half-sobbing, and only in stanza three do we learn why: because "she knows what I have to tell." The central paradox of the poem—that the forlorn girl is so love-struck she must come promptly to meet her lover, though she knows she is coming for "the inevitable farewell"—is also Hardyesque. It doesn't suggest the almost cosmic irony that Hardy concerned himself with in a poem like "In the Night She Came," nor does it imply the social bitterness of, say, Hardy's "The Conformers," or some of his later *Satires of Circumstance*,[6] but it is based on the perversity of character that Hardy, too, found so engrossing, and that he explored most fully in (among works likely to have influenced Lawrence) such poems as "A Tramp-Woman's Tragedy" and the "love-lyrics" from *Time's Laughingstocks*.

Because it is more Hardyesque than Lawrentian, however, "A Winter's Tale," skillful and succinct though it is, is not

[6] Most of the *Satires of Circumstance* were first published in 1914, too late for them to have influenced much of Lawrence's early verse, but a few appeared in 1909 in the *English Review*, where the poet may have read them.

one of the best of Lawrence's early poems. As a poet, Hardy excelled at summing up social and metaphysical bitterness in one compact, ironic perception:

> So savage winter catches
> The breath of limber things,
> And what I love he snatches,
> And what I love not brings.[7]

But Lawrence's great talent as a novelist and as a poet was for leaving things inconclusive, "in the dark"; his genius was for suggesting rather than summarizing. As Graham Hough notes, especially "in writing of human relations [Lawrence] often leaves a residue of the unobjectified. A situation is suggested, it is illuminated in one or two brilliant flashes, and for the rest—a frank confession of the residual mystery." [8] Hardy's poetry, together with his own fictional impulses, may have focused the young poet's attention upon the poetic possibilities of character, but he had to find his own ways of dealing with those possibilities.

iii

Lawrence the novelist mediated most effectively between the young man and the demon in those poems where he directed the poet toward the hidden mysteries of a situation, rather than distracting him with dramatic twists of plot. Understandably enough, the more personally involved Lawrence was with a subject, the more intensely his novelist-self—and through the novelist his poetic demon—attended to it. Thus while *The Trespasser* and the Helen poems associated with it tended to be derivative and sentimental or affected, many of the poems Lawrence wrote in conjunction with such novelistic self-explorations as *Sons and Lovers* and, to a lesser extent, *The White Peacock,* can be included abong the best of his early works in verse.

[7] "The Farm-Woman's Winter," *Time's Laughingstocks.*
[8] Hough, p. 43.

"Discord in Childhood" is a fragment of a longer work, Lawrence revealed in his unpublished introduction to *Collected Poems* 1928, "probably . . . good" but "destroyed [because it] had the demon fuming in [it]." [9] Still, it is by no means a mere byproduct of *Sons and Lovers,* though in its final form it deals with a scene described at greater length in the book.[10] While using the same images, and even some of the same phrases as the passage in the novel—"shrieking," "booming," "silence of blood"—the poem accomplishes an entirely different purpose. Not concerning itself with plot or character or the filling in of "background" (the main function of the passage in the novel), it attends to the pure violence that is the essence of this particular dramatic situation. That some (though not all) particulars of the situation are unknown to the reader only adds to the poem's power of suggesting "residual mystery."

Like most of Lawrence's best fictionalized poems, "Discord in Childhood" makes its point about mysteries through the use of specific physical details. "The ash tree with its terrible whips," the "slender lash/Whistling she-delirious rage" and the "male thong booming and bruising" suggest both the human and the inhuman violence of the world as it appears to one child, a world convulsed with the destructive violence of its own blood, hung with both outer and inner whips. "[All] mysteries and possibilities lies in things and happenings," wrote Lawrence to Blanche Jennings in 1908, "so give

[9] Lawrence, unpublished Preface to *Poems, CP,* p. 850.

[10] Cf. *Sons and Lovers,* ch. 4: "Having such a great space in front of the house gave the children a feeling of night, of vastness, and of terror. This terror came in from the shrieking of the tree and the anguish of the home discord. Often Paul would wake up, after he had been asleep a long time, aware of thuds downstairs. . . . Then he heard the booming shouts of his father . . . then the sharp replies of his mother. . . . And then the whole was drowned in a piercing medley of shrieks and cries from the great, wind-swept ash-tree. . . . There was a feeling of horror . . . and a sense of blood. . . . The wind came through the tree fiercer and fiercer. . . . And then came the horror of the sudden silence. . . . What was it? Was it a silence of blood?"

us the things and happenings, and try just to show the flush of mystery in them." [11] This sounds like a statement about writing novels, but the young writer was discussing his taste in poetry, and it is plain that even this early in his career he saw that, for him, the most successful poetic technique would be to start with a "thing" or a "happening," as in "Discord in Childhood," and then, through concentrated attention, to "show the flush of mystery."

"Piano" might also at first glance seem like a byproduct of the novelist's career, but it, too, concentrates upon mystery, going far beyond "Discord in Childhood" in developing a coherent but "suggestive" poem out of the germ of an idea that occurs in one of the novels. "The little, old-maidish piano began to sing a tinkling Victorian melody, and I fancied it must be some demure little woman with curls like bunches of hops on either side of her face who was touching it," writes Cyril, the narrator of *The White Peacock*. "The coy little tune teased me with old sensations, but my memory would give me no assistance." [12] Here the same connection is set up between the piano and nostalgia as in the poem. Indeed, though the setting of the poem is perhaps a concert at which the poet is listening to a "great black piano appassionato," Lawrence was surely thinking back to the same little Victorian upright in both works.

In *The White Peacock* we learn that "the vocal chords behind the green silk bosom . . . had become as thin and tuneless as a dried old woman's. Age had yellowed the teeth of my mother's little piano. . . . The prim, brown lips were always closed." And in the first draft of "Piano" we are told about "my mother's piano, little and brown, with the back/That stood close to the wall, and the front's faded silk both torn/ And the keys with little hollows, that my mother's fingers had worn." But in the final draft of the poem many of these extraneous details were eliminated, and only the essential as-

[11] Letter to Blanche Jennings, 20 January 1909, *Letters*, pp. 47–48.
[12] *The White Peacock*, Part 1, ch. 1.

pects of things and happenings were described. The weak "shaking" of the first draft gave way to the precision of "the boom of the tingling strings," which suggests, like many of the details in "Discord in Childhood," the overwhelming nature of the child's universe, the way it can "master" his emotions through a relatively trivial object, a "tinkling" piano that seems to "tingle." And "the small, poised feet of a mother who smiles as she sings" suggest, again, the powerful poise of small things in a child's world.

The rest of the poem reveals the "flush of mystery" behind the piano and the singing, in this case the mystery of sentiment, to use a word that was not fashionable even in Lawrence's day. For as John Jones puts it, "Piano" shows, "as does a lot of Lawrence's early verse, that he is unafraid of sentiment to an extent that makes it impossible to fit him into modern poetic categories. He faces up to traditionally 'romantic' subjects without a trace of misgiving and without the paralysing sense that you can't write about daffodils or the moon unless you stand them on their heads." [13] Lawrence at his best was capable, in other words, of sentiment undistorted by either sentimentality or irony, and he indicated in "Piano" that his talent was to develop in the direction of the anti-ironic act of attention. For though "Piano" does deal with an ironic discrepancy between past and present, and with the paradox that the voice of the great black piano of the present is overwhelmed by the melodies of the little Victorian upright of the past, Lawrence responded to this irony without ironic detachment. Betrayed back into the past "in spite of myself," he yielded wholly to "the flood of remembrance," showing that he was capable of surrendering himself to emotion without embarrassment—"my manhood is cast/Down in the flood of remembrance, I weep like a child for the past"—while maintaining the sort of strict control over his material—"the tingling strings," "the small poised feet of the mother"—that would keep it from ballooning into a sentimental effusion

[13] John Jones, *New Statesman*, 23.

48

like "Guelder Roses." He showed, finally, that through the influence of the novelist, whose attention was focused with increasing precision on things and happenings, the young man had learned how to admit the perceptions of his demon, who saw the flush of mystery in ordinary reality.

"Hueffer . . . likes to 'sark' me because I am 'a serious person at grips with life,'" Lawrence wrote to Garnett in 1912.[14] Already his anti-ironic seriousness made him seem odd to the fashionable literary *monde* on whose fringes he moved. Yet in the service of his art he felt he had more and more to cast away the young man's derivative artifice and strive for such seriousness, even at the cost of painful confrontations with emotions most men would rather ignore. And again, just as novelistic self-explorations had led the maturing poet to deal with fruitful personal material that he might otherwise have overlooked, so most painful emotional confrontations occurred through the mediation of novelistic activity.

iv

The terse but powerful "Cherry Robbers" is related to a scene that recurs in both *The White Peacock* and *Sons and Lovers* in the same way "Discord in Childhood" and "Piano" are related to passages in *Sons and Lovers* and *The White Peacock*.[15] But in "Cherry Robbers" we have the sense that the demon's attention has been turned to matters a good deal more complex than the simple though intense emotion of the other two poems. "Piano," after all, succeeds because of its

14 Letter to Edward Garnett, 10 February 1912, *Letters*, p. 99.
15 Cf. *The White Peacock,* Part 1, ch. 6: "She thrust the stalks of the berries under her combs . . . Then, with the ruby bunches glowing through the black mist of curls, she looked up at me, brightly, with wide eyes." *Cf.* also *Sons and Lovers,* ch. 11: "Cherries touched [Paul's] ears and his neck as he stretched forward . . . Beside [Miriam] on the rhubarb leaves, were four dead birds, thieves that had been shot . . . He threw a handful of cherries at her . . . She ran for shelter, picking up some cherries. Two fine red pairs she hung over her ears, then she looked up again . . ."

naiveté, because of the poet's willingness to "wring the neck of sophistication" and, in surrendering himself to the tide of his nostalgia, to become like a child again. Childlike, he doesn't question his emotions; he plumbs no depths beyond the (seemingly) clear depths of a single feeling. In "Discord in Childhood," too, he writes from a child's point of view, and the universe he apprehends is purely violent, the child's emotion one of undiluted terror. But in "Cherry Robbers" Lawrence penetrates, though without deliberate irony, to the ambivalent feelings that seethe beneath the intensity of surface emotions. The mystery with which he invests things and happenings is no longer the flush of feeling, pure and simple, but the shadow of tensely conflicting impulses.

The narrative itself is deceptively naive and straightforward, but from the first stanza it depicts a deadly tableau:

> Under the long dark boughs, like jewels red
> In the hair of an Eastern girl
> Hang strings of crimson cherries, as if had bled
> Blood-drops beneath each curl.

Only the two inversions mar the simplicity of the style, and neither is particularly obtrusive. For once the young poet is at his ease in a strict form, for its artifice only sets off his honesty the more. "Blood-drops beneath each curl," however, is the crucial line in this stanza, for besides expanding the metaphor of "the hair of an Eastern girl" into a kind of conceit, it strikes the chord coupling pain and beauty (or love) which is to be the theme of the poem.

In stanza two we penetrate further to what is literally as well as figuratively "under" the cherries:

> Under the glistening cherries, with folded wings
> Three dead birds lie:
> Pale-breasted throstles and a blackbird, robberlings
> Stained with red dye.

This is almost like the progression in a child's poem: under the boughs are cherries—blood-drops; under the blood-drops, death. "Red dye" provides a significant ambiguity: are the dead birds stained with the juice of the cherries, or with their own blood? The central association of the poem is obviously reinforced by this whole stanza, and in stanza three we discover the human equivalent of the tableau of the cherry tree.

> Against the haystack a girl stands laughing at me,
>   Cherries hung round her ears,
> Offers me her scarlet fruit; I will see
>   If she has any tears.

The fruit the girl offers, the poem implies, is more than the innocent cherries she hangs round her ears; and the young man who plucks the fruit of her sexuality—her virginity—will draw blood in more ways than one. But the speaker's hostility—"I will see/If she has any tears"—was of greatest interest to Lawrence's demon, for it is the most unexpected aspect of the situation as well as the most intense and mysterious. We might expect, if the logic of the poem were consistent, that the speaker, the human parallel to the dead robberlings, would be the one to bleed or weep. But on the contrary, it is the girl who will suffer from his sexual maraudings. The cherries, the poem seems to say—the fruit of life, its blood, ripeness, passion, love—bring pain indiscriminately to those who trifle with them.

But more than pointing this not exactly original moral, "Cherry Robbers" establishes the profound connection between love and hate, life and death, pleasure and pain, sex and sadism, the will of the victor and the desire of the victim, which was for years to be a major Lawrentian subject in both prose and poetry. Not only would the emerging novelist deal with this matter in *Sons and Lovers* and, especially, in *The Rainbow* and *Women in Love,* but some of the most successful early poems, like "Lightning," "Wedding Morn," "Scent of Irises," "Last Words to Miriam," "Snapdragon," "Love on the Farm," and, in *Look!,* "Bunny," and "A Young Wife," gain their power from what we might call the love and hate, or perhaps better, the sex and death polarity. As Conrad Aiken noted quite early in Lawrence's career,

Look, Amores and *New Poems* contain more than a handful of uniquely captivating poems. They have a curious quality—tawny, stark, bitter, harshly coloured, salt to the taste. The sadistic element in them is strong . . . [Lawrence ventures] among moods and sensations which no poet has hitherto attempted.[16]

These poems of searing honesty are works in which the demon is always present, works in which Lawrence was first able to integrate his three poetic selves—the young man, the novelist and the demon—into a single, whole and productive artistic self.

[16] Aiken, p. 101. Lawrence was quite conscious of this element in himself as well as in his work. "Some savage in me would like to taste your blood," he wrote to Louie Burrows in 1910. (Boulton, p. 65.)

—4
The Demon

i

As his integrated poetic personality fitfully emerged, Lawrence grew gradually easier with the skill of verse. He himself recognized this. "It is only in the less immediate, the more fictional poems," he wrote, years later, "that the form has to be played with. The demon, when he's really there, makes his own form, willy-nilly, and is unchangeable." [1] Many of the most successful early poems of emotional realism, such as "Snapdragon," "End of Another Home Holiday" or "Love on the Farm," are therefore the most formally liberated. When he did not allow literary convention or novelistic invention to muffle the voice of the part of himself that was his demon, Lawrence had known from the first what he wanted to do in poetry. "Before anything I like sincerity, and a quickening, spontaneous emotion," he wrote to Blanche Jennings in 1908. "I do not worship music." And in 1909 he added that "I want to write live things, if crude and half-formed, rather than beautiful, dying, decadent things with sad odours." [2]

The conventional young man, the apprentice poet, did produce a few beautiful, dying, decadent things, but many of Lawrence's best poems *were* crude and half-formed. Their often Hardyesque crudeness, however, was associated with their life. "Marsh will hold it as a personal favour if I will take more care of my rhymes," the young poet wrote to Cyn-

[1] Lawrence, unpublished Preface to *Poems, CP,* p. 851.
[2] *Letters,* p. 21 and pp. 47–48.

thia Asquith in 1913. "Poor things, they go cackling round like a poultry farm . . . He thinks I'm too Rag-time." But the next day he wrote defensively to Marsh himself that "I think . . . my rhythms fit my mood pretty well in the verse." [3] And while Lawrence had by no means found his *métier* in any of the "Rhyming Poems," there is no doubt that the more honest and live his poems became, the more the young poet attempted to fit his form to his moods. Crude his verse may have been, but for him the way to skill led ultimately through such crudeness rather than through music.

"Love on the Farm," for instance, though a poem Lawrence called "fictional" in his preface to *Collected Poems* of 1928,[4] is surely one of the most live and emotionally realistic of these early verses, and it exhibits a degree of formal looseness unusual among the "Rhyming Poems." It has a number of awkward rhymes and awkward phrases leading up to rhymes, such as "Or should he my tears surmise." But some of the rhymes are the kind of casual half-rhymes (home/come, hood/flood, window/wind) that, since Owen and Auden, are considered a sign of technical sophistication and not of aesthetic clumsiness. There is a Blakeian naiveté in the style, moreover, especially in the opening, that almost vindicates the occasional syntactical awkwardness. The picture of the woodbine in the third stanza, for instance, might come straight out of the *Songs of Innocence:*

> She woos the moth with her sweet, low word;
> And when above her his moth-wings hover

[3] *Letters,* pp. 220–221.

[4] According to Jessie Chambers (E.T.", p. 116) it was originally two separate poems, but though the situation may have been "fictionalized" enough reminiscent fragments of it occur throughout *The White Peacock* (see ch. 2, especially) to suggest that it had its basis in fact. As Hough remarks, "the lover . . . is manifestly . . . George Saxton. . . . The girl in the novel is his sister; she shrinks from him in just this way [though] it is not an amorous shrinking." (Hough, p. 198) And George Saxton is based on Will Chambers, just as his sister Emily is Jessie.

Then her bright breast she will uncover
And yield her honey-drop to her lover.

But behind this innocence, as behind the innocence of Blake's "darkening green," looms the darkness, the wound, of experience. "In the west/I see a redness suddenly come . . . Tis the wound of love goes home!" And as darkness gains on "the golden light" of the opening, the style grows progressively less lyrical and more gnarled. The central section, in which the man kills the rabbit, is cast in breathless tetrameter. In the final, sensual confrontation between the man and the woman, the lines lengthen, though unevenly, into a rough but more relaxed pentameter. Throughout, the poem quivers with the tense ambivalence of its theme.

A few crucial symbols transmit that theme, recurring like leitmotifs. The "large, dark hands" of stanza one become "the large, hard hands" of stanza five, in which the rabbit dies, and finally, in stanza six, "the uplifted sword/Of his hand against my bosom," a hand whose "fingers . . . still smell grim/Of the rabbit's fur." Breasts and throats are uncovered, vulnerable, to the pleasure-pain of love and death: first "the evening's anxious breast," then the "bright breast" of the woodbine, the warm throat of the swallow and the choked throat of the rabbit; at last the bosom of the woman, whose throat is choked with desire and the terror of desire as the rabbit's was choked with a relentless wire ring. Finally "scarlet," for "the wound of love" that is the poem's theme, permeates the imagery like a stain of blood. The evening "reddens," the swallow makes "warm display/Of red upon the throat," the water hen exhibits "quaintly scarlet blushes," and in the end "a flood of sweet fire sweeps across" the speaker—the sensual fire of life, of the blood, which is also, in a paradox going back at least to the Renaissance, the fire of death.

Interestingly, in striking out for himself as a whole poet, Lawrence at first accommodated the unconventional observations of his demon to a traditional framework. The studious young man still had his part to play, just as the novelist did. The latter focused Lawrence's attention on dramatic events and on the depths of character. The former played his part in the choice of genre—a Browningesque dramatic monologue—and contributed, perhaps, the central trope, based on an Elizabethan pun of which even Eliot would have approved. But it was the demon, Lawrence himself would have said, who brought to bear on this material, this form, this style, the intensity of attention that lifts it above a conventional literary exercise, charging it with the ambivalent immediacy of physical life, its joy ("the nest's warm busy ball") and its nausea ("fingers that still smell grim," "I let him nose like a stoat"). In finding precise images for those "allotropic states" of feeling through which all people pass,[5] the young poet demonstrated his special sensitivity to an *emotional* universe pulsing with such violent ambivalence, a universe characterized, in the words of the poem's original title, by "Cruelty and Love" together.

"Snapdragon," another of the most successful of the early "Rhyming Poems," also deals with this central ambivalence of life, though less directly. And here again, the young poet made a tentative effort to liberate himself from what had begun to seem the confining symmetry of conventional stanza form. As in "Love on the Farm," however, he was not yet ready to discard rhyme, traditional meter, and stanzaic patterning entirely, but contented himself with a crude attempt to fit his rhythms to his mood. To do this, he worked out a verse structure in which a basic, six-line, rhymed stanza in roughly iambic pentameter formed a kind of ground bass against which stanzas of varying lengths, meters, and rhyme patterns could be played. The basic stanzas contained most of the essentials of the narrative, while the varying stanzas contained the poet's flights of fancy, the symbolic or expressionistic material.

This freer symbolic material was the more innovative part

[5] Cf. *Letters*, pp. 281–282.

of the poem and accounts for the work's frequently being considered "one of Lawrence's most 'modern' poems" of this period.[6] Yet in the last analysis these "fanciful" sections are not the most successful parts of "Snapdragon," though they exhibit the young poet in a mood for technical experimentation. It is not a series of rather strained metaphors like

This bird, this rich,
Sumptuous, central grain,
This mutable witch,
This one refrain,
This laugh in the fight,

which strikes the casual reader leafing through *Georgian Poetry 1911–1912* as something so very much out of the ordinary. Rather, it is the more penetratingly realistic stanzas of the poem that are most striking when one comes upon them after a bout with Brooke or Abercrombie. We hardly need "This clot of night,/This field of delight" to clarify the meaning of the confrontation between the narrator and the girl.

As in "Love on the Farm," this confrontation is charged with sexual energy, its intensity and its ambivalence. Like the former work, "Snapdragon" could have been titled "Cruelty and Love," though it tends to emphasize desire slightly more than "Love on the Farm" did. The main action of the poem is essentially the same, however. An act of cruelty to a non-human creature—real cruelty in "Love" (the killing of the rabbit) and symbolic cruelty in "Snapdragon" (the throttling of the flower)—reveals the cruelty that is a latent but inescapable element in most human sexuality.[7] Furthermore, just as "Love" was skillfully held together by a series of linked sym-

[6] Moore, p. 75.

[7] The killing of the rabbit is also a natural part of life on the farm, whereas the throttling of the flower is perverse. Perhaps for this reason "Snapdragon," more than "Love," recalls the "Rabbit" chapter of *Women in Love,* in which Gudrun and Gerald are brought by their struggle with a pet rabbit to a moment of "mutual hellish recognition." Though "Love" also involves cruelty to a rabbit, it seems to lack such perversity.

bols, "Snapdragon" is unified by a network of symbols or leit-motifs.

Except for the irrelevant flights of fancy noted earlier, "Snapdragon" uses this material economically. A number of the major symbols or implements of the action are mentioned in the first stanza (cups, eyes, windows, birds, "sin") and the rest (flower, throats, blood, darkness) appear soon after. The remainder of the poem skillfully varies these basic elements. "My windows of discovery" become "the windows of my mind." "The mellow sunlight stood as in a cup" foreshadows the "wine-skin of my heart," which leads to "my Grail, a brown bowl twined/With swollen veins" and "I longed to turn/My heart's red measure in her cup;/I longed to feel my hot blood burn/With the amethyst in her cup." "Her bright eyes like sparrows" are harbingers of the way she sinks "into my sight like a settling bird" with "her bosom couched in the confines of her gown/Like heavy birds at rest there," all setting the scene for the almost surrealistic dream-vision in which desire is personified as "a brown bird" settling on the lover's heart.

> Again I saw a brown bird hover
> Over the flowers at my feet;
> I felt a brown bird hover
> Over my heart, and sweet
> Its shadow lay on my heart.

The "crimson throat" of the flower reminds the lover of his "own throat in her power." Later he himself puts his "hand to the dint/In the flower's throat" and achieves a triumph over the girl that renders him oblivious even to the possibility that "the large hands of revenge" (mysteriously related to the large hands of his sweetheart) may "get" his "throat at last."

But while "Snapdragon" is unified by the same sort of leit-motifs that unify "Love on the Farm," it differs from the earlier poem [8] in one very important respect: while "Love" is

[8] Lawrence's placement of "Love" before "Snapdragon" in *Poems 1928* is significant, since he claimed to have arranged the collection

told from the female point of view, "Snapdragon" is related from the male point of view. The speaker of "Love" can only conjecture about the part of cruelty in her lover's desire for her, but the narrator of "Snapdragon" experiences directly the electric charge of sadism and of masochism with which his desire seethes. "There in the dark," he tells us, "I did discover/Things I was out to find." The dark—"the dark of my heart," "the dark of her eyes"—always a favorite Lawrentian questing or resting place, reveals his desire to be a victim ("I longed to turn my heart's red measure in her cup") as well as her desire to be a victim ("I opened her helpless eyes to consult/Their fear, their shame, their joy that underlies/Defeat in such a battle"). It reveals her desire for victory ("She laughed, she reached her hand out to the flower,/Closing its crimson throat") and his final victory ("Her pride's flag, smitten, cleaved down to the staff"). It reveals, in short, the narrator's desire for *being*, for "death I know is better than not-to-be." "Being," as Lawrence implied in "Love on the Farm" and "Cherry Robbers," contains death as well as life, just as it contains cruelty as well as love. "Not-to-be" means not to experience, not to attend, not to know. Knowledge of life necessarily involves knowledge of death, and to attend to life is to attend to the death at the heart of life, to physical death as well as the spiritual death that is, as we shall see, a kind of precondition for heightened life.

ii

Death alone, however, "the long haunting of death in life," as Lawrence wrote in his preface to *Collected Poems* 1928 and "the drift towards death," [9] as he phrased it in a letter to Edward Garnett, became a major subject for the integrated poet, young man-novelist-demon in one, toward the end of his early

----

chronologically. Though see Marshall, *The Psychic Mariner* (New York, 1970), p. 62, for further discussion of the composition of "Snapdragon."
  [9] Lawrence, Preface to *Poems, CP,* p. 28. *Letters,* p. 161.

manhood when his mother's illness and death was the central fact in his experience. Lawrence had always been a confessional poet, as he himself was the first to point out. "Many of [my] poems are so personal," he wrote, "that in their fragmentary fashion they make up a biography of an emotional and inner life." [10] Indeed, much of his best work in verse was produced when his novelist-self turned his demon's attention to the profound drama of his personal life. "Cherry Robbers" was included among what Lawrence called "the Miriam poems," a group of verses dealing with the writer's first major extrafamilial love relationship, the one with Jessie Chambers, and "Love on the Farm" was apparently inspired by Jessie Chambers too. "Snapdragon" dealt with Louise Burrows, "the big and dark and handsome" girl to whom Lawrence got himself briefly engaged in 1910 in what was evidently an attempt to escape from the increasingly pervasive shadow of his mother's illness.[11]

But if these poems about the young writer's early sweethearts gained a dimension of intensity from being so firmly rooted in personal reality, how much more intense would be poems, if he could write them, about the center of his emotional existence, the mother, of whom, so long as she lived, all other women were merely vague reflections. Most writers would not be able to deal directly with a subject so psychologically significant. They would have to sublimate the material, somehow to disguise it, even—perhaps especially—from themselves. The extraordinary thing about Lawrence, however, is that he seems to have accomplished a kind of self-psychoanalysis, a confrontation of some of the subtlest and most perverse forces in himself, which enabled him to write quite frankly about subjects that would constrain or constrict most writers. "One sheds one's sicknesses in books," he told

[10] *CP*, p. 27.
[11] "When I think of her I feel happy . . . she is big and dark and handsome." *Letters*, p. 70.

his old friend A. W. McLeod in 1913, "repeats and presents again one's emotions, to be master of them." [12]

Because he believed this, he was able in *Sons and Lovers* to analyze an Oedipal situation so freely that psychiatrists still find it hard to believe the young novelist had perceived the nature of his feelings almost entirely on his own, and he was able, in the days when his mother lay dying and in the months following her death, to produce the series of so-called "mother poems" which, because of their naked attention to feeling, have been found embarrassing by some readers perhaps not so well equipped to encounter raw emotions as he himself was. Yet these poems are among the best of the early verses: the least cluttered with extraneous material; the most direct, the most intense and attentive; the least formally awkward. Moreover, "painful and eccentric" as they may seem,[13] they are poems in a confessional tradition that goes back at least as far as Wordsworth, and which also numbers among its practitioners Meredith, Hardy, Yeats, and, more recently, Robert Lowell, Sylvia Plath, and Anne Sexton.

Lawrence actually began writing these confessional poems about his mother and the fluctuations in his relationship with her a little before he knew she was seriously ill. "Monologue of a Mother" and "End of Another Home Holiday" [14] both deal with the adolescent and post-adolescent crisis of separation, the first from the mother's point of view, the second from the son's. Both, because they confront their subject matter so attentively, can be counted among the more successful of the early verses. Still, young man and novelist play a part in both poems slightly out of proportion to the demon's role. "Monologue of a Mother" is a little too "fictionalized" and at the same time too dependent on information we can only get from knowledge of Lawrence's biography or from reading *Sons and Lovers*. And "End of Another Home Holiday" is perhaps a

[12] *Letters*, p. 234.   [13] See Hough, p. 196.
[14] For an excellent analysis of this, see Alvarez, *Stewards*, pp. 144–49.

little too long; some of the more philosophical passages ("Oh! but the rain creeps down to wet the grain/That struggles alone in the dark") might have been omitted.

Several of the other "mother poems," notably "The End" and "The Virgin Mother," are quite as unsuccessful as some critics think the whole series is. These weak poems fail, though, not because they are painful and eccentric, but rather because they are maudlin and banal. The lines

If I could have put you in my heart,
If but I could have wrapped you in myself
How glad I should have been!
And now the chart
Of memory unrolls again to me
The course of our journey here, here where we part,

are merely outpourings of sentiment. None of Lawrence's various *literary* selves seems to have had any part in producing them. But then it can certainly be said of Lawrence, as Marius Bewley has said (with much less justification) of Wallace Stevens, that he published far too many "practice poems." [15] Yet, as in Stevens' case, the practice verses served their purpose. The raw material brought to the surface in these failed poems was honed and refined to brightness in successful poems on the same subject.

The best of the later "mother poems" approach a lyric perfection that Lawrence was never even to attempt again. These works, which include "Brother and Sister," "Listening," "Troth with the Dead," "Sorrow" and "The Bride" are comparatively short and quite traditional, even derivative, in form. The well read young man contributed his literary background, though not his sentimentality, to their style. And for once the rhymes and rhythms work smoothly. It is hard to be-

[15] Marius Bewley, "The Poetry of Wallace Stevens," included in Brown and Haller, ed., *The Achievement of Wallace Stevens* (New York, 1963), p. 158. Alvarez has remarked that "Lawrence wrote too much verse, like Hardy and Whitman, the two poets who influenced him most." *Stewards*, p. 141.

lieve that the same Lawrence who confessed that "my verse is often strained and malformed" and who warned Marsh that "skilled verse is dead in fifty years" [16] could have written a stanza like this, from "Brother and Sister":

> Some say they see, though I have never seen,
> The dead moon heaped within the new moon's arms;
> For surely the fragile, fine young thing had been
> Too heavily burdened to mount the heavens so!
> But my heart stands still, as a new, strong dread alarms
> Me; might a young girl be heaped with such shadow of woe?

The cool control of these lines, the disciplined stanza pattern against which the conversational voice of the poet is set, are qualities that may remind us (even more than "Tarantella") of Yeats, that master technician whose work the young Lawrence had at one point found "vapourish, too thin." [17]

But if "Brother and Sister" is in some respects Yeatsian, "Troth with the Dead" is metaphysical.

> The moon is broken in twain, and half a moon
> Beyond me lies on the low, still floor of the sky:
> The other half of the broken coin of troth
> Is buried away in the dark, where the dead all lie.

> They buried her half in the grave when they laid her away,
> Pushed gently away and hidden in the thick of her hair
> Where it gathered towards the plait, on that very last day;
> And like a moon unshowing it must still shine there.

> So half lies on the sky, for a general sign
> Of the troth with the dead that we are pledged to keep;
> Turning its broken edge to the dark, its shine
> Ends like a broken love, that turns to the dark of sleep.

Watching his mother die had left the young poet tense with attention to his own grief and, more, to the paradox of death-in-life. It had left him, as he indicated in "Listening," aware of a terrible silence.

---

[16] *Letters*, p. 221.   [17] *Ibid.*, pp. 47–48.

My words fly off a forge
　The length of a spark;
I see the silence easily sip them
　Up in the dark.

Yet he was able to generalize his grief into the skillful conceits of "Troth with the Dead" and "Listening."

Lawrence's poems were still, though, most successful when they were apparently simplest, and when they began with things and happenings. "Sorrow," for instance, is a moving lyric, which, by lifting certain details mentioned in passing in Chapter Thirteen of *Sons and Lovers* from the dramatic context of the novel, transforms them from casual contingencies to independent symbols.

Why does the thin grey strand
Floating up from the forgotten
Cigarette between my fingers,
Why does it trouble me?

Ah, you will understand;
When I carried my mother downstairs,
A few times only, at the beginning
Of her soft-foot malady,

I should find, for a reprimand
To my gaiety, a few long grey hairs
On the breast of my coat; and one by one
I watched them float up the dark chimney.

It is the *intensity* of attention to these precisely observed realistic details that gives the poem its power: "the thin grey strand" of smoke evolves into the mother's "long grey hairs" which, evanescent as smoke, float smokelike "up the dark chimney"; "her soft-foot malady" is cancer, but also death, which overwhelms its victim with a silence as savage as the silence of the heavens is perfect.

But even more than the versification of "Brother and Sister," the form of "Sorrow" is beautifully realized too, enhancing the work's attentive strength. As Alvarez remarks, in

Lawrence's "Rhyming Poems" the "fainter the chime, the more remote the echo, the more convinced the poetry seems," [18] and "Sorrow" is a good example of the justice of this comment. Not only are the lines unrhymed within the individual stanzas, the interstanzaic rhymes are for the most part casual half rhymes—fingers/downstairs/hairs, forgotten/beginning/one by one—that loosely but effectively link the poem into a unified whole. All three aspects of Lawrence's poetic personality must have been involved in writing this poem: the young man who tinkered with literary forms; the novelist who was driven to examine a comparatively ordinary human situation—a man smoking a cigarette; and the demon whose extraordinary power of attention transfigured the details of the situation.

"The Bride," perhaps the most brilliant of these early grief-driven acts of attention, was similarly produced by the integrated poet, his demon acting as a lens of deep perception for the whole man. Again, the poem is related to a passage from *Sons and Lovers* (in Chapter Fourteen), and again the casual details of the prose are intensified into poetic metaphor.

> My love looks like a girl tonight,
>> But she is old.
> The plaits that lie along her pillow
>> Are not gold,
> But threaded with filigree silver,
>> And uncanny cold.

The Hardyesque stanza pattern is exactly right for conveying the poet's point. The innocence of "My love looks like a girl tonight" is immediately undercut by the frighteningly terse "But she is old." Discovery follows on discovery: like many of Lawrence's best poems, this is a poem of discovery through attention, and as the poet attends ever more closely to his subject we discover truths ever more terrible. Thus we learn first that "my love" is not a girl, but—the revelation is somehow

---

[18] Alvarez, p. 143.

sinister—"she is old," and this discovery is followed quickly by the chilling discovery that she is dead: her plaits are "uncanny cold."

Yet in death, we learn in stanza two,

> She looks like a young maiden, since her brow
>> Is smooth and fair;
> Her cheeks are very smooth, her eyes are closed,
>> She sleeps a rare,
> Still, winsome sleep, so still, and so composed.

Death has smoothed away the lines of age from the aged woman, "my love," whom we know is Lawrence's mother (though the information is not essential). It has, in a way, perfected her, returning to her the fairness and winsomeness of her youth. As for Rilke, death for Lawrence—at least in his most religious and philosophical moods, and increasingly so as he grew older—was not a tragic interruption of life, but rather the final stage in the *process* of life, the final ripeness. "Und ihr Gestorbesein/erfüllte sie wie Fülle," wrote Rilke of Eurydice in the poem "Orpheus. Eurydike. Hermes." "Wie eine Frucht von Süssigkeit und Dunkel,/so var sie voll von irhem grossen Tode." Moreover, just as the woman of the Lawrence poem has had her maidenhood restored to her by death, so in the Rilke work Eurydice "war in einen neuen Mädchentum/und unberührbar." [19] The principal difference between the women of the two poems is that where Rilke uses the metaphor of maidenhood or virginity to represent the effect of death, Lawrence in his third and final stanza goes beyond the imagery of maidenhood to the bridal imagery that gives the work its title.

[19] . . . And her deadness
was filling her like fullness.
Full as a fruit with sweetness and with darkness
was she with her great death . . .
She had attained a new virginity. ["Orpheus. Eurydike. Hermes," from *Neue Gedichte*, tr. J. B. Leishman, *New Poems* (London, 1964), p. 145.]

Nay, but she sleeps like a bride, and dreams her dreams
    Of perfect things.
She lies at last, the darling, in the shape of her dream,
    And her dead mouth sings
By its shape, like thrushes in clear evenings.

Of course there is an element of bitterness, even of irony, in the fact that this woman has only achieved "the shape of her dream" in death, and that for her the perfect marriage is the inescapable, cold bridal with death. Hardy, for one, might even have built his poem around this irony. But Lawrence, like Rilke, seems able to dismiss the bitterness: it is part of life, not worth protesting, that dreams are unattainable, and life, perhaps for this reason, is too wonderful, death too mysterious, too full of sweetness and dark for bitterness. Indeed, the tone of the whole poem, though it begins by undercutting itself and is full of minor ironies, is, as in most of Lawrence's best poems, anti-ironic.

In Lawrence's anti-ironic stance can be found the main difference between his confessional poems and those of more recent writers in this genre. We need only compare Sylvia Plath's "Daddy" to "The Bride" to see how Lawrence's work diverged from what has become a central tradition in contemporary verse. Sylvia Plath, also in a sense mourning the death of a parent of the opposite sex to whom she had an unusually intense attachment, loses no opportunity of pointing out the ambiguities and ironies of her own feelings. "Daddy" is a "black shoe/In which I have lived like a foot/ For thirty years," but he's also "the black man who/Bit my pretty red heart in two." Even as she betrays herself in lines almost rigid with passion and anguish:

At twenty I tried to die
And get back, back, back to you.
I thought even the bones would do,

she laughs at herself:

But they pulled me out of the sack,
And they stuck me together with glue.[20]

Her situation, as she sees it, is too terrible, but also too grotesque, to bear. "Ogden Gnash," one critic has labeled this style.

Lawrence, however, is serious; like Rilke, he is at every moment "a serious person at grips with life." His poem builds intently to the final revelation: "Her dead mouth sings/By its shape, like thrushes in clear evenings." Significantly, this figure is the only one not even implicit in the details of the *Sons and Lovers* passage. We may consider this serious last discovery a product of purely poetic attention and not in any sense a byproduct of fictional activities. And it is, ultimately, his capacity for metaphorical vision of this order that indicates the main direction Lawrence's poetic talent was to take: away from fashionable wit and irony, from the balanced grace of the traditional lyric, toward the less well charted paths of vatic attention.

Again, as in the stanza as a whole, there *is* an irony in these last lines of "The Bride," an irony—or paradox—some critics might consider crucial: that, dead, the woman "sings" perhaps more beautifully than she did in life, that beneath the appearance of death there is a more significant reality. Yet Lawrence is not primarily interested in this irony. He is more concerned with his visionary perception of something stirring beneath the crust of the obvious than he is with the ironic discrepancy between appearance and reality. Where he had failed in "A Man Who Died" to encompass the meaning of the dead man as Rilke did in "Leichen Wäsche," he succeeded in "The Bride," perhaps because of his tragic involvement with his mother, in achieving an anti-ironic act of attention comparable to Rilke's vision in "Früher Apollo" of the god's mouth

[20] Sylvia Plath, *Ariel* (London, 1965), pp. 54–56.

der jetzt noch still ist, niegebraucht und blinkend
und nur mit seinem Lächeln etwas trinkend
al würde ihm sein Singen eingeflösst.[21]

But whereas for Rilke such penetration of an object was, if not easy, part of the work he had consciously defined for himself, for the young Lawrence it was still extraordinarily difficult. He was not yet certain of his goals as a poet, nor even of what poetic style would be most congenial to him. Worse, he had, as we have seen, to master three contending poetic selves, all urging him in different directions. The wonder is that he was able, at this stage, to write as much good poetry as he did. Yet steadily, though with many intermittent failures, he advanced toward self-knowledge and control, and toward the delicate poetic discipline that was to become uniquely his. In a poem like "The Bride," for instance, the three selves momentarily became one.

[21] . . . the mouth below
   as yet still silent, sparkling and unused,
   just drinking something with its smile, as though
   its singing were being gradually infused. [*Neue Gedichte*, tr. Leishman, *New Poems*, p. 47.]

PART II

THE NEW LIFE

The creative, spontaneous soul sends forth its prompt-
ings of desire and aspiration in us. These promptings
are our true fate, which is our business to fulfill.

Foreword to *Women in Love*

—5

The Burden of Self-Accomplishment: Preparation for Change

i

Although the process of integrating Lawrence's three poetic selves into a single poetic personality was slow, it went forward with a certain inevitability. Because he was a poet-novelist with a symbolic turn of mind, however, Lawrence needed a dramatic action to signify the death of his old, disintegrated self and the entrance of his new, unified self into a new life. The death of his mother had effectively cut him off from childhood and young manhood, but it did not usher in a new existence. On the contrary, it left the poet sick, "silence-haunted," and "drifting towards death." "The sun immense and rosy/Must have sunk and become extinct/The night you closed your eyes forever against me," he declared in the "Elegy" for his mother which, along with "Moonrise," opened *Look! We Have Come Through!* For Lawrence, as for Dante, the new life had to begin not with death (though that was a part of it), but with love, with the love of a woman who was not—at least overtly—a mother figure, but a mysterious "other." Thus though there had been flashes of a "new" style in even the earliest poems, for Lawrence, the new life (and with it a new style) began most decisively when he met Frieda Weekly-Richthofen in April 1912, and *Look! We Have Come Through!*, his book about those first years with Frieda, is both record and evidence of the changes that took place.

The story of Lawrence's first meeting with Frieda need not be labored, for it is already a classic in the annals of literary biography. The jobless and sickly young man who goes to see an old teacher for advice because his life is at such loose ends and meets instead the teacher's beautiful wife sounds almost like a character in a novel. Certainly Frieda Weekly-Richthofen, reckless and aristocratic, seems at first more fictional than real. Everything about her was alien to the young man Lawrence had been: her social class, her nationality, her age, her experience, her unconventionality, her slight anti-intellectualism, even her coloring—those extraordinary green " 'Tartar' eyes flecked with brown!" [1] In marrying Frieda, Lawrence would be accepting and assimilating all these new traits, liberating himself from his old self, and beginning a new life as a new man. *Look!*, he later noted, reveals "the intrinsic experience of a man during the crisis of manhood, when he marries and *comes into himself*" (italics mine), for through his relationship with his wife, "she who is the other," the protagonist (Lawrence) is made aware of "the burden of self-accomplishment!/The charge of fulfilment!" [2] "I deliver myself over to the unknown in coming to you," Birkin, the Lawrence-figure in *Women in Love,* tells Ursula, partly modeled after Frieda. "Only there needs the pledge between us, that we will both cast off everything, cast off ourselves even, and cease to be, so that that which is perfectly ourselves can take place in us."

Significantly, one of the earlier poems in *Look!* bears the title "And oh—that the man I am might cease to be—," a quotation from Tennyson's "Maud." Self-weariness, almost self-loathing, must precede the new awareness and the new life. In his trance of grief the son-lover knows "the stream of

[1] Moore, *The Intelligent Heart* (New York, 1954), p. 154.
[2] See Lawrence's Preface to *Look! We Have Come Through!* See also Moore, *Op. Cit.,* p. 165: Lawrence's "involvement with Frieda . . . made it possible for him to get beyond . . . his past and . . . to come through."

my life in the darkness/Deathward set." Yet though Lawrence himself was conscious, in this crucial period, chiefly of an overwhelming emotional exhaustion following the death of his mother—"Day wearies me with its ostentation and fawnings"—and later, after the meeting with Frieda, of an undefined thirst for new life, the forces of transformation had been working in him all along. The "new man" he was to be was in most important ways the man he had always moved toward becoming, as a novelist and as a poet.

ii

Frieda's unconventionality may have intensified the young poet's courage to experiment, but his interest in experimentation had always been there. "I have a wicked delight in smashing things which I think I can make better," he had written to Blanche Jennings in December 1908, four years before meeting Frieda.[3] And in the best of the early poems, works like "Love on the Farm" and "Snapdragon," Lawrence had allowed his demon at least to crack the neat stanzas and regular rhythms of conventional form. Though as late as 1913 he apologized to Marsh because "my verse is often strained and malformed,"[4] he had already begun to formulate an aesthetic far different from Marsh's. An exchange between Paul and Miriam in *Sons and Lovers,* which the writer was just completing during those first months on the continent with Frieda, summarizes this emerging theory. Miriam is admiring one of Paul's pictures. Finally she asks him "Why do I like this so?" adding that "It seems so true." "It's because—it's because there is scarcely any shadow in it," [he replies]. "It's more shimmery, as if I'd painted the shimmering protoplasm in the leaves and everywhere, and not the stiffness of the shape. That seems dead to me. Only this shimmeriness is the real living. The shape is a dead crust. The shimmer is inside, really."[5] And by 1912 Lawrence had expressed this emerging

[3] *Letters,* pp. 43–44.   [4] *Letters,* p. 230.
[5] *Sons and Lovers,* Ch. VII.

aesthetic practically as well as theoretically, for he had written at least one poem that strikingly foreshadows his mature free verse. The poem, "A Man at Play on the River," was not published in either book or periodical form in his lifetime, yet it is one of the best of the early poems and certainly the most stylistically prophetic.[6]

As in some of the *Look!* and in all of the *Birds, Beasts and Flowers* works, there are no rhymes in the piece and no fixed meters. Instead, it is unified by a kind of incantatory repetition that was eventually to become as essential to Lawrence's versification as to his prose style. "In point of style," Lawrence wrote in a retrospective introduction to *Women in Love,* "fault is often found with the continual, slightly modified repetition. The only answer is that it is natural to the author, and that every natural crisis in emotion or passion or understanding comes from this pulsing frictional to-and-fro which works up to culmination." Lawrence himself was conscious, though, that such repetition in his free verse (as in his prose) could take many forms, not merely literal but structural and figurative as well.

In "A Man at Play," for instance, almost every phrase has its grammatical parallel:

> Like a fly that weaves through the shadows,
> Like a bee that plays with the reflection of flowers
> Darts a man at play,

or

> Up the river, under the trees
> Down the river, in the gleam of the sun,
> Across the river, bending low.

[6] If Pinto and Roberts had not verified that it comes from Ms. 1479 (Univ. of Nottingham Library), it would be hard to believe the young writer had produced this poem. Yet it is surrounded by "dateable" poems, and Pinto records Ada King's testimony "that during . . . the winter of 1910–1911 [Lawrence] had this notebook with him." (*CP,* p. 1026)

But the repetitions and parallels are not simply mechanical: they have a movement that is organic and evolutionary. With the self-evolving flow of the river itself, the poem's central ideas grow, through subtle changes and additions, out of its pattern of parallels. For example, the lines

> A swift, dexterous man, plying the slender pole,
> His body pulsing with play
> His full, fine body bending and urging like the stress of a song,
> Darting his light punt with the quick-shifting fancy of verse,

casually introduce the comparison of the man's play to a song or a poem which is the work's chief perception. Similarly, "continual slightly modified repetition" of the word "joy" helps establish both "the ever-changing joy" of the man's body and the exuberance of the poem.

"A Man at Play" has an underlying metaphorical logic, however, that is perhaps belied by its fluid and casual surface. The central comparison of the man's play to a song is so carefully embedded in the imagery of the piece that it is almost a conceit. In combination with another recurring simile—"Like a bee that plays with the reflection of flowers"—it brings the poem to a witty and polished conclusion. After his rhythmic, playful journey up the river, the man reaches his destination, a houseboat on which a laughing girl awaits him, and

> the soft caress of her hidden laughter
> Plays round him, as colour-ripples played
> Round his bright joyful body
> When he swung like the rhythm of a poem over the river
> That made shadows and shimmering ripples the soft notes of a song,
> And now hangs like the fragrant close of the measure
> Over her strewn, white, laughing form.

The slight confusion we may feel about exactly *what* "hangs like the fragrant close of the measure" (study of the syntax suggests that the missing subject is still "the soft caress of her hidden laughter") does not detract from the neatness of this conclusion. Not only does it cleverly unite the poem's two chief similes into one figure, but with its faint hint of rhyme (river/measure, song/form) it gracefully closes the measure of the poem itself.

It is surprising, especially when we consider this work in the light of the many awkwardly versified "Rhyming Poems," to find Lawrence suddenly handling a poem's technical requirements with such skill. The wit in "A Man at Play" is never obstructed by formal clumsiness, and even the shape of the piece, with its lapsings and lingerings, seems expressive:

> Over the surface of a shadow-colour floats
> His little punt, an autumn-brown beech-leaf,
> Playing with the eddies
> Hither and thither
> Anywhere;
> Playing with the soft-slipping water.

Just two long, complicated sentences, the poem—to quote from Lawrence's attentive description of the river Trent in *Sons and Lovers*—"[slides] by in a body . . . intertwining among itself like some subtle, complex creature."

The explanation seems to be that the intensity of Lawrence's attention to his subject determined the form of this poem. Concentrating on the playful man, whose body was "pulsing" like a poem, Lawrence himself felt free to play, to experiment, to innovate; and the openness of the verse into which his thoughts naturally flowed allowed him, as his mature *vers libre* did, to attend even more closely to his subject. Like the form, the subject here foreshadowed his future development in several ways.

First, the comparison of the man's exuberantly playful body to a poem suggests that Lawrence, in spite of his apologies to Marsh, was continuing to develop a belief that poetry, rather than consisting of "scraps sweetly moulded in easy Plaster of

Paris sentiment," [7] was an organic process equivalent to the pulse and play of a healthy body. Such a poetic, though it had not yet profoundly influenced the young writer's verse technique, would eventually lead him to reject what he considered the "dead shell" of conventional form in favor of what he regarded as the more living technique of free verse, a technique in which the style seems almost a natural emanation of the subject, part of its organic "shimmeriness" rather than a superimposition upon it.[8]

But if in this piece the young poet expressed his emerging sense that a poem is a "living body," he also, significantly, explored the converse of that notion: he suggested that the human body is like a poem. And in this simile he was expressing a conviction which, especially after his meeting with Frieda, was to become one of the great themes of his life. He was declaring his faith in "the ever-changing joy" of the body itself, his belief "that perfect bright experience never falls/To nothingness." [9] In arriving at this conviction Lawrence was joining the ranks of what we might call the poets of the body, the poets of incarnation. He was joining Keats, who at one point called for "a life of Sensations rather than of Thoughts," and Wallace Stevens, who was to declare, using a metaphor interestingly reminiscent of the central figure of "A Man at Play," that "the body is the great poem." [10] Above all, however, he was joining Whitman, the only one of these writers who played an important part not only in his choice of this theme but in his development of a poetic style.

iii

"Whitman, the great poet, has meant so much to me," wrote Lawrence in the essay on his American precursor with

[7] *Letters,* p. 21.
[8] Cf. Goodheart, p. 42: "Wherever [Lawrence] finds a passion for form . . . he senses an animus against life."
[9] *Look,* "Moonrise."
[10] Keats, Letter to Bailey, November 22, 1817. Stevens, "Adagia," *Opus Posthumous* (New York, 1957), pp. 157–182.

which he concluded *Studies in Classic American Literature:* Whitman, with "his wide strange camp at the end of the great high-road"; Whitman, "the first white aboriginal"; Whitman, who "was the first heroic seer to seize the soul by the scruff of her neck and plant her down among the potsherds."

"There!" he said to the soul. "Stay there!" Stay there. Stay in the flesh. Stay in the limbs and lips and in the belly. Stay in the breast and womb. Stay there, O soul, where you belong.

And at about the same time that he wrote this essay (1919), Lawrence finally attempted a definitive statement of his poetics, making specific reference to Whitman. "The quick of all the universe, of all creation," he wrote in "Poetry of the Present," the introduction to *New Poems*, "is the incarnate, carnal self. Poetry gave us the clue [to this self]: free verse: Whitman." For "the clue to all [Whitman's] utterance lies in the sheer appreciation of the instant moment, life surging itself into utterance at its very well-head." For Lawrence, as for Whitman, there was a necessary connection between a philosophy that affirms life in the body and an "organic" aesthetic that repudiates all laws except its own. The specific stylistic implications of this ultimately Coleridgean aesthetic become clear when we compare "A Man at Play" with Whitman's "The Dalliance of the Eagles," a work Lawrence much admired.[11]

Where "A Man" was two long sentences, "The Dalliance" is only one, a sentence that is not even, as Lawrence's were, grammatically complete. Yet through a complex structure of interlocking parallels the piece, like "A Man at Play," achieves an effect that is onomatopoetic in the sense that it *imitates* its subject. The headlong plunging movement of swift participial repetitions like "In tumbling turning clustering loops, straight downward falling" is balanced, for instance, by the static noun clauses, without verbs or participial modifiers, of

11 See Daleski, footnote, p. 195. Also letter to Godwin Baynes, Nehls, V. 1, pp. 500–501.

"the twain yet one, a moment's lull,/A motionless still balance in the air." The importance of parallel structure in the two poems supports Sir Herbert Read's theory that both Lawrence and Whitman write what is essentially a "poetry of grammar." [12]

Yet if one reads their poems aloud, it becomes apparent that neither Lawrence nor Whitman has completely eschewed rhythm or meter as a poetic device. Rather, their lines move with a more natural, less artificially regular rhythm than that of conventional metric. Both Lawrence and Whitman have done, without much theoretical fanfare, something like what Hopkins did in "inventing" sprung rhythm.[13] They play off the flexible against the regular, combining a sense of natural, totally variable stress, with a sense of regular recurrence. Lines like

> His full, fine body bending and urging like the stress of a song,
> Darting his light punt with the quick-shifting fancy of verse,

or

> The rushing amorous contact high in space together,
> The clinching interlocking claws, a living, fierce, gyrating wheel,

are obviously rhythmic, though one hardly knows where to mark off the feet, and neither Lawrence nor Whitman went to the trouble of indicating "outriders."

In a letter to Edward Marsh on this subject, Lawrence indicated that he was himself keenly aware of the ways in which his meter deviated from the norm. "I think I read my poetry more by length than by stress—as a matter of movements in space [rather] than footsteps hitting the earth," he told Marsh.

[12] See Herbert Read, "The Figure of Grammar: Whitman and Lawrence," *The True Voice of Feeling* (New York, 1953), pp. 87–100.

[13] Hopkins himself conceded that Bridges was right in sensing a relationship between his own versification in "The Leaden Echo and the Golden Echo" and Whitman's verse. *Cf.* Read, p. 93.

I think more of a bird with broad wings flying and lapsing through the air than anything, when I think of meter . . . it [rhythm or meter] all depends on the *pause*—the natural pause, the natural *lingering* of the voice according to the feeling—it is the hidden *emotional* pattern that makes poetry, not the obvious form . . . the ear gets a habit and becomes master, when the ebbing and lifting emotion should be master and the ear the transmitter. [But] if your ear has got stiff and a bit mechanical, *don't* blame my poetry . . . I don't write for your ear. This is the constant war, I reckon, between new expression and the habituated, mechanical transmitters and receivers of the human constitution.[14]

That last line, with its conscious rebellion against the traditional, the "habituated," the "mechanical," is perhaps most Whitmanesque, for Whitman, too, spoke grandiosely of the innovative "poet of the future." [15] Still, the entire metric Lawrence describes, as well as the vision of poetry that it implies, is clearly Whitmanesque.

Because they believe in the body, both Lawrence and Whitman work with the body's natural rhythms: against the regular blood pulse they set the varying rhythms of movement and breath and feeling to produce what Harry Moore has called Lawrence's "kinetic line" and what the recent Black Mountain school of American poets, led by the theorist Charles Olson, call the "breath unit." [16] "A Man at Play" and "The Dalliance," for example, get much of their rhythmic power from onward-moving repeated participles. Lacking both subject and verb, "The Dalliance" concentrates upon pure movement (and, in the midst of that, pure stasis). Similarly, the accretion of participles in "A Man at Play" implies action-in-progress, immediate action—life—which is going on right now, rather

[14] *Letters,* pp. 242–244.

[15] See Whitman, *Democratic Vistas,* Vol. II in the series *Complete Poems and Prose of Walt Whitman* (New York, 1948), p. 301.

[16] See Moore, *Life & Works,* p. 57, and Isidor Schneider, review of *Last Poems, The New Republic* 75 (June 7, 1933), comparing Lawrence's verse lines to "breaths." See also Charles Olson: "Verse now . . . must . . . put into itself certain . . . possibilities of the . . . breathing of the man who writes." ("Projective Verse," *Poetry New York* No. 3, 1950.)

than action that is finished, perfected, historical. Through both grammar and rhythm, the two poems suggest the vitality of bodies in motion, rather than fixed or decorated artifacts.

There is, however, a stylistic difference between Lawrence's free verse and Whitman's, a difference that perhaps depends more on the dissimilar backgrounds of the two writers than on any philosophical differences between them.[17] For one thing, because Lawrence is, as W. H. Auden notes, more personal than Whitman, his poems tend to be shorter and more lyrical than those of the American writer. Though Whitman wrote a number of brief lyrics like "The Dalliance" (especially the "Calamus" poems, *Drum Taps* and *Sands at Seventy*), his major works are ambitious in length as well as in scope, physically as well as spiritually expansive. His short poems—taken separately—often seem fragmentary, like parts seeking a whole, "sparkles from the wheel." Lawrence, on the other hand, wrote comparatively few really long poems after the two extravagant works that conclude *Look!*—"New Heaven and Earth" and "Manifesto"—and these are perhaps the most Whitmanesque poems he ever wrote.[18]

The relatively short poems Lawrence did write, moreover, though they frequently make use of Whitmanesque organic meter, often have certain conventional or traditional qualities absent from, say, "Song of Myself." Some of the poems in *Birds, Beasts and Flowers,* for instance, owe more to Lawrence's early reading in English Romantic poetry than they do to his reading of Whitman. Similarly, such works as "Gloire de Dijon" in *Look!,* or "Southern Night" in *Birds,*

[17] See, however, Lawrence's attack in *Studies* on "this awful Whitman . . . with the private soul leaking out of him," and his complaint in a 1913 letter that Whitman is a "man rougé with unsatisfiedness . . . pouring his seed . . . into the idea of humanity." (*Letters,* p. 257.)

[18] Though some of the *Birds, Beasts and Flowers* poems tend to be longer than the conventional lyric, they are more nearly overgrown *lyrics* than Whitman's long poems are. "Fish," for instance, is formally discrete in a way "Passage to India" and "Crossing Brooklyn Ferry" are not.

Beasts and Flowers, depend more upon the young man's brush with Imagism than they do upon his admiration for Whitman: the lines, like the poems themselves, are often shorter than Whitman's lines, with more of the Imagist tendency to concentrate on a single image or idea rather than catalogue a host of images and ideas.

Though "Leaves of Grass" was one of the young man's "great books," then, Lawrence was never dominated by Whitman. Rather, through an independent evolutionary process, he came to a point comparable to that at which Whitman began, and then adopted the aspects of Whitman's style toward which he felt most sympathetic—the use of parallel structure, the "organic" rhythm, and so forth. And it seems certain that it was his "new life" with Frieda that finally revealed the possibilities of Whitmanesque literary liberation to the young poet in transition.

iv

Despite its increasingly conscious use of Whitmanesque or Imagistic free verse, *Look!* still contains a good deal of conventional versification. Though the poet classed the collection among his "Unrhyming Poems," it includes a number of pieces technically indistinguishable from work that appeared in earlier volumes. While "Moonrise," the opening poem, is one of the few extant examples of a Lawrence poem written entirely in blank verse—Lawrence was notably bad at the form—"Martyr à la Mode," two poems later, is a strange combination of blank verse and rhymed couplets. "The Sea," another poem early in the volume, contains passages of blank verse along with lines more crudely versified. The book also includes ballads ("Ballad of a Wilful Woman") and ballad-like poems ("Hymn to Priapus") along with "songs" and the sort of self-invented forms—"icy kaleidoscopics," in Conrad Aiken's phrase—that Lawrence did not always manage well.

But a number of these apparently conventional rhyming poems are really a good deal more transitional than they appear. "Hymn to Priapus," for instance, might at first seem comparable to a successful rhyming poem like "Tease" and to some of the other early poems. Yet in "Hymn" Lawrence has come far from the smooth artifice of "Tease," and even from the conversational roughness of the dialect works. The skillfully irregular rhythms and unobtrusive rhymes in

> My love lies underground
> With her face upturned to mine,
> And her mouth unclosed in a last long kiss
> That ended her life and mine,

or

> Now I am going home
> Fulfilled and alone,
> I see the great Orion standing
> Looking down,

suggest that he is now consciously trying to write a poem that will, as he later advised Catherine Carswell, "use rhyme accidentally, not as a sort of draper's rule for measuring lines off." [19]

Perhaps, as in "Love on the Farm" and "Snapdragon," the two early poems to which "Hymn" is closest, the love-death tension that charges the work focused the poet's attention on a substance from which the style arose naturally, as if this particular form were implicit in the subject matter from the first. "Design in art," Lawrence was to write some years later, "is a recognition of the relation between . . . various elements in the creative flux. You can't *invent* a design [though he had tried to in some of the early "Rhyming Poems"]. You recognize it, in the fourth dimension, that is, with your blood and your bones, as well as your eyes." [20] Certainly the best of the rhymes that link the uneven lines of "Hymn" seem not to have been imposed on the poem but rather "recognized" by

[19] Letter to Catherine Carswell, January 11, 1916, *Letters*, p. 413.
[20] "Art and Morality," *Phoenix* (I), p. 525.

the poet as a part of his attentive meditation on "faithless and faithful" grief.

The same kind of apparently accidental design characterizes several unpublished early poems that either predate or are concurrent with the composition of "Hymn." "She Was a Good Little Wife" and "Pear-Blossom" are both shaped and unified as much by repetition as by rhyme. The rhymes tend to be either naively simple or faintly dissonant (blood/good, bosom/blossom), and, like the metrical scheme, the rhyme scheme (in "Pear-Blossom" a modified *terza rima*) is not consistent or regular in either poem. In both works the elasticity of the form, with its subtly varied repetitions, permitted the poet to attend to his subject matter with an intensity that was unusual even for this transitional period.

In "She Was a Good Little Wife," "the hum of the bees in the pear-tree bloom" becomes, as the speaker looks into the eyes of the woman, the hum of life in all things, the hum of desire in his own body.

> And the bustle of bees in the pear-tree bloom,
> And their subtle, eager booming,
>> Like a murmur of fire
>> Passed into my blood.

In "Pear-Blossom," a few necessary details are sketched in with selective simplicity, and the occasional substitution of repetition for rhyme, as well as the uneven line–lengths—lapsing and lingering with the poet's *feeling,* as Lawrence was to write to Marsh—reinforce the attentive intensity of the piece.

> The pear-blossom is a fountain of foam
> At your cottage-end; it falls back again
> In sprays and spurts of foam.
>
> The flowers against your window pane
> Are a 'poppy-show.' Peep, while you comb
> Your hair, peep out on the lane!—

That year, when the pear was out, my delight
As you crawled naked over me,
Your small breasts clumps of white

Pear-blossom hanging! And one small knee
Dug firm in my breast as you reached out right
To the window and the white pear-tree!

And you climbed back naked over me
As I lay on the bed, and you sat with the flowers on your thighs,
And looked at me;

And as I lay and looked in your eyes
You wept, and the bed trembled under me.
I was faint with surprise—

I am terrified of the pear-blossom
Round and white as a small bosom
With a nipple centre of red:

My God, to think it is gone for ever,
To think that you are gone for ever,
I am terrified you are dead.

Like "Piano," "Pear-Blossom" is elegiac in tone, a poem about nostalgia as well as a poem about the flower-like evanescence of perfect moments of love and sensual pleasure; and, as in "Piano," Lawrence is not afraid to surrender himself entirely, without irony, to his emotion. Yet, "cast down in the flood of remembrance," he skillfully fits his style to his mood. His ability to use rhyme "accidentally," together with his capacity for precise attention to feeling, suggests that he is already becoming "sufficiently sophisticated to wring the neck of sophistication."

—6
The Mystic Now:
Poetry of the Present

i

More than any other work, "Bei Hennef" may be the first truly "Lawrentian" poem Lawrence wrote; it is therefore fitting that when he revised *Look!* for inclusion in *The Collected Poems* of 1928, the mature poet added this piece—originally published in *Love Poems* (1913)—using the work as a prominent bridge between poems in his earlier ("Rhyming") and later ("Unrhyming") style. In "Bei Hennef," Lawrence cast caution to the winds, both emotionally and stylistically. Waiting to change trains at Hennef, en route from Trier to Waldbröl; sitting on the deserted station platform in the twilight, with "the little river twittering" by over its cold stones and the familiar shapes of the world going dark—"all the troubles and anxieties and pain/Gone under the twilight"—he wrote to Frieda that "Now for the first time during today, my detachment leaves me, and I know I only love you. The rest is nothing at all. And the promise of life with you is all richness. Now I know." [1] He committed himself absolutely to his emotion, in other words, and this intense attention to feeling perhaps made the poem's formal liberation inevitable.

Certainly Lawrence himself believed that "Bei Hennef" was a turning point for him. "The first few poems [of *Look!*]," he wrote years later, "belong to England and the end of the death-experience, but "Bei-Hennef," written in May 1912 by a river in

[1] Letter to Frieda Weekley, [?10] May, 1912, *Letters,* p. 117.

the Rhineland, starts the new cycle." [2] "And at last I know my love for you is here," he declared in the poem. "I can see it all, it is whole like the twilight." The "new cycle" begins with love and with attention to love's nuances. Now that everything is "shut up and gone to sleep," ordinary reality in shadow, the poet at last can attend both to his emotion, which is "large, so large I could not see it before,/Because of the little lights and flickers and interruptions," and to the scene of his emotion, the outer world that reflects the inner world of his feelings: "The wan, wondering look of the pale sky . . . and the soft 'sh!' of the river/That will last for ever."

Under pressure of suddenly intensified consciousness, the poem emerges gently, tentatively from what Lawrence saw as the hard shell of "coherent thought," the elaborate tortoise shell of technical artifice. Throughout, the crutch of rhyme is cast away, except for a few echoes naturally implicit in the material (river/ever, interruptions/pains). Rhythms are flowing and irregular, determined by the stress of feeling rather than the "dead" stress of the shell. "We are all like tortoises who have to smash their shells and creep forth tender and overvulnerable, but alive," Lawrence was to write J. O. Meredith three years later.[3] He might have been remembering himself on the station platform at Hennef, consciously abandoning the moral and aesthetic scruples of his young manhood and, the detachment of the artificer gone, setting out to attend completely to the great emotion of his new life, an emotion which, though forbidden, was "whole like the twilight."

Attending, he discovered that what he felt was "almost bliss," and this total honesty, this—to quote Alvarez again—"complete truth to feeling," was what finally gave the poem its form as well as its passional substance. The statement

> You are the call, and I am the answer,
> You are the wish, and I the fulfillment,
> You are the night, and I the day,

[2] *CP,* p. 28.
[3] Letter to J. O. Meredith, 2 November 1915, *Letters,* p. 374.

would have been rather banal, had not the young man, through the honesty of his attention, qualified it with "strange, how we suffer in spite of this!" And the poem might have been a shapeless emotional effusion had not the quality of Lawrence's attention produced the strongest rhyme in the work: "This is almost bliss" at the end of the first stanza, which rhymes with the last line, "Strange, how we suffer in spite of this!" Though this poem may be a creature that has smashed its shell, it has bones where bones are needed—to define from within its beginning and its end.

If Lawrence did write "Bei Hennef" on the station platform at Hennef, attending to his emotion even as he was in the grip of it, it is possible that his memory of this experience may have helped determine the poetics he was to outline in "Poetry of the Present," two years after *Look!* had appeared. He himself recognized the relevance of this essay to the poems in *Look!* "All this should have come as a preface to *Look! We Have Come Through!*," he remarked.[4] But in fact "Poetry of the Present" seems more than relevant to *Look!*; it seems to be a direct outcome both of the book and of the new life the book represents.

"Bei Hennef," for instance, like the ideal free verse Lawrence describes in this essay, was evidently "instantaneous like plasm" both in composition and in technique, "a direct utterance from the . . . whole man" in a way that the other poems we have so far discussed were not. Even "Pear-Blossom" is carefully shaped by rhyme and repetition; its mood is reminiscent; in Lawrence's sense it is poetry of the past. "Love on the Farm," "Snapdragon," and the best of the "mother poems" attend to situations that are already fixed, accomplished; they penetrate what has been and what is, rather than what is in the process of becoming. Only "A Man at Play," of all the poems we have so far examined, reflects in style as well

4 All references to "Poetry of the Present" are to the text in *CP,* pp. 181–186.

as substance something of the "seething" mutability of "the Now." Yet insofar as it is a fictionalized poem, a third person description of someone else's moment, "A Man at Play" would not be for Lawrence the sort of direct utterance that "Bei Hennef" is.

Such a distinction between first person and third person poetry may appear merely a quibble, especially since I have stressed the organic vitality of "A Man at Play." It might be argued, moreover, that Lawrence uses the man at play as an object of attention in the same way that he was later to use birds, beasts and flowers: as a vehicle for a certain kind of meditation. In *Birds, Beasts and Flowers,* however, there is a direct and overt involvement on the part of the speaker with his subject which, despite the immediacy of "A Man at Play," does not occur in the earlier poem; in *Birds, Beasts and Flowers,* as in "Bei Hennef" and a group of the most significant *Look!* poems, not only is the poem, like "A Man at Play," evolving before our eyes, but the poet himself is evolving, discovering. In "Bare Fig-Trees," for example, he gropes toward accurate perception:

> Fig-trees, weird fig-trees,
> Made of thick smooth silver,
> Made of sweet, untarnished silver in the sea-southern air—
> *I say untarnished but I mean opaque* (italics mine),

and in "Bei Hennef" he moves toward self-understanding:

> And at last I *know* [italics mine] my love for you is here;
> I can *see* it all . . .
> It is large, so large, I could not see it before. . . .
>
> What else? it is perfect enough.
> It is perfectly complete,
> You and I
> What more—?
>
> Strange, how we suffer in spite of this!

This sort of evolutionary process is the technique Lawrence first formulated in "Poetry of the Present"—"life surging itself into utterance at its very well-head." "Any man of real individuality," Lawrence wrote in his foreword to *Women in Love,* "tries to know and to understand what is happening, even in himself, as he goes along. This struggle for verbal consciousness should not be left out in art. It is a very great part of life. It is not superimposition of a theory. It is the passionate struggle into conscious being."

In *Look!,* then, Lawrence's effort of attention came together with the idea that the poem itself *happened* in a single moment of attention, or perhaps, rather, that it happened or became itself in a series of moments of attention. "The utterance is like a spasm, naked contact with all influences at once," Lawrence wrote in "Poetry of the Present," elaborating an idea he may have discovered in writing the *Look!* poems. "It does not want to get anywhere. It just takes place." But such an emotional or intellectual event cannot in his view be confined within the shell of conventional form. "The lovely form of metrical verse" requires a plan; the poet must have a rhyme scheme and a metrical structure in which to channel his thoughts.

But the essence of poetry of the present, as Lawrence conceives it, and as he wrote it in some of the *Look!* poems and in *Birds, Beasts and Flowers,* is its planlessness. Since the poem is at every moment discovering itself, "any externally-applied law would be mere shackles and death. The law must come each time from within." If it happens that "bliss" and "this" rhyme, that is simply a fact implicit in the nature of the material, Lawrence would say. In his poetry of the present "there is no rhythm which returns [deliberately] upon itself, no serpent of eternity with its tail in its own mouth." Such artificial recurrence would imply a kind of prior knowledge that Lawrence wants entirely to disavow. For him the poem is a perceptual experience that the poet himself—and the reader along with him—must undergo, an act of attention whose purpose is epistemological: discovery through a certain process of attention, and the process or experience of discovery is as much the subject of the poem as the ostensible subject itself. "The living plasm" of the present "vibrates unspeakably" and the poet's task is to speak the unspeakable. He does not recollect emotion in tranquillity; he discovers emotion in "the creative quick" of the moment of experience.

ii

Total absorption in the quick of experience, though it was to become a central tenet of Lawrence's thought by the time he had finished writing *Look!*, might not even have seemed possible to the young poet a few years earlier. He had to break free from his own past in order to form a new poetic allegiance, not to the "flood of remembrance" that informed so many of his novels, but to the moment of the present. At last, caught up in the quick of the new life, he was able to take a new look at life itself. Where he had felt himself abandoned in an incoherent universe, with no purpose but the purposeless "drift towards death," he now felt that "the most superb mystery we have hardly recognized: the immediate, instant self." The discontinuity of experience became a virtue for him, as it was for Walter Pater: [5] "Eternity is only an abstraction from the actual present. Infinity is only a great reservoir of recollection, or a reservoir of aspiration: man-made. The quivering, nimble hour of the present, this is the quick of Time. This is the immanence. The quick of the universe is the pulsating, carnal self, mysterious and palpable."

But just as this new vision of things affected Lawrence's poetic technique, confirming him in his originally almost in-

[5] See Conclusion to *Studies in the History of the Renaissance:* "Those impressions of the individual mind to which . . . experience dwindles down are in perpetual flight . . . each of them is limited by time, and . . . as time is infinitely divisible, each of them is infinitely divisible also; all that is actual in it being a single moment, gone while we try to apprehend it. . . . Our one chance lies in expanding that interval. . . . Great passions may give us this quickened sense of life."

stinctive movement toward free verse, so it had a profound thematic effect on the poems in *Look!*, influencing the writer to attempt ever more direct encounters with the quick of his own experience. Here again, however, we must confront a number of the objections to Lawrence's confessional poetry that were also leveled at some of the mother poems. For a poet to elevate his personal "moments" to art has seemed foolish as well as presumptuous to many readers. "They may have come through but I don't see why I should look," asserted Lawrence's one-time intellectual companion, Bertrand Russell; and even Aldous Huxley, who was to become one of the writer's most perceptive and positive critics, chimed in, complaining that "reading these poems was like opening the wrong bedroom door." [6]

If we view much of *Look!* as a mode of confessional or, in A. Alvarez' phrase, "extremist" poetry, however, these attacks seem needlessly dogmatic. Huxley and Russell appear to be demanding that Lawrence's poetry be public in a sense in which we no longer ask that poetry be public. As Alvarez has remarked, private or subjective verse has come to seem perhaps the most viable sort of poetry. In a world of violently changing moral and aesthetic values, "internal confusion transmuted into new kinds of artistic order becomes the most possible form of coherence." [7]

Yet more recent critics, even those who theoretically approve of confessional verse, are still bothered by some aspects of the autobiography in *Look!* What disturbs them most, however, is not the confessional nature of Lawrence's material but his way of dealing with it. Rather than approaching his experience ironically, standing back from emotion and handling it with surgical detachment as, Alvarez approvingly notes, Sylvia Plath handles her despair—"objectively, accurately and with a certain contempt" [8]—Lawrence surrenders himself to his feelings. "His relations with Frieda were too

[6] See John Jones, *The New Statesman, loc cit.*
[7] A. Alvarez, *TLS* (3/23/67), 232.   [8] *Ibid.*

94

much on top of him," John Jones concluded in 1957, and an anonymous writer in *TLS* added eight years later that "almost the whole of . . . *Look!* . . . crucial material though it may be for the biographer, is vitiated as poetry by an inability in Lawrence in any way to stand outside, to detach himself from the immediate pressure of experience." [9]

But detachment is precisely what Lawrence did not want. If his poems are "dramatization[s] of the experience of the moment," that is because he consciously attempted to enact rather than examine his experience. "Lawrence forced himself to be *exposed* to his experiences," Richard Hoggert remarks. "He refused to accept the second-rate compromise or the comfortable near-truth." [10] This is certainly true of the best poems in *Look!*. Given Lawrence's particular genius and the approach to poetry he evolved at least in part as a result of that genius, the poems in *Look!* that are least successful are usually those in which he is most "detached" from his experience, either because he tries to channel it into a predetermined form (as in "Roses on the Breakfast Table," "Lady Wife" or "Paradise Re-Entered") or because the experience itself is a failure of honesty (as in "She Looks Back") or a failure of discovery (as in "Manifesto").

In such cases, Lawrence himself might explain that the whole man has not been attending to the subject of the poem. The best poetry of the present, he had specified, is "a direct utterance from the instant, whole man. It is the soul and the mind and body surging at once, nothing left out." But in unsuccessful poetry of this sort something *is* left out—"detached." "She Looks Back," with its "curse against all mothers," is soulless in its failure of sympathy for the agony of Frieda and her children. "Manifesto" and, to a lesser extent, "New Heaven and Earth," are in a sense mindless in their inability to find a language that can fittingly express the soul's discoveries. Meaningless or banal phrases like "the unknown

---

[9] Jones, *loc. cit.* Also *TLS* (6/26/65), 725.
[10] Richard Hoggert, *The Listener* (Oct. 29, 1964), 673.

unknown" (in "New Heaven and Earth") or "man's sweetest harvest of the centuries, sweet, printed books," "so far, so good" and "these are my red-letter thanksgivings" (all in "Manifesto") indicate not that Lawrence was too close to his experience but rather that he was not close enough, that, since the poet's intellect was making no real effort of attention, the whole man was not participating in the utterance of the poem. Conversely, then, the most successful poems in *Look!* are generally those which most carefully attend to that immediate pressure of experience many critics have considered destructive of Lawrence's art.

"Frohnleichnam," for instance, though not the best of the works in *Look!*, succeeds because it attends wholly to the moment of experience: the existential moment becomes not only the occasion of the poem but also its theme. The style of the piece, like that of "Bei Hennef," is free, flowing "according to [the poem's] own laws," in directions that are at every moment newly found. Its only deliberate recurrences are a few subtle rhymes (balcony/slowly/birchtrees/Christi; first/birch; meet you/see you; communication/repudiation) that seem to be accidents of the material, and a series of those grammatical parallels which, rather than forcing the poem into preordained patterns, allow the poet to discover his experience, and thus himself, through a process of "continual, slightly modified repetition."

The poem begins with an incantatory exploration of the past, and with an attempt to understand the relevance of the past to the moment of the present:

> You have come your way, I have come my way;
> You have stepped across your people, carelessly, hurting them all;
> I have stepped across my people, and hurt them in spite of my care.
>
> But steadily, surely, and notwithstanding
> We have come our ways and met at last
> Here in this upper room.

The past must be confronted with honesty. It cannot be ignored, or, as in "She Looks Back," cursed. It must be taken into consideration, even if it is eventually to be repudiated. Only after such self-examination can "the mystic Now" be fully experienced.

The exploration of the present, too, is a process of discovery through "modified repetition" rather than artificial recurrence. As in "Bei Hennef" the "sensational immediacy" [11] of the physical world cannot be ignored.

> Here the balcony
> Overhangs the street where the bullock-wagons slowly
> Go by with their loads of green and silver birch-trees
> For the feast of Corpus-Christi.

> Here from the balcony
> We look over the growing wheat, where the jade-green river
> Goes between the pine-woods,
> Over and beyond to where the many mountains
> Stand in their blueness, flashing with snow and the morning.

The Bavarian scene is simple, idyllic, almost like a fairy tale. "Die Frieda und ich haben unser Zusammenleben in Beuerberg im Isartal angefang in Mai 1912—und wie schön es war," Lawrence was to write to Max Mohr in 1929, seventeen years later.[12]

But the physical setting, as in "Bei Hennef," is most significant as a reflection of the poet's subjective experience:

> I have done; a quiver of exultation goes through me, like the
>   first
> Breeze of the morning through a narrow white birch.
> You glow at last like the mountain tops when they catch
> Day and make magic in heaven.

The phrase "I have done" is perhaps most striking. What has the poet done? Obviously he has experienced; he has made

[11] J. Middleton Murry, "The Poems of D. H. Lawrence," in *D. H. Lawrence: Two Essays* (Cambridge, 1930).

[12] Quoted by Harry Moore, in *Heart*, p. 128.

love to his wife; he has in some sense done "the deed of life." [13] In another sense, though, he has done with the past; he has come to terms with it; he is ready to commit himself, as he did in "Bei Hennef," to the present, to this valley in the Bavarian tyrol which is also a valley in time, a moment of experience that, as we can see from the letter to Max Mohr, Lawrence wanted to preserve.

Even as he wrote the poem he must have realized, however, that the incarnate moment must elude all attempts to preserve it; that, in fact, the moment was precious because of its transiency:

> At last I can throw away world without end, and meet you
> Unsheathed and naked and narrow and white;
> At last you can throw immortality off, and I see you
> Glistening with all the moment and all your beauty.

"World without end"—the famous "heaven/haven" of lovers —must be rejected. This is the feast of Corpus Christi, of the *body* of Christ ("Frohnleichnam" literally means joyful corpse or joyful body), and so for Lawrence it becomes a feast of incarnation. The mortal body of his wife is "glistening with all the moment and all [her] beauty," but that beauty and the moment are identical, for the beauty with which Frieda "glistens" is the beauty of the moment.

Unlike Yeats's "Ledaean" Maud Gonne or Dante's angelic Beatrice, both neo-Platonic types of eternal, transcendent beauty, Frieda is for Lawrence entirely a mortal woman. In committing himself to the flesh, in doing the deed of life and having done with the abstract burden of the past, he has committed himself and his wife to the process, the movement, the *dance* of time.

> Shameless and callous I love you;
> Out of indifference I love you;
> Out of mockery we dance together,
> Out of the sunshine into the shadow,

[13] See Julian Moynahan, *The Deed of Life* (Princeton, 1963).

98

Passing across the shadow into the sunlight,
Out of sunlight to shadow.

As opposed to the perfectly symmetrical dance described in "Poetry of the Present," however, "where the hands link and loosen and link for the supreme moment of the end," this dance moves onward to no purpose, no end.[14] Each motion, like each moment of life, exists purely for itself. Sunshine and shadow alternate as light and darkness, day and night alternate, in a natural rhythm, for no reason except that they are part of the whole process.

As we dance
Your eyes take all of me in as a communication;
As we dance
I see you, ah, in full!
Only to dance together in triumph of being together
Two white ones, sharp, vindicated,
Shining and touching,
Is heaven of our own, sheer with repudiation.

Caught up in the rhythm of the dance, the lovers are at last fully able to attend to each other. In "First Morning," Lawrence had complained that when he was unable to "free myself from the past, those others—/ . . . our love was a confusion," but now that he has committed himself to the process of the present he realizes that "I see you, ah, in full!" just as his wife's eyes are now able to "take all of me in as a communication." Dancing together "in triumph," the lovers at last discover their true selves, their "instant, incarnate selves," and dancing in the joy of discovery they are assumed into the only heaven Lawrence can imagine, the heaven of the moment, a paradise "sheer"—purely itself—"with repudiation" of the past and of the future.

For Lawrence—and this idea becomes the theme of *Look!* and of some of the novels too—the moment of love is impor-

[14] This dance combines elements of two dances in *The Rainbow:* the pregnant Anna's dance of pride in Ch. VI, and the dance of life at Fred Brangwen's wedding in Ch. XI.

tant because a man best knows his own being through his knowledge of another. Such knowledge enables him to slough off the twin burdens of past and future, and to affirm the "creative quick" of the present when the lovers are together in the heaven of their momentary love. While for Dante his beloved was a messenger of immortality, and "the new life" to which she led him was that life of the spirit which transcends the temporal limitations of the flesh, for Lawrence, whose new life almost parodies Dante's, the beloved is a guide to the heaven immanent in the incarnate moment, and a messenger of that unknown which does not transcend but is implicit in the known.

iii

The relationship between the self, representing the known, and the other, incarnating the unknown, was to become, like the primacy of "the Now," a central Lawrentian preoccupation. The two ideas, however, are not just coincidentally but essentially related. The "love of man for a woman," Lawrence had written to Blanche Jennings in 1908, is next in importance to religion; "one should feel in it the force that keeps the menagerie on the move." By the time he and Frieda had set up house together he had elaborated this theory. Love had become not only the mysterious *primum mobile* of things, the life force, but also a mode of discovery. "It's astonishing how barbaric one gets with love," he wrote to Edward Garnett on 11 June 1912. "One finds oneself in the *Hinterland der Seele* . . . I never knew I was like this. What blasted fools the English are, fencing off the big wild scope of their natures."

By January 1913, about seven months later, his ideas of love, life, the lover or "other," and the unknown had become even more explicit. "A woman that I love sort of keeps me in direct communication with the unknown, in which otherwise I am a bit lost," he told Ernest Collings. And finally, "I believe there is no getting of a vision," he wrote to Gordon

Campbell in 1914, "before we get our souls fertilized by the *female*"—and "female" is "not necessarily woman but most obviously woman." [15] Only after such fertilization by the female, the incarnation of the moment, can one realize, in every sense, all "the tremendous unknown forces of life, coming unseen and unperceived as out of the desert to the Egyptians, and driving us, forcing us, destroying us if we do not submit to be swept away." Thus in "Humiliation," another typical *Look!* poem of discovery through gradually modified repetition and increasingly focused attention, the poet's fear that his beloved will leave him leads him to confront a truth that constitutes perhaps the major discovery of the book:

> God, that I have no choice!
> That my own fulfilment is up against me
> Timelessly!
> The burden of self-accomplishment!
> The charge of fulfilment!
> And God, that she is *necessary!*
> *Necessary,* and I have no choice!

Not only is Frieda necessary for her own sake, she is necessary because without her Lawrence cannot wholly become himself; he cannot wholly experience "the moment" of his life. If she—the other—left him, he would no longer, paradoxically, be himself: "The thing with my body that would go on living/Would not be me." Only when he can answer to his "blood, direct," through communion with his wife, can he, in the words of a famous letter to Ernest Collings, encounter "the mystery of the flame forever flowing, coming God knows how from out of practically nowhere, and being *itself*" [16]—can he, that is, encounter the mystery of selfhood. *Look!*, in short, is not only a book about the new life of the

[15] *Letters*, pp. 16, 132, 179, 291.
[16] Letter to Collings, *Letters*, p. 180. This is the letter which includes the (often misinterpreted) statement that "My great religion is a belief in the blood . . . as being wiser than the intellect." And here again Lawrence opts for *being* rather than (or as a form of) *knowledge*.

moment, but also a book about how the new life was achieved through the relationship with the poet's wife, and Lawrence, who at one time planned to call the collection *Poems of a Married Man,* celebrates marriage not only as the feast of life, but as the wedding of the self to the not-self, the known to the unknown, the spirit to the flesh.

Images of Frieda in which, significantly, she is seen as flower-like, an emblem of the natural world in all its mysterious vitality—her green eyes "clear like flowers undone/For the first time, now for the first time seen"; her body golden in the morning light, "her swung breasts . . . like full-blown/ Gloire de Dijon roses"—lead inevitably to the poet's own self-fulfillment: "I am myself at last; now I achieve/My very self." And this perfected, sexually ripened self is also flowerlike:

> No rose-bush heaving
> Its limpid sap to culmination has brought
> Itself more sheer and naked out of the green
> In stark-clear roses, than I to myself am brought.

Yet "the perfect rose" is, in the words of "Poetry of the Present," "only a running flame, emerging and flowing off, and never in any sense at rest, static, finished," so that, awakening from a night of love, the poet must discard the past once more. "There was something I ought to remember: and yet/I did not remember. Why should I?" The immediate present, charged with life, is more than enough. "The running lights/ And the airy primulas, oblivious/Of the impending bee," a "hairy big bee" who might be said to represent the doom of the future that continually threatens the moment of the present, are "fair enough sights."

Though *Look!* is filled with such celebrations of marriage and of "the mystic Now" marriage makes possible, the poems that most successfully explore these matters are the companion pieces "Song of a Man Who Is Loved," "Song of a Man Who Is Not Loved," and "Song of a Man Who Has Come

Through," especially the latter two. Not surprisingly, therefore, these are among the most successful poems in the volume.

"Song of a Man Who Is Not Loved" is rhymed and shaped into rigidly patterned stanzas, as if Lawrence meant to suggest that the fluid act of attention, the poetry of the present which discovers its own form as it confronts its meaning, cannot take place without love, the wedding to the unknown. And this inability to deal with the "tremendous unknown forces of life" that sweep into the psyche like a great wind "out of the desert to the Egyptians," this impotence, is the true subject of the poem. To the man who is not loved, "the space of the world is immense, before me and around me;/ If I turn quickly, I am terrified feeling space surround me." Without the communion that transfigures every moment, a man must be overwhelmed by the "insanity of space" that had horrified the poet in "Humiliation." Where the man who is loved, becoming serenely himself ("I am that I am"), has attained this sure selfhood because of his relationship with his lover, the unloved man sees himself as "isolated in the universe," and he wonders "what effect I can have." Lacking a vital connection with what is outside him, he is unable to perceive coherence in anything, least of all in himself. "My hands wave under/The heavens like specks of dust that are floating asunder."

Not only is he unable to harness the creative forces of his own psyche, however; he is in imminent danger of being destroyed by them. "I hold myself up, and feel a big wind blowing/Me like a gadfly into the dusk." Incoherent and helpless in the grip of the disintegrating winds out of the desert of the soul, the man who is not loved inevitably loses all sense of selfhood and purpose.

> So much there is outside of me, so infinitely
> Small am I, what matter if minutely
> I beat my way, to be lost immediately?

> How shall I flatter myself that I can do
> Anything in such immensity? I am too
> Little to count in the wind that drifts me through.

In the "Song of a Man Who Has Come Through," on the other hand, Lawrence uses the same wind imagery to show how love can transform destruction to creation, how the principle of death and the principle of life are merely two aspects of the same mystery. "Coming through," as distinct from being loved, is the next step in the process that both creates selfhood and enables the established self to "get" ("have" and "beget") a "vision." In the argument of *Look!* Lawrence had said that

After much struggling and loss in love and in the world of men, the protagonist throws in his lot with a woman who is already married. Together they go into another country, she perforce leaving her children behind. The conflict of love and hate goes on between the man and the woman, and between these two and the world around them, till it reaches some sort of conclusion, they transcend into some condition of blessedness.

Love, in other words, is not an automatic cure for the diseases of the soul; it is a hard-won "condition of blessedness" [17] that one can attain only intermittently and after much struggle. One must struggle to cast off the abstractions of past and future, the burdens of guilt and grief. One must exorcise the terrors of egotism (which fears the loss of self that precedes the discovery of a new self) and scepticism (which doubts the existence of the unknown in the known). It was this struggle to which Lawrence referred when he wrote to Garnett in June 1912 of "the inner war which is waged between people who love each other, a war out of which comes knowledge." [18]

Where the "Song of a Man Who Is Loved," therefore, deals

[17] It is noteworthy that Lawrence deleted the phrase "condition of blessedness" from the *Poems* version of this Argument. Perhaps after years of marriage he no longer believed so fervently in the beatitudes of his youth.

[18] Letter to E. Garnett, 29 June 1912, *Letters,* p. 132.

with the peace that can be redeemed from the chaos in which the loveless man is drifting, the "Song of a Man Who Has Come Through" defines a more mystical experience. Because "the one quality of love is that it universalizes the individual," [19] the man who has come through is able to transcend the limitations of his former self. "Not I, not I, but the wind that blows through me!" he exults, surrendering himself to the unknown forces of life, the "fine, fine wind" that "is blowing the new direction of time." For this wind of creativity is the wind of "the moment, the immediate present," and the "new direction of time" is the future that issues from the present, from "the source, the creative quick," just as the "unrestful, ungraspable poetry of the sheer present . . . sweeps past forever, like a wind that is forever in passage and unchainable."

In the "Song of a Man Who Has Come Through," as in "Poetry of the Present," complete submission to this unknown force of life (the opposite, again, of the detachment demanded by some critics) is the necessary prelude to that discovery which is simultaneously love and knowledge, and incidentally art, the creative vision:

> Not I, not I, but the wind that blows through me!
> A fine wind is blowing the new direction of Time.
> If only I let it bear me, carry me, if only it carry me!
> If only I am sensitive, subtle, oh, delicate, a winged gift!
> If only, most lovely of all, I yield myself and am borrowed
> By the fine, fine wind that takes its course through the chaos
>   of the world
> Like a fine, an exquisite chisel, a wedge-blade inserted;
> If only I am keen and hard like the sheer tip of a wedge
> Driven by invisible blows,
> The rock will split, we shall come at the wonder, we shall find
>   the Hesperides.

Unlike the constricted song of the unloved man, this song is a perfect illustration of the technique as well as the theory

[19] *Letters*, p. 374.

of poetry of the present. Focusing on the strength of the wind within the soul, the poem is "wind-like in its transit," as Lawrence thought such verse should be, a structure of swiftly and skillfully modified parallels and repetitions. Unrestrained by conventional rhymes and rhythms the long first stanza sweeps forward to its climax: the (projected) moment of discovery. "The rock will split, we shall come at the wonder, we shall find the Hesperides."

"The wonder" is at the heart of the poem just as in Lawrence's view wonder—the mystery—is at the heart of life, the "wonder-journey." Significantly, Lawrence substituted "wonder" in proof for "word." For him, wonder inheres in knowledge of the unknown while the word simply involves the formulation of that knowledge, and, writing in a tradition of visionary attention rather than craftsmanly discipline, he consistently preferred to emphasize the mystery of such paradoxical knowledge rather than the mastery of its formulation in language.

> Oh, for the wonder that bubbles into my soul,
> I would be a good fountain, a good well-head,
> Would blur no whisper, spoil no expression.

The word exists to express the wonder, rather than wonder to generate the word. Here, as the poet anticipates his moment of transformation, the stanzas become shorter, the lines terser. Having been swept this far by the inspiring wind of the unknown present, he waits for some final revelation. "One has only to say to one's soul, be still, and let be what will be," Lawrence was to write to Lady Ottoline Morrell in 1916. "One can do absolutely nothing any more, with one's will. Yet still one can be an open door, or at least an unlatched door, for the new era to come in by." [20]

Even in this "condition of blessedness," however, he is attacked by the oldest human fears, fears of the destructive unknown:

[20] *Letters*, p. 412.

What is the knocking?
What is the knocking at the door in the night?
It is somebody wants to do us harm.

But the mysterious, frightening visitors are part of the "condition of blessedness."

No, no, it is the three strange angels.
Admit them, admit them.

From the "heaven of our own, sheer with repudiation" into which the lovers danced at the end of "Frohnleichnam," from the paradise they re-entered through the "strait gate of passion" in "Paradise Re-Entered," these angels of the unknown appear to transfigure not only the private world of the lovers but their vision of all reality, and to lead them to a "New Heaven and Earth."

That they are *three* strange angels suggests these visitants are the celestial messengers who visited Abraham in Genesis 18, bringing—appropriately enough in terms of Lawrence's poem—word of Sarah's renewed fertility.[21] But then they may also be the Hesperides, mentioned earlier in the piece, the three guardians of the isles of the blessed.[22] In any case, their exact identity is less significant than the mystery of their sudden appearance out of the unknown and the nature of their blessedness. No matter what allusions Lawrence may have intended, they are, like Rilke's angels, "almost deadly birds of the soul," [23] harbingers of the creative-destructive mystery implicit in every moment of life. Admitting them, affirming them, the poet admits and integrates the unknown into himself. He admits the demon against whom he had so frequently struggled in his young manhood; he admits the "magnificent ghosts of the darkness," the "powers of night," to whom he

[21] Cf. *Genesis* 18, 1, 2.
[22] See Robert Hogan, "Lawrence's 'Song of a Man Who Came Through,'" *Explicator*, XVII (1959), item 51.
[23] Rilke, *Duino Elegies*, tr. J. B. Leishman and Stephen Spender (N.Y., 1939), p. 29.

had prayed in "Mutilation." And admitting all these forces, he at last becomes, as he told Ottoline Morrell, "a oneness"; [24] he reaches "the source, the issue" of creativity in himself, the wellsprings of wonder that make love and utterance possible. For the process is self-renewing: through love the poet "knows" the mystery, and through the force of the mystery he is able to utter—to commune—and thus to love.

Like many of Lawrence's later poems, then, the "Song of a Man Who Has Come Through" is a poem about the process of healing and making whole that Jung called "integration." The poet's loving relationship with another has made possible his confrontation of a second, even more significant other, the other who is also, paradoxically, himself; for the unconscious (the well of wonder, the source of the mysterious wind) is both self and not-self. Lawrence felt, like Jung, that one becomes most fully oneself when one is in touch, through whatever means, with this unconscious not-self ("Not I, but the wind") which is at the same time, in a mystical sense, one's truest self.[25]

[24] *Letters,* p. 428.
[25] "Wholeness of the personality is achieved [in Jung's system] . . . when . . . consciousness and the unconscious are linked together in a living relation." Jolande Jacobi, *The Psychology of C. G. Jung* (Yale, 1962), p. 102. An analogous process described by Jung is that of "coming to consciousness" (*Bewusstwerdung*), which involves "the unfolding of a deeper, wider . . . more receptive consciousness [with an] unobstructed connection with the unconscious." (Jacobi, p. 45)

—7
She Who Is the Other:
The Substance of Change

i

Because this integration of the other into the self entails at least a momentary loss of familiar daytime consciousness, a number of the poems in *Look!* deal not only with the themes of love, otherness, and the mystery of the moment, but also with the cycle of spiritual and emotional death and rebirth that was another characteristic Lawrentian theme.[1] "New Heaven and Earth" most obviously follows this pattern. "Weary of the world," of ordinary reality in which "everything was tainted with myself," in which, in a kind of perversion of all Lawrence's theories of love and knowledge, "I kissed the woman I loved,/And God of horror, I was kissing also myself," the poet dies—dies of a surfeit of himself, presumably—and is "trodden to nought in the sour black earth/ Of the tomb."

Yet when he has surrendered himself completely, when he is "nothing," then, as in the "Song of a Man Who Has Come Through," he is suddenly "everything . . . myself, the same as before, yet unaccountably new." Risen, renewed, he com-

---

[1] See *Women in Love*, ch. 3, in which Birkin speaks of "the great dark knowledge you can't have in your head," a remark reminiscent of Jacobi's comment that *bewusstwerdung* "is not equivalent to [rational] consciousness in the usual sense." (*loc. cit*) Later Birkin adds that "You've got to learn not-to-be, before you can come into being." And in ch. 14 he tells Ursula that he wants "love that is like sleep, like being born again."

munes with the unknown new world of his wife's body, and in the course of this sexual communion the whole cycle of dying and rising recurs, only this time it is "oblivion of uttermost living" that mysteriously destroys and recreates the lover.

> Sightless and strong oblivion in utter life takes possession of
> me!
> The unknown, strong current of life supreme
> drowns me and sweeps me away and holds me down
> to the sources of mystery, in the depths,
> extinguishes there my risen resurrected life
> and kindles it further at the core of utter mystery.

Though it is the most obvious, "New Heaven and Earth" is not the only poem that deals with this pattern of death and resurrection. In "And oh—that the man I am might cease to be," one of the first poems in the book, Lawrence had wished "the sunshine would stop" and the daytime world "would be crushed out/between two valves of darkness," and in "In the Dark" he had admonished his wife that it "rests/One to be quenched, to be given up, to be gone in the dark." In "A Young Wife" the speaker, caught up in "the pain of loving," notes how

> The darkness starts up where
> You stand, and the night comes through
> Your eyes when you look at me.
>
> Ah never before did I see
> The shadows that live in the sun!

He (or she, for the speaker may be the young wife) sees that

> At the foot of each glowing thing
> A night lies looking up

and knows that "the faint fine seethe in the air"

> is death still seething where
> The wildflower shakes its bell
> And the skylark twinkles blue,

and the peculiar electricity of the relationship between love and death in this piece recalls the compounding of love and death in such early poems as "Love on the Farm," "Cherry Robbers" and "Snapdragon."

In the poems toward the end of *Look!* where he had more fully developed his ideas about the self and the other, the known and the unknown, Lawrence elaborated this almost instinctive perception into an even richer theory about the relationship of love and death, a theory that is perhaps comparable to the ideas that underlie some versions of the Tristan and Isolde story. In fact, *Look!* fits both dramatically and philosophically into what we might call the "Tristan tradition" in a number of ways.

Dramatically, the basic situation is the same, though in some details it differs from the legend of Tristan. Like Tristan, Lawrence usurps the wife of an older mentor—Ernest Weekley, his teacher at the University of Nottingham. Burdened with guilt at having betrayed a man who has been kind to both, the lovers escape to another country (in Gottfried's *Tristan* another part of the forest), where, through treachery or misunderstanding in most early versions of *Tristan* and through the nature of the situation in *Look!*, they eventually fall out with one another: in the Tristan legend they are separated, while in *Look!* "the conflict of love and hate goes on between the man and the woman, and between these two and the world around them." In the end, however, they are united (in Gottfried literally, in Wagner literally and figuratively, in Lawrence figuratively) by a *Liebestod* which in Lawrence, and to a certain extent in Wagner, represents a death to ordinary life and a mystical renewal in oblivion.

It is not likely that Lawrence had any conscious intention of following the Tristan story, just as he undoubtedly had no intention of parodying *La Vita Nuova*. Yet just as he must have been familiar with Dante, he was familiar with Tristan: he had seen Wagner's *Tristan und Isolde* and certainly knew the medieval legend itself. "I do like Cornwall," he wrote to J. D. Beresford in January 1916. "It is still something like King Arthur and Tristan. It has never taken the Anglo-Saxon civilisation, the Anglo-Saxon sort of Christianity." [2] He does not, then, need to have alluded to these works for us to find that there is a real relationship between them and *Look!*.[3]

Like Gottfried, Thomas, Wagner and Dante, Lawrence was contributing his vision of the sexual mystery to the European literature of love. Like Wagner, he saw this meeting of man and woman as an encounter of the known with the unknown, the self with the not-self, a drowning of the self in "sightless and strong oblivion." Like Gottfried, whose "Cave of Lovers" is a shrine dedicated to the moment and mystery of love, he approached the powerful sexual and generative force with religious reverence. As for Gottfried the heaven of the lovers was "heaven on earth," so for Lawrence the lovers in their dance of incarnation achieve the only heaven that has meaning, a heaven that is, unlike the eternal heaven to which Beatrice guides Dante, purely momentary. "What better food could they have for body or soul?" writes Gottfried of the lovers in their cave of earthly bliss. "Man was there with woman, woman there with man. What else should they be needing? They had what they were meant to have, they had reached the goal of their desire." [4] And for Lawrence, too, the new world of his wife's flesh is the end of his desire, the goal of all knowledge.

ii

It might be objected that though *Look!* is thematically comparable to works like *Tristan* or *La Vita Nuova*, it is so much

[2] *Letters*, p. 409. Cf. letter to Catherine Carswell, 11 January 1916, *Letters*, p. 413; also Boulton, pp. 44, 119.

[3] Though he did allude once in *Look!* to the Tristan legend, significantly in "Elysium," the poem which follows "New Heaven and Earth," where he wrote (echoing Hardy) "I have found a place . . . Lonelier than Lyonesse." (*CP*, p. 261).

[4] Gottfried von Strassbourg, *Tristan,* tr. A. T. Hatto (Penguin, 1960), p. 263.

inferior in structure and execution as to vitiate the comparison. Lawrence did attempt, through the arrangement of the poems and through the formulation of an "argument," to convince the reader that, as he said in the original Foreword to the book,

These poems should not be considered separately, as so many single pieces. They are intended as an essential story, or history, or confession, unfolding one from the other in organic development, the whole revealing the intrinsic experience of a man during the crisis of manhood, when he marries and comes into himself.

But though he managed to sketch what we might consider a prototype of novels like *Women in Love* and *The Rainbow,* and though *Look!* included a number of innovative and successful poems, the work as a whole never actually became more than what Graham Hough calls "a long verse-journal in which we are to expect neither completeness in the parts nor an Aristotelian plot, but simply the development of an intelligible train of feeling through a number of fragmentary occasions." And since many of the poems are failures either of knowledge or technique, one might conclude with Hough that the volume "shows a decline from the earlier work" and that "the series survives as a biographical document; otherwise only by a few beautiful and incidental poems." [5] It would seem, in other words, that Lawrence's poetic art, except in a few cases, was not equal to his ambition, and that therefore the *Tristan* and *La Vita Nuova* parallels are specious. Conrad Aiken, indeed, goes so far as to wonder "whether the theme of *Look!* had better not have been treated in prose."

The story, such as it is, emerges, it is true, and with many deliciously clear *moments,* some of them lyric and piercing, but with a good deal that remains in question. It is the poet writing very much as a novelist, and all too often forgetting that the passage from the novel to the poem is among other things a passage from the cumulative to the selective. [6]

[5] Hough, pp. 195, 200.   [6] Aiken, p. 103.

Yet it is possible to answer most of these objections and to show that, despite its relatively modest means, *Look!* shares some of the intensity of *Tristan* and *La Vita Nuova*. The ratio of failure to success in Lawrence's early "rhyming poems," after all, is quite high—no lower, certainly, than in *Look!*. More important, it is for once futile to speculate that Lawrence might better have handled the subject of a group of poems in prose because, as I have tried to show, the theme of *Look!* was one, in terms of his aesthetic, especially suited to poetry: the theme of knowledge, of discovery. The fragmentary "verse-journal" form was inherent for him in the theme of knowledge through love as the music of the *Liebestod* was implicit for Wagner in the death of Tristan and Isolde, and it is significant that the title Lawrence finally chose for the book was one which stressed perception, an epistemological imperative—*Look! We Have Come Through!*—for the entire work is, ultimately, an extended act of self-discovery. Through poetry, Lawrence thought, the poet discovers himself, his style, and the nature of his subject, just as the lover, through sexual communion, discovers the unknown within the known, the divine within the human.

If, wearied by the subjective trap of his own "sole self," the poet must eventually turn away from himself, it is his experience of love that enables him, finally, to turn outward, away from the subjective mode. For Lawrence, then, the knowledge gained through *Look!* goes beyond the mystical knowledge of the *Liebestod,* and becomes a form of self-knowledge that permits important artistic as well as emotional growth. Though the writer was accused by some critics of yielding to excessive subjectivity in *Look!,* it was precisely because of his commitment to subjectivity in so many of these poems that he was eventually able to attain greater objectivity in *Birds, Beasts and Flowers.* Having once learned how to yield himself and be "borrowed by the fine, fine wind" that whirled out of the deeper recesses of his psyche, he was finally able to attempt "self-accomplishment" not merely through self-knowledge and through the direct experience of love, but through indirect knowledge of a kind of absolute otherness, the otherness of non-human life. "It is one life which is passing away from us, one 'I' is dying," Lawrence wrote to Katherine Mansfield in 1915, about the process *Look!* records, a process of what Keats would have called "soul-making." "But there is another [self] coming into being, which is the happy, creative you." [7] We might say of him, using the same metaphor, that he himself had to undergo the subjective love-death of *Look!* in order to become "the happy, creative" poet who reached full maturity in *Birds, Beasts and Flowers.*

In the meantime, as Aiken admits, a number of "deliciously clear moments" remain in the book, a few of them moments which for the poet were instants of almost miraculous discovery and which for the reader are instances of very fine poetry. "Never, never, never could one conceive what love is, beforehand, never," Lawrence wrote to Sally Hopkin shortly after his honeymoon.[8] Already he was groping toward the discovery that inspires and informs the best of the poems in *Look!* "Life *can* be great—quite godlike. It *can* be so. God be thanked I have proved it."

[7] *Letters,* p. 401.   [8] *Ibid.,* p. 130.

PART III

THE OTHER SIDE
OF SILENCE

One may see the divine in natural objects.
                                    "Making Pictures"

—8

Life into Art: The Biographical
Background of *Birds, Beasts and Flowers*

i

Though the war plays little overt part in Lawrence's cre-
ative work of the period,[1] much of the personal drama of
Look! was played out against the social darkness of a world
that seemed to him convulsed with self-hatred. It is in such
a world that we can best imagine the unloved man blown into
the abyss of nihilism, for only through the support of an af-
firmative "other" can the luckier man who is loved resist the
chaos that "rattles like shrapnel" through a disintegrating
society. "The War finished me: it was the spear through the
side of all sorrows and hopes," Lawrence wrote to Lady
Cynthia Asquith on January 31, 1915, six months after fight-
ing had broken out.[2] Having deliberately sensitized himself to
experience, he saw perhaps more quickly than most people
that the life before the war was "like another life—we *were*
happy," and he felt almost at once that "it breaks my heart,
this war (but) it is the business of the artist to follow it home
to the heart of the individual fighter . . . the desire of war—
the *will* to war." [3]

[1] Lawrence made little use of his wartime experience before he wrote
Kangaroo. "England, My England" was an exception to this rule, as was
the small group of war poems he wrote.
[2] *Letters*, p. 309.
[3] Letter to Harriet Monroe, 17 November 1914, *Letters*, p. 295.

Yet just as he was able to draw personal and artistic strength from the idea of death and rebirth through love, so Lawrence was sometimes able to see the war as "a necessary autumnal process of disintegration" that would hasten the inevitable destruction of the old order and clear the way for "a new heaven and a new earth." When he was in this mood even the image of a zeppelin "high up like a bright golden finger, quite small, among a fragile incandescence of clouds," could take on visionary radiance, and it was no doubt this concept of war as a terrible necessity that enabled him finally to come through these years as a man and a writer.[4] "Homer was wrong in saying, 'would that strife might pass away from among Gods and men!' He did not see that he was praying for the destruction of the universe; for, if his prayer were heard, all things would pass away," Lawrence was eventually to write in the epigraph to the "Reptiles" section of *Birds, Beasts and Flowers*.[5]

Even without, however, so Yeatsian a dogma as "in the tension of opposites all things have their being," the writer was able to derive creative energy from the European cataclysm. Certainly the contrast between the "corpse-cold" world of wartime England and the relative freedom of postwar Italy, to which the Lawrences escaped as soon as possible, must have been at least as great as the contrast between the death-haunted young poet-novelist of 1911 and the "godlike" lover that he became in 1912. During the war *The Rainbow* and *Women in Love* were suppressed or unpublished in England; Lawrence and Frieda were harassed by civil and military authorities even to the verge of arrest on espionage charges; and, unable to leave the country, they were also unable to live decently in it. His liberation from the "long, ashy-grey coffin" [6] of such a life, as much as his earlier liberation into an interior universe

[4] *Letters,* pp. 375, 366.

[5] He was paraphrasing John Burnet's *Early Greek Philosophy* (London, 1892, 1908, 1920), p. 164: "War . . . is the father and king of all things, in the world as in human society; and Homer's wish that strife might cease was really a prayer for the destruction of the world."

[6] *The Lost Girl,* ch. XIV: "The Journey Across."

of love, must have provided Lawrence with a new experience of coming through.

The composition of *Look!* had in several ways prepared the poet to write *Birds, Beasts and Flowers:* it gave him a style—free verse, the poetry of the present—and a technique—attentive, anti-ironic submission to the "tremendous unknown forces of life." Now the war and postwar experiences modified his view of things in another way: they transformed his subject matter, confirming him in a temporary but violent hostility to warring humanity ("I hate humanity so much I can only think with friendliness of the dead") [7] and at the same time focusing his attention on the peace of an inhuman natural order—Italy with its primal sea and raging flowers; Australia with its antediluvian bush; New Mexico with its pride of mountains—that had reassuringly endured.

Coming through after the long struggle to be truly married, after the long death-in-life of the war, Lawrence and Frieda found that they had stepped from a human world of dead shapes and hard edges into a universe alive with radiant objects. "Living in Sicily after the war years was like coming to life again," [8] Frieda wrote years later, in *Not I, But the Wind,* and living once more with enough to eat and the "dawn-coast" of the Mediterranean at his feet, it was only natural that Lawrence should begin to turn from his wartime preoccupation with the flaws of western society to a celebration of the natural world, just as it was inevitable that having achieved a "oneness" in his marriage, he should be able to turn away from the subjectivity of *Look!* to a consideration of the kingdom of otherness inhabited by all that is non-human (birds, beasts and flowers), no longer human (dead men, dead cultures) or not yet human (the future, and by extension the creative mystery that forms the future).

"The very fact of established polarity between the two," Lawrence wrote in *Psychoanalysis and the Unconscious* of the

[7] Letter to Cynthia Asquith, 1 September 1916, *Letters,* p. 470.
[8] Frieda Lawrence, *Not I, But the Wind,* p. 100.

relationship between mother and child, "maintains that corre-
spondence between the individual entity and the external uni-
verse which is the clue to all growth and development." [9] The
phrase can be applied equally to that "established polarity"
between Lawrence and Frieda which enabled him to with-
stand the trials of the war years and after the war to write a
book of poems charged with life in all its energy and its variety,
a book where despite the occasional bitterness of the poet but
because of his reverent attention, each thing in "the external
universe," as G. M. Hopkins had said, "selves—goes itself."

ii

Lawrence's bitterness cannot be discounted, for it was one
of the wellsprings of *Birds, Beasts and Flowers*. Out of his
wonder at the inhuman otherness of the creative mystery
within himself, the young poet had written to Gordon Camp-
bell in 1914 that "we want to realise the tremendous *non-
human* quality of life—it is wonderful." [10] But it was only
during the war that he learned the contempt for humanity and
the compensatory respect for non-human nature that was to
become one of the central themes of much of his work from
about 1918 to 1926.

I watch, in the morning when I wake up, a thrush on the wall
outside the window—not a thrush, a blackbird [he wrote in 1915 to
Lady Ottoline Morrell] and he sings, opening his beak. It is a
strange thing to watch his singing, opening his beak and giving
out his calls and warblings, then remaining silent. He looks so re-
mote, so buried in primeval silence, standing there on the wall
and bethinking himself, then opening his beak to make the strange,
strong sounds. He seems as if his singing were a sort of talking to
himself, or of thinking aloud his strongest thoughts. I wish I was a
blackbird, like him. I hate men.

Already a habit of close attention to the non-human had been
established, and it had been established in conjunction with a

[9] *Psychoanalysis and the Unconscious*, p. 28.   [10] *Letters*, p. 291.

rejection of humanity. "There is a wagtail sitting on the gate-post," Lawrence wrote to Lady Ottoline. "I see how sweet and swift heaven is. But hell is slow and creeping and viscous and insect-teeming: as is this Europe now, this England." [11]

No doubt it was this feeling for the fundamental innocence of non-human nature, as opposed to the guilt of "this crawling, sniffling, spunkless brood of humanity," [12] that motivated Birkin's well-known, anti-human declaration in *Women in Love:* "You yourself [he is addressing Ursula], don't you find it a beautiful clean thought, a world empty of people, just un-interrupted grass, and a hare sitting up?" Earlier in the book he had attempted a fuller exposition of the idea.

If mankind is destroyed, if our race is destroyed like Sodom, and there is this beautiful evening with the luminous land and trees, I am satisfied. That which informs it all is there, and can never be lost. After all, what is mankind but just one expression of the in-comprehensible. And if mankind passes away, it will only mean that this particular expression is completed, and done. That which is expressed, and that which is to be expressed, cannot be dimin-ished. There it is, in the shining evening. Let mankind pass away —time it did.

By "the incomprehensible" Lawrence meant at this point the creative-destructive mystery, that mystery he was later to identify as "the Living God"; and to approach, to revere, in some sense to comprehend this "incomprehensible" had always been the aim of his best art. But now, because the war had accelerated what might have been an inevitable process, the maturing writer moved from his earlier consideration of the mystery as it is manifested in mankind to an engagement with the mystery itself as it more purely appears in the otherness of birds, beasts and flowers. Like Ursula, he learned to love "best of all the animals that were single and unsocial as [he himself] was. [He] loved the horses and cows in the field. Each

[11] *Ibid.,* pp. 339, 338.
[12] Letter to Earl Brewster, 2 November 1921. *Ibid.,* p. 669.

was single and to itself, magical. It was incapable of soulfulness and tragedy which [he] detested so profoundly." [13]

But if, in the later war years and early postwar years, we repeatedly hear from Lawrence that "I am terribly weary in my soul of all things in the world of man," and that consolation is only to be found in the inhuman otherness of nature, we cannot help feeling that such an attitude, though understandable, is not the healthiest one for a practicing novelist whose subject is "the whole man alive." Perhaps inevitably, this anti-human attitude, more than the suppression of *The Rainbow* and the unpublishability of *Women in Love,* led directly to Lawrence's temporary loss of interest in the novel and the consequent weakness of *The Lost Girl, Aaron's Rod,* and *Kangaroo.* "I find people ultimately boring," he told Murry in a letter in 1917, and added, logically enough, that "you can't have fiction without people. So fiction does not, at the bottom, interest me any more." [14]

Although he had rejected both fiction and humanity, however, Lawrence did not abandon his literary engagement with the "mystery." But in letters to Murry and Mrs. Carswell he revealed that "philosophy interests me most now." [15] He was working on *Studies in Classic American Literature,* and later in this period would turn to *Psychoanalysis and the Unconscious* and *Fantasia of the Unconscious,* all of which, though philosophical and expository in form, were essentially creative efforts to comprehend the "incomprehensible." "That which is expressed, and that which is to be expressed, cannot be diminished," Birkin had concluded, and certainly that which Lawrence had to express did not diminish, despite his changing attitudes. Rather, his literary energy flowed into new channels. Thus it is that in a period when his novelistic abilities seemed to falter, he was able to produce *Studies,* his finest

[13] *Women in Love,* Chs. XI: "An Island," V: "In the Train," and XIX: "Moony."
[14] *Letters,* pp. 558, 514.   [15] *Ibid.,* pp. 514–515.

volume of literary criticism; *Sea and Sardinia,* some of his most brilliant travel-writing; and, most important for our purposes, *Birds, Beasts and Flowers,* his best volume of poetry so far.

iii

The puzzle of Lawrence's so-called "leadership" novels has long preoccupied critics, many of whom find the question of why the author's novelistic art failed between *The Lost Girl* and *The Plumed Serpent* almost more challenging than an exploration of the success of such works as *The Rainbow* and *Women in Love.* That Lawrence violently rejected humanity in these years does not seem as significant to some of these critics as one specific form his rejection took, the form of a contempt for humanity which logically required that the novelist (and a few Calvinistically favored others) exercise a natural right, even an obligation, to guide inferior mankind. Despairing of humanity as he did, Lawrence wrote that "I don't believe either in liberty or democracy. I believe in actual, sacred, inspired authority: I believe in the divine right of natural aristocracy . . . the sacred duty to wield undisputed authority." [16] Like Carlyle or Nietzsche, two writers with whom he is often (and rightly) compared, he developed a concept of "superhuman" heroism that was a key element in his thought at least until the middle twenties.

But such a belief, even more than the vehement but vague misanthropy out of which it grew, might seem seriously to have impaired the writer's *general* creativity; for creativity must depend, as Lawrence himself decided, on an ability to intuit the truth of another being. A man who can write in all seriousness (and though he is speaking through the mask of Lilly, it is Lawrence who is speaking), "I can't do with folk who teem by the billion like the Chinese and Japs and orientals . . . the flea-bitten Asiatics. Even niggers are better than Asiatics, though they are wallowers," seems certainly to be in a state of

[16] Letter to Mabel Luhan, 10 April 1922. *Ibid.,* p. 700.

hysteria that must blind him to reality and preclude real creative attention.[17]

Paradoxically, though, Lawrence's leadership obsession, as much as his temporary but keen misanthropy, rather than impairing his poetic abilities, made possible the success of *Birds, Beasts and Flowers*. The novel, as historians of the genre have often observed, is essentially a bourgeois, democratic art form. Characters in a novel must seem to be self-propelled; they must always retain at least the illusion of freedom that characters in tragedy inevitably lose. The tragic hero has to come to terms with his fate; the protagonist of a novel must in a sense create his fate. Thus the central obligation of a character in a novel is the obligation of self-achievement, "the charge of fulfilment" as Lawrence put it in "Humiliation," a burden implicitly laid on all the major characters in Lawrence's novels from *Sons and Lovers* to *Women in Love*. But the leadership obsession of the post-war years not only supplanted Lawrence's earlier, novelistic concern with self-achievement, it precluded such a concern. If some men are "natural kings," born with "the right, the sacred duty to wield undisputed authority," then everything has already been predetermined, the fate of both leaders and followers already established, and the struggle for self-achievement becomes, as in *Aaron's Rod*, a mere meaningless drifting from place to place and person to person in search of some external "force of life," human or divine, to take the place of that creative sense of self-determination no longer felt within.

Yet when the leader is found, the relationship between leader and follower that is established (the relationship, for instance, of Aaron and Lilly), because of the fixedness of the characters—the one authoritative, the other submissive—can never really provide material for a successful novel. As Lawrence pointed out, the job of the novel is to explore the "subtle inter-relatedness" of all things. But in the leader-follower

[17] *Aaron's Rod,* Ch. 19: "Low-Water Mark."

polarity such inter-relatedness is limited or merely perfunctory, reduced almost by definition to the barest minimum: the one commands, the other submits; there are no complex reciprocal pressures to record. Even if the follower rebels, he is doomed, once he has been typed by the novelist, either to learn once more to submit, and be saved, or to refuse to submit, and be lost. In either case there is no question of independent or even of contingent self-achievement, and therefore no chance for the fluid relativity that an exploration of the many forms of human self-achievement entails. The submission of the follower must be complete, without qualification or variation; the power of the leader is pure, in a sense single rather than multiple in its manifestations, and absolute.

But this concept of power that is inherent and predetermined like a tragic fate, while it may be antithetical to the novel, is an idea that has always been compatible with the writing of poetry, particularly the sort of anti-ironic, visionary poetry Lawrence wrote best. The poet, as Lawrence sees him, is not simply an ordinary person who happens to have mastered a particularly difficult craft. Rather, like the aristocrat—the leader, the hero or the priest—he is a special kind of being, set off from other men by a power which, like the power of the aristocrat, is mysteriously his—the power of *in*sight, of visionary attention. To this power he surrenders himself absolutely, and insofar as it radiates out of him, marking him off from other men, it is to this power in him that other men submit, or should submit, awe-stricken.

> Weave a circle round him thrice
> And close your eyes with holy dread,
> For he on honey dew hath fed
> And drunk the milk of paradise,

wrote Coleridge of the artist-seer, and "Accept it, recognise the natural power in the man . . . and give it homage," wrote Lawrence of the aristocrat, who might be the visionary artist as well as the heroic master. "Then there is a great joy, an up-lifting, and a potency passes from the powerful to the less powerful." [18]

Homage to the mystery of power, in other words, is as essential to Lawrence's extremely Romantic concept of poetry as to the relationship of leader and follower. And such homage necessarily precludes irony, just as the leadership novels precluded any real exploration of the complexities of self-achievement. The profound egalitarianism which, as Lawrence recognized, is an absolute prerequisite of true democracy, permits the sort of relativism that leads to an ironic—Prufrockian—qualification of experience: "Who am I to ask the overwhelming question? Why not so-and-so?" In the aristocratic Lawrentian system, however, both leader and follower must commit themselves, without ironic reservations, to the power both apprehend as mysteriously fluent in the leader. And therefore the world-vision of both is not ironic, like that of most modern, egalitarian men, but anti-ironic, wholly concentrated on the wonder of power. There is "Ich dien [I serve] in all the weary irony of his mien," writes Lawrence in "Elephant" of the Prince of Wales, who is enduring a Pera Hera in Ceylon, for the contemporary non-leader is weary, diffident, unable to commit himself wholly to any special magic in himself. But he himself would be different, the aristocratic poet declares. He would "stand and hold . . . three feathers above the world,/And say to them . . . *Serve me, I am meet to be served,/Being royal of the gods.*"

But if the anti-ironic ideas of singleness and wonder inevitably developed out of tendencies that made it natural that Lawrence's poetry would be more successful than much of his fiction in this period, they brought him to *Birds, Beasts and Flowers* in another way, too, for one of the things that most fascinated him about birds, beasts and flowers was what he called their "singleness." Like Ursula in *Women in Love* he appears to have loved the "horses and cows in the field" be-

[18] *Apocalypse*, pp. 24–25.

cause "each was single and to itself, magical," because each had a quality of possessing itself completely, without any "soulfulness" or any "detestable social principle."

All things non-human seem to have the quality of being, as Sartre puts it, *en soi;* [19] they seem totally *in themselves,* incapable of knowing or imagining that which negates themselves. In a sense they *are* so fully that they cannot imagine *not being.* Only man, who is in Sartre's system *pour soi* rather than *en soi,* can imagine, and therefore create, nothingness, and thus only man is capable of "soulfulness and tragedy." ("Nor hope nor dread attend a dying animal," Yeats, more succinctly than Sartre, declared; "Man has created death.") More, only man is capable of irony, for his vision, a vision simultaneously of being and not-being, is in this respect inevitably ironic (though the visionary poet, like the leader, attempts to suppress his ironic tendencies), whereas one of the qualities that give the non-human its distinctive otherness is its purely anti-ironic selfhood, for to be single and to oneself, to be *en soi,* is necessarily to be incapable of irony.

In a way, then, Lawrence's bitterness about the war both directly and indirectly made possible the writing of *Birds, Beasts and Flowers,* and, more, the success of the poems in that volume. His bitterness inspired a temporary but intense misanthropy, resulting in a contempt for the mass of mankind and a belief in the "sacred right" of a specially chosen few to guide the many. Such a leadership obsession, however, incompatible as it was with the writing of successful novels, led to the composition of visionary, anti-ironic poetry. More, it necessitated content as well as form, not only the genre of *Birds, Beasts and Flowers* but also its subject matter.

[19] Cf. *Being and Nothingness,* tr. Hazel E. Barnes (New York, 1953), esp. "Introduction," and ch. VI. Sartre has always dealt with non-human *objects* (rather than *creatures*) as examples of the *en soi,* but the distinction between men and objects implied by the categories of *en soi* and *pour soi* seems inevitably to extend itself into a distinction between human and non-human life. (I am indebted to Marjorie Grene for illuminating discussions of Sartre.)

Yet it would be overstating the case to explain *Birds, Beasts and Flowers* solely as an expression of Lawrence's reaction against certain forms and ideas, for there was a real relationship, too, between the success of his marriage and his ripening poetic abilities. "Whatever happened on the surface of everyday life," Frieda recalled in the preface to *Not I, But the Wind*, "there blossomed the certainty of the unalterable bond between us, and of the ever-present wonder of the world around us."[20] Like Birkin, after he and Ursula had pledged themselves to each other, Lawrence, coming through with Frieda, may have found in himself "a strange new wakefulness, the tension of his consciousness broken . . . a simple glimmering awareness, as if he had just come awake, like a thing that is born, like a bird when it comes out of an egg, into a new universe." [21] That universe, inhuman and full of wonder, is the universe of *Birds, Beasts and Flowers.*

[20] Frieda Lawrence, p. vi.
[21] *Women in Love,* Ch. XXIII: "Excurse."

—9

The Natural Flowering:
Style as Process

i

Just as in the earliest years of his literary career there had been an important relationship between the various forms in which Lawrence worked, so at this point in the middle of his career his poetry was deeply affected by his prolonged experimentation with the essay. As Graham Hough has pointed out, the poems in *Birds, Beasts and Flowers* are "closely related to a prose form, the imaginative essay, in which fragments of external reality—things, people, places—appear, and the effort is to present them with the maximum of objectivity and vividness—yet to offer them as objects of contemplation in themselves, not as elements in a narrative or exercises in self-revelation." [1]

It is not often enough noted that Lawrence was among the best contemporary writers of the personal essay, but once we recall his mastery of that form, the nature as well as the success of *Birds, Beasts and Flowers* becomes clearer. The aesthetic presuppositions behind both Lawrence's essays and his free verse of this period have much in common. For one thing, the writing of essays, unlike the writing of novels, ap-

[1] Hough, pp. 205–206. Though Hough also suggests that these poems "are not lyrics . . . not verse as song," a strong case might be made for the *ode*-like nature of some, e.g. "Medlars and Sorb Apples." Harold Bloom discusses this quality in an excellent article, cited earlier. But the essay-analogy seems to me the most consistently useful approach.

pears to be an activity specially suited to the aristocratic temper Lawrence was cultivating in these years. As Lawrence interprets his role, the essayist, like the Romantic poet, must feel himself capable of extraordinary insight into an object or problem. Like the leader, he must have a special power to deal with things, and because of the limitations of the form in which he works, he must deal with things in their singleness rather than in their "inter-relatedness."

Accordingly, Lawrence's best essays are not primarily informational (though the literary and travel essays alike depend on certain basic structurings of fact). Their central purpose is knowledge through meditation: they *essay* to know something, not wholly and extensively, in all its parts and implications, but intuitively, often obliquely, fragmentarily; not through orderly ratiocination, but through emotional perception. As Lawrence's style evolved, the style of his essays became increasingly idiosyncratic, increasingly elliptical, spontaneous and jazzy, as though reflecting the process rather than the product of thought. Perhaps the most notable characteristic of *Studies* or *Fantasia* is that their author seems himself to be in the process of discovering his ideas as he writes. But Lawrence's developing hostility to formalism, to "the aesthetic quality . . . which takes the edge off everything and makes it seem 'boiled down,' " tended inevitably to such elliptical, unfinished-seeming attempts at intuitional understanding rather than to ordered and balanced artistic wholes.[2]

Correspondingly, the style of the *Birds, Beasts and Flowers* poems is from the first casual, improvisational, unfinished: a style that functions not only as a means of communication but as a process of discovery. The beginning of a piece does not contain the end, or even necessarily imply it, though, as Lawrence asserts, "the end cracks open with the beginning."

[2] *Etruscan Places,* p. 174. Cf. also Birkin's remark in *Women in Love* (Ch. XXIV) that "You must leave your surroundings sketchy, unfinished, so that you are never . . . confined, never dominated."

> You tell me I am wrong.
> Who are you, who is anybody to tell me I am wrong?
> I am not wrong,

he declares in the first lines of "Pomegranate," and

> Would you like to throw a stone at me?
> Here, take all that's left of my peach,

he offers in the opening of "Peach," and in both passages he admits the reader into the intimacy of his own meditations so that the sort of implicit dialogue out of which his essays often evolve can be set up between them.

Such a dialectic is one of Lawrence's chief stylistic devices in *Birds, Beasts and Flowers.* "In Syracuse . . . no doubt you have forgotten the pomegranate trees in flower," he tells the reader almost contemptuously in "Pomegranate," making him an unseen antagonist, a foil in the dialectic of discovery, "whereas at Venice," he continues, the pomegranates were "actually growing" and "now in Tuscany" there are "pomegranates to warm your hands at . . ."

> And, if you dare, the fissure!

> Do you mean to tell me you will see no fissure?
> Do you prefer to look on the plain side?

> For all that, the setting suns are open,
> The end cracks open with the beginning:
> Rosy, tender, glittering within the fissure.

Not only do such imaginary objections enable him to move dramatically to his conclusion, but if no one looked "on the plain" or static side of nature, the poems themselves would not be processes of thought but rather what Lawrence disliked at this point: "mere" representations of static truths.

Lawrence does not use only the reader, however, as a foil in his dynamic evolution of the poem, though he almost always involves his audience in some kind of struggle. In a number of the *Birds, Beasts and Flowers* pieces, he addresses his subject.

"When did you start your tricks,/Monsieur?" he asks the mosquito, for instance, or "Tuscan cypresses,/What is it?" he inquires, and "you know what it is to be born alone,/Baby tortoise!" he exclaims, setting up an implicit dialogue between himself and the inhuman object of his attention. This sort of dialogue even at times becomes explicit, as at the end of "Man and Bat," when the bat is made to "chirp," seeing the poet

> on this terrace, writing:
> *There he sits, the long loud one!*
> *But I am greater than he . . .*
> *I escaped him,*

a comment that neatly puts the problem of otherness into a simultaneously terrifying and amusing perspective.

A third kind of dialectic Lawrence occasionally constructs in these poems is the dialogue within himself, the debate between one aspect of himself and another. Such an internal struggle seems, of course, by definition ironic. Yet, as always, Lawrence deals with the irony of his subject straightforwardly, anti-ironically. In "Snake," for instance, the poet relates his own conflicting attitudes toward the godly but deadly serpent:

> The voice of my education said to me
> He must be killed . . .
>
> And voices in me said, If you were a man
> You would take a stick and break him now, and finish him off.
>
> But must I confess how I liked him,
> How glad I was he had come like a guest in quiet to drink at my water trough.

Then he turns to the reader to include *him* too (though as judge rather than adversary) in the dialectical process:

> Was it cowardice, that I dared not kill him?
> Was it perversity, that I longed to talk to him?
> Was it humility to feel so honoured?

But his conclusion—"And so, I missed my chance with one of the lords/Of life"—implies no ironies. His final position is one to which he is wholly committed, though it is the dialectic that charges the words "I felt so honoured . . . he seemed to me again like a king" with special meaning. Had the lordliness of the snake not been opposed by the "voices of my accursed human education," were the snake not "a king in exile, uncrowned in the underworld," he would be less a king, too static a creature to represent the vital dialectic of nature— "for in the tension of opposites all things have their being."

ii

It is especially significant that Lawrence uses this dialectical process in his attempt to "comprehend" nature in these poems, because the natural world as it emerges throughout *Birds, Beasts and Flowers* is itself a world of processes rather than appearances, of inexorable motion rather than stillness. Ultimately every step in the process of the pomegranate, for instance, is of equal importance, just as every step in the poet's essay to comprehend the pomegranate is as important as every other. There is no *final* knowledge, no real epiphany.[3] "The end cracks open with the beginning," which is why no step in the process of discovery can be left out. The pomegranate trees flower and produce fruit; the fruit ripens and cracks open— and it is its germinal brokenness that Lawrence takes as emblematic of himself and of this book, which is to be a series of processes of exploration into the mysterious inhuman process of nature. "For my part," the poet tells his invisible listener, "I prefer my heart to be broken./It is so lovely, dawn-kaleidoscopic within the crack."

This emphasis on natural as well as artistic process had been characteristic of *Look!*, too, but there it was specifically on the creative achievement of the self through love that Lawrence concentrated his energies, for until he had become himself he

[3] "Man is always sold in his search for final KNOWLEDGE," Lawrence declared in his Poe essay (*Studies*, p. 81).

135

could not actively engage the external world. As a corollary of this, the fluidity of the poems in that volume, their "wind-like transit" from thought to thought and discovery to discovery was essentially a process of self-knowledge, a "struggle into verbal consciousness." In writing *Birds, Beasts and Flowers,* however, with the experience of *Look!* behind him like a fire he need no longer fan but from which he could now draw warmth, Lawrence not only used poetry as a kind of essay-like process of discovery more consistently and objectively, but also, obliquely, elliptically, and fragmentarily, affirmed the good of process itself, of flux rather than fixity.

For this reason, it is noteworthy that many of the epigraphs in the book are taken from John Burnet's *Early Greek Philosophy.* There are no Platonic or Neoplatonic absolutes in the poet's thought of this period (except perhaps the absolute image of the philosopher or poet-king); rather, nature in exactly Hopkins' sense, is "an Heraclitean fire," and each living object must be seen not as an expression of any one form but rather in terms of every stage of its existence. The peach, for instance, like the pomegranate, is at once bloom, flesh and stone. It is not "round and finished like a billiard ball," the poet scornfully assures his reader, though "it would have been if man had made it." On the contrary, like that of the pomegranate, its essence consists of all the accidents of its development and can only, therefore, be grasped through a temporal process that reflects its own nature.

Like all the other fruits and flowers, trees and animals of *Birds, Beasts and Flowers,* the peach is not, then, as Graham Hough suggests it is, an object of "timeless contemplation," but rather an object of contemplation in time, knowledge of which is never "finished" or perfected because it is itself never finished or perfected.

Why the groove?
Why the lovely, bivalve roundness?
Why the ripple down the sphere?
Why the suggestion of incision?

Lawrence asks, half-parodying Blake, but unlike Blake he literally holds the answer in his hand: "all that's left of my peach"—the stone. Even after the poet has almost completely assimilated the peach, after he has eaten it, something remains, that central mystery which is

> Wrinkled with secrets
> And hard with the intention to keep them.

Nothing in nature is ever finished—"the end cracks open with the beginning"—and there is, ultimately, no comprehending the incomprehensible, no fixing the flux.

iii

This essential process of nature is not merely reflected in the dialectical movement of some of the essay-poems in *Birds, Beasts and Flowers,* but also in a newly witty use of the kind of "continual, slightly modified repetition" that we first noticed on a large scale in *Look!* "Now the emotional mind, if we may be allowed to say so, is not logical," Lawrence was to write some years later in a preface to his translation of Verga's *Cavalleria Rusticana* which elaborates the ideas of the earlier foreword to *Women in Love.*

It is a psychological fact that when we are thinking emotionally or passionately, thinking and feeling at the same time, we do not think rationally: and therefore, and therefore, and therefore. Instead, the mind makes curious swoops and circles. It touches the point of pain or interest, then sweeps away again in a cycle, coils round and approaches again the point of pain or interest. There is a curious spiral rhythm, and the mind approaches again and again to the point of concern . . . as [it] stoops to the quarry, then leaves it without striking, soars, hovers, turns, swoops, stoops again, still does not strike, yet is nearer, nearer, reels away again, wheels off into the air, even forgets, quite forgets, yet again turns, bends, circles slowly, swoops and stoops again, until at last there is the closing in and the clutch of a decision or a resolve.[4]

4 *Phoenix* (I), pp. 249–250.

A fuller and more precise description of the repetitive, meditative process of many of the *Birds, Beasts and Flowers* poems can hardly be imagined. "Bare Fig-Trees," for instance, is, like many of the *Look!* poems, a structure of repetitions, the poet's aim in it a discovery or "verbal consciousness" of his subject. Because thought and feeling become one, however, in this process of knowing, Lawrence gradually and wittily blends emotion and perception in a central conceit discovered through the spiraling repetitions of the mind in action. The fig-tree, he tells us, is made of "thick, smooth-fleshed silver, dull only as human limbs are dull/With the life-lustre,/Nude with the dim light of full, healthy life." But "smooth-fleshed silver" leads through "slightly modified repetitions" to "nude with the dim light of full, healthy life," which in its turn spirals outward to a vision of the "great, complicated, nude fig-tree" as "rather like an octopus . . . flourishing from the rock in a mysterious arrogance," while the octopus complication naturally develops into that central conceit of the tree as a live and "many-branching candelabrum" that is to have so many ramifications.

Lawrence's "abstract thought is always deep reaching," Anaïs Nin perceptively remarks, because "it is really concrete; it passes through the channels of the senses." [5] Certainly in this case his equation of the tree with democracy seems inevitable because of the immediacy of his description of the tree itself. We do not feel that Lawrence has in any way forced his material to take this direction, but rather that his mind and the material, in their "churning, spiraling interaction," inevitably brought forth this discovery. We feel, moreover, because of the completeness of what Miss Nin calls Lawrence's "sensorial penetration," that this discovery of the nature of the tree is most significant not because it reveals that democracy is like a bare fig-tree (a mechanical, allegorical point), but rather because it reveals that a fig-tree is like democracy, "each [twig]

[5] Nin, p. 63.

imperiously over-equal to each, equality over-reaching itself."

Lawrence's idea, in other words, like his form, is implicit in the nature of his material, and his style, whether dialectic or repetitive, is a technique for penetrating to some central image that reveals the essence of his subject. The final implication of the candelabrum–democracy conceit is reached, interestingly, through the slightest verbal modification of all: a kind of punning repetition not as often associated with Lawrence's style as it should be, though such purely verbal wit is, of course, a primary form of "slightly modified repetition." "Oh weird Demos, where every twig is the arch twig," the poet exclaims, and a concentration on the word itself—"Demos, Demos, Demos!"—leads him inevitably to "Demon, too," a moral judgment that what he is encountering is a "wicked fig-tree, equality puzzle, with your self-conscious secret fruits." [6]

Like the dialectical processes discussed earlier, this witty, punning, subtly repetitious style was a mode increasingly natural to Lawrence in prose as well as verse, especially in the improvisational prose of essays and letters. *Studies* glitters with such passages of verbal play; the section on Hawthorne's characterization of little Pearl, for example, aptly illustrates the style:

> She will be blameless, will Pearl, come what may.
>
> And the world is simply a string of Pearls to-day. And America is a whole rope of these absolutely immaculate pearls, who can't sin, let them do what they may. . . .
>
> By Hawthorne's day it was already Pearl. Before swine, of course. There never yet was a Pearl that wasn't cast before swine. It's part of her game, part of her pearldom. . . .
>
> And yet, oh, Pearl, there's a Nemesis even for you.
>
> There's a Doom, Pearl.
>
> Doom! What a beautiful northern word. Doom.

[6] Similarly, Lawrence's comic insight into the "libidinous" she-goat—that "she is brittle as brimstone"—evolves with witty inevitability from his observation that "she looks back . . . with a cold, sardonic stare" and is therefore "sardonic, sardonyx, rock of cold fire."

The Doom of the Pearl.
Who will write that Allegory? [7]

The letters, too, are full of witty miniature essays like the virtuoso letter of January 9, 1924, to Willard Johnson that begins "Yesterday came the Horse [the magazine *The Laughing Horse* edited by Johnson] capering a trifle woodenly" and continues through a spiraling series of discoveries through repetition to the "final clutch of a resolve": "I've got to ride, centaur, on a blue stallion." [8]

It might be objected, however, that some of the assumptions underlying this style-process analogy are fallacious, that such writing is only apparently spontaneous process, and that this "anti-rhetorical style," as Robert Langbaum has remarked, "is itself a rhetoric." [9] Certainly much modern criticism is based upon an opposite vision of the poem as object: a "well-wrought urn," a "little world made cunningly." A poem, in this more prevalent view, is accomplished, perfected; it is, in a sense, as Wyndham Lewis asserts in *Tarr,* already dead. Yet, as Father Walter Ong reminds us, "all verbalization, including all literature, is radically a cry . . . a modification of one's exhalation of breath which retains the intimate connection with life which we find in breath itself," and it is clear that this was Lawrence's belief.[10] To the extent, though, that a cry or sound is also a process—sound waves moving in time as well as in space—all poetry is process rather than object, unfinished rather than finished, and our use of the present tense in synopsis and paraphrase is a tacit acknowledgment that though a writer may himself be dead, his work is still *happening.*

[7] *Studies,* p. 113.
[8] See *Letters,* pp. 767–770: "Dear old Azure Horse, Turquoise Horse, Hobby Horse, Trojan Horse with a few scared heroes in your belly: Horse, laughing your Horse Laugh, you do actually ramp in with a bit of horse sense" and so forth.
[9] See Langbaum, *The Poetry of Experience* (New York, 1957), p. 33.
[10] Walter J. Ong, "A Dialectic of Aural and Objective Correlatives," in John Oliver Perry, ed. *Approaches to the Poem* (San Francisco, 1965), pp. 242–243.

For Lawrence, then, as for Walter Pater, who may well have helped shape his ideas on this matter, "not the fruit of experience, but experience itself" is in a sense "the end" of art,[11] and both his mature poetic style (which he finally evolved in *Birds, Beasts and Flowers*) and his attempts at spontaneous composition (which may have determined that style) [12] clearly indicate this belief. Even as objects independent of their creator, the dialectic or repetitive essay-poems in *Birds, Beasts and Flowers* preserve the gestures of their composition in the way that action-painting retains the movements of the artist. Moreover, insofar as a poem is for Lawrence a *body*—and we saw earlier the importance of this analogy—it is both an object and a process, an existent and his existence. Yet just as the existent and his existence are inseparable, so for Lawrence body and process are inseparable. Just as there is no moment in the life of a body when it is not somehow in motion, so there is no moment for Lawrence when a poem ceases to participate in the process of its creation, when it ceases to be not only an essay or attempt at discovery, but, indeed, an *act* of attention.

iv

So far this discussion of the stylistic technique of *Birds, Beasts and Flowers* has emphasized the act or process of percep-

---

[11] Walter Pater, "Conclusion" to *The Renaissance*. Like Pater's, Lawrence's thought stresses the *flux* of experience, as I noted in Pt. III, and the young Lawrence must have known his Pater as well as he knew his Swinburne. Pater's metaphor of a "hard, gemlike flame," however, suggests a potential interest in *fixing* the flux which Lawrence didn't have, but which many of Pater's disciples in the "aesthetic" nineties elaborated upon, converting the "gemlike flame" to a "flamelike gem."

[12] Like Rilke (who reported writing the *Sonnets to Orpheus* in "a single breathless act of obedience" and some of the *Duino Elegies* in the same way) and Keats (who apparently wrote the "Ode to a Nightingale" in two or three hours), Lawrence often attempted spontaneous composition. "The demon . . . makes his own form . . . and is unchangeable," he wrote in his Foreword to *Poems*. "And *Birds, Beasts, and Flowers* are practically untouched."

tion that gives distinctive quality to most of the poems in the volume. That it is a process primarily of *attention* should not, however, be overlooked. As in earlier poems, where Lawrence's attention to his subject falters or fails, his poem almost invariably fails. More specifically, his "essays" on birds, beasts and flowers fail when they become polemical expositions of the writer's own social and metaphysical theories rather than penetrations of the object or creature he is contemplating.

The volume's flaws, then, are inherent in the prose form to which its verses are most closely allied, just as the flaws of some of Lawrence's early novelistic poems were inherent in the young man's tendency to over-fictionalize. Insofar as the *Birds, Beasts and Flowers* poems are polemical essays, almost mechanical impositions of ideas on their subjects, their poetic energy is vitiated by what should more properly, in terms of Lawrence's own concept of poetry, be prose concerns. Insofar, however, as they are attempts at a kind of attention "so intent and so submissive," as Graham Hough puts it, "to the real nature of the external objects that all mere subjective effusion is burned away," they are the most consistently successful poems Lawrence ever wrote. But when Lawrence "uses animal life or nature to illustrate some human principle or emotion, his plants and animals lose their identities, and his abstractions are made no clearer." [13]

Lawrence himself recognized this often obstructive conflict between the polemic and the mystic in his own nature. "There was his wonderful, desirable, life-rapidity," he writes of himself-as-Birkin in *Women in Love,* "and there was at the same time this ridiculous, mean effacement into a Salvator Mundi of a Sunday-school teacher, a prig of the stiffest type." [14] If it was "life-rapidity," the ability swiftly and almost mystically to apprehend life essences, out of which the wonderfully attentive "Peach" and "Pomegranate," "Sicilian Cyclamens," "Medlars and Sorb Apples," "Almond-Blossom," and many others

[13] Hough, pp. 205–206. Nin, p. 102.
[14] *Women in Love,* Ch. XI: "An Island."

flowered, we can surely blame "Figs," "Hibiscus and Salvia Flowers," "Purple Anemones," "Bibble," and "Elephant" on the often inattentive and stridently theoretical "Salvator Mundi."

"Figs," for instance, after a precise description of the fruit itself

> Folded upon itself, enclosed like any Mohammedan woman,
> Its nakedness all within walls, its flowering forever unseen,
> One small way of access only, and this close-curtained from the light,

imposes on the female analogy what J. Middleton Murry calls a "hard, bleak quality of dogmatic asseveration" [15] that has nothing to do with the fig, but everything to do with the poet's own antifeminist preoccupations:

> [When] the fig has kept her secret long enough.
> . . . it explodes, and you see through the fissure the scarlet.
> And the fig is finished, the year is over.
>
> That's how the fig dies, showing her crimson through the purple slit
>
> Like a wound, the exposure of her secret, on the open day.
> Like a prostitute, the bursten fig, making a show of her secret.
>
> That's how women die too.
> The year is fallen over-ripe,
> The year of our women.
> The year of our women is fallen over-ripe.
> The secret is laid bare.
> And rottenness soon sets in.
> The year of our women is fallen over-ripe.

Some readers might note that in many of the poems in *Birds, Beasts and Flowers,* Lawrence seems to use his subject merely as a starting-point for the consideration of some larger prob-

[15] Murry. *Two Essays,* p. 3.

lem. His conclusions often seem like emotional abstractions from the specific material of the piece:

> For my part, I prefer my heart to be broken.
> It is so lovely, dawn-kaleidoscopic, within the crack.

or

> Demos, Demos, Demos!
> Demon, too,
> Wicked fig-tree, equality puzzle, with your self-conscious secret fruits.

But general as these conclusions are, they both develop directly from the material of the poem, and apply as surely to that material as to anything else. Each is a culmination of that process of descriptive attention which constitutes the body of the poem; neither is discontinuous from the main line of the work. We saw, for instance, that the central point of "Bare Fig-Trees" was that the fig tree was like a democracy, rather than that a democracy was like a fig tree. But in "Figs" Lawrence seems far more interested in the notion that women are like figs than in the idea that figs are like women. Thus "Bare Fig-Trees" concludes with a reference essentially to the *tree,* while "Figs" ends with a question about women:

> What then, when women the world over have all bursten into self-assertion?
> And bursten figs won't keep?

The terms in which Lawrence views the fate of the fig, moreover—"the secret is laid bare/And rottenness soon sets in . . . Ripe figs won't keep"—almost directly contradict the judgment with which he concludes "Pomegranate": "I prefer my heart to be broken./It is so lovely, dawn-kaleidoscopic, within the crack." In "Pomegranate" the poet sees the process of nature as a positive good because he is writing of it for its own sake: the flowering, the fruiting, the ripening and the rupture are natural, inevitable. Lawrence knows, attending to

144

reality rather than intending morality, that it would be absurd to object on some human ground to so mysterious and uncontrollable a process. "Do you mean it is wrong, the gold-filmed skin, integument, shown ruptured?" he asks mockingly.

In "Figs" however, the rupture of the fig becomes an obscenity because the writer is not attending to his real subject, the fig as it is in nature, but rather imposing a puritanical, human horror on nature.

> The fig dies, showing her crimson through the purple slit,
> Like a wound, the exposure of her secret, in the open day,
> Like a prostitute, the bursten fig, making a show of her secret.

There is death and rebirth in nature, but no prostitution; there is mystery, but no morality: so that, especially in Lawrence's terms, to see nature in such a way is merely to label (or libel) the "incomprehensible."

"Purple Anemones," too, after a wonderful vision of Persephone returning to earth and surrounded by

> Caverns,
> Little hells of colour, caves of darkness,
> Hell, risen in pursuit of her; royal, sumptuous
> Pit-falls,

reduces the inhuman by making it no more than an emblem for the narrowly human. Between cuteness—

> You, Madame Ceres . . .
> You thought your daughter had escaped?
> No more stockings to darn for the flower-roots, down in hell?

and bitterness—

> *At 'em, boys, at 'em!* . . .
> Those two enfranchised women,

the nature of the purple anemones is almost entirely lost sight of. Flowers and fields are virtually personified out of existence, and Lawrence's little tale of "Poor Persephone and her rights for women . . . the bit of husband-tilth she is," though told with a nervously jazzy wit, seems a poor substitute for the vision the poet might have had.[16]

Again, in "Bibbles," despite the precision, affection, and wit of the poet's description of his little dog "like a little black dragon" with a "Chinese puzzle-face," abstract and, within the terms of the poem, irrelevant political theories intervene between the poet and his subject. Poor Bibbles, not smart enough to distinguish one human being from another, becomes a "democratic little bull-bitch, dirt-eating little swine." But of course when he sees her like this, though he may even mean to view her comically, Lawrence is not attending to Bibbles as she is in herself, just as he was not seeing the fig in itself when he described it in terms of prostitution. Instead, he is seeing a horror out of his own mind, substituting a kind of basically unfunny paranoia ("You miserable little bitch of love-tricks,/I know your game") for perception, righteousness ("All right, my little bitch,/You learn loyalty rather than loving,/And I'll protect you") for awareness. What started out as a captivating sketch of his pet becomes instead a series of assertions that have little or nothing to do with the tiny, black, dragon-like dog. "The world of art is only the truth about the real world, that's all," Lawrence had had Ursula say in *Women in Love*,[17] but like most other artists, he sometimes forgot central points of his own dogma.

[16] "Hibiscus and Salvia Flowers" similarly imposes political dogma on nature. Attending to the flowers, Lawrence notes their "native royalty," but when he describes the "loutish commonness" of the socialists we feel he is not attending to them as they really *are*.
[17] Chapter XIX: "Continental."

—10
Blood-Knowledge: Intuition
versus Intellection

i

It may seem odd to contrast the polemical assertiveness of the least successful *Birds, Beasts and Flowers* poems with the mystical submissiveness of the best poems in this volume. In what sense can acts of attention be considered either "mystical" or "mystically submissive"? What sort of mystical knowledge characterizes Lawrence's most successful poems in this collection? To answer these questions we must explore the distinctions Lawrence frequently made between what he considered the two principal modes of consciousness—the dark, instinctive or intuitive consciousness that is the mode of the "blood-self" and the clear, intellectual awareness that is the mode of the "nerve-brain self." [1]

"You can idealize or intellectualize," Lawrence wrote in his study of "Crèvecoeur," or, on the contrary, "you can let the dark soul in you see for itself." [2] One can, in other words, attempt to formulate a kind of rational, objective truth about experience—a truth that is in a way abstracted from the creature or thing to which it applies—or one can attempt in a less conscious way to penetrate to the essence of an object through a process of mystical attention—a process mystical because "based upon intuition, insight or similar subjective experi-

---

[1] *Studies*, p. 124.　　　　[2] *Ibid.*, p. 35.

ence." [3] The blood-self, metaphorically blind, achieves knowledge in this second way, by so far submitting itself to an object that it, in a sense, becomes the object. And as a mode of knowledge, such mystical being or becoming increasingly—for Lawrence—replaced the more scientific process of observation and ratiocination that has been traditional in the west at least since the Renaissance. Like the Dionysian poet of whom Nietzsche wrote, Lawrence aimed, certainly in those acts of attention that constitute his best *Birds, Beasts and Flowers* poems, "to be the eternal Joy of Becoming itself," [4] to penetrate to the process at the heart of all forms by mystically being each thing-in-itself.

A passage in *Women in Love* provides an excellent illustration of this process of mystical submission through which the artist intuits the essence of an object. Gudrun, sketching by the side of Willey Water,

had waded out to a gravelly shoal and was seated like a Buddhist, staring fixedly at the water-plants that rose succulent from the mud of the low shores. What she could see was mud, soft, oozy, watery mud, and from its festering chill, water-plants rose up, thick and cool and fleshy, very straight and turgid, thrusting out their leaves at right angles, and having dark lurid colours, dark green and splotches of black-purple and bronze. But she could feel their turgid fleshy structure as in a sensuous vision, she *knew* how they rose out of the mud, she *knew* how they thrust out from themselves, how they stood stiff and succulent against the air . . . absorbed in a stupor of apprehension of surging water-plants, [she] sat crouched on the shoal, drawing, not looking up for a long time, and then staring unconsciously, absorbedly, at the rigid, naked, succulent stems.[5]

The process of attention described here begins (as in many of the *Birds, Beasts and Flowers* poems) with a descriptive list-

[3] From the definition of "mystical" in Webster's *Seventh New Collegiate Dictionary* (G. & C. Merriam, 1950).
[4] Nietzsche, "Ecce Homo," *The Philosophy of Nietzsche,* p. 868. Quoted by Goodheart, p. 73.
[5] *Women in Love,* Ch. X: "Sketch-Book."

ing of the attributes of the object or objects to be known. Thus Gudrun (and Lawrence) almost force themselves to notice aspects of the plants to which one might not normally attend: their thickness, coolness, fleshiness, straightness, turgidity, and dark, lurid colours. Most people, Lawrence would say, don't normally see the various accidents of reality; usually they see (as he himself does in his lesser poems) only their own conceptions or corruptions of reality. When we see a rose, we generally apprehend it, Lawrence would say, as no more than a sketch of a rose, for we are so accustomed to the idea of roses that we no longer need to concentrate on all the accidents of a plant in order to get at its essence. But for this reason we fail to apprehend the flower in its fullness; our sense of reality is diminished, for we "see" merely the green line and the blob of red that denote "rose." Only by an effort of intense attention, Lawrence would add, can we make ourselves aware of the rose in all its solidity, its dimension, its complicated structure, its shadings of color. Yet it is only when we do this—when we see the rose more wonderingly, as Lawrence might put it—that we see *this* rose at all.

Gudrun, however, is enabled, through a deliberate fixing of her mind on the attributes of the water-plants, to transcend these accidents and intuitively to *know* the essence of the plants "as in a sensuous vision." [6] Her intellectual consciousness is then replaced by "a stupor of apprehension" in which knowledge of the plants becomes so overwhelming that it goes beyond ordinary consciousness to that "dynamic centre of first consciousness" Lawrence described in *Psychoanalysis and the Unconscious,* where "the child knows beyond all knowledge. It does not see with the eyes, it cannot perceive, much less con-

[6] "Intuiting essences" suggests Husserl's concept of the "eidetic reduction." Husserl would doubtless have accepted Lawrence's intuitional method of perception; in writing of the "eidetic reduction" he declares that "we can . . . profit from . . . the gifts of art and particularly of poetry" in the attempt to "clarify" essences, for "free fancy" occupies "a privileged position." "On Eidetic Reduction," in *Phenomenology,* ed. Joseph J. Kockelmans (New York, 1967), p. 111.

ceive . . . yet from the belly it knows, with a directness of knowledge that frightens us and may even seem abhorrent." [7]

In an equally important passage about the paintings of Cezanne, Lawrence elaborated his description of this knowledge.

It is the appleyness of the portrait of Cezanne's wife that makes it so permanently interesting: the appleyness, which carries with it the conviction of knowing the other side as well, the side you don't see, the hidden side of the moon. For the intuitive perception of the apple is so *tangibly* aware of the apple that it is aware *all round,* not only just of the front. The eye sees only fronts, and the mind, on the whole, is satisfied with fronts. But intuition needs all-roundedness, and instinct needs insideness. The true imagination is for ever curving round to the other side, to the back of presented appearances.

This process of intuitional knowledge is strikingly analogous to the process of inseeing (*Einsehen*) Rilke described in his letters.

I love inseeing. Can you imagine with me how glorious it is to insee, for example, a dog as one passes by—*insee* (I don't mean inspect, which is only a kind of human gymnastic by means of which one immediately comes out again on the other side of the dog, regarding it merely, so to speak, as a window upon the humanity lying behind it, not that)—but to let oneself precisely into the dog's very centre, the point from where it begins to be dog, the place in it where God, as it were, would have sat down for a moment when the dog was finished, in order to watch it under the influence of its first embarrassments and inspirations and to know that it was good, that nothing was lacking, that it could not have been better made . . . Laugh though you may, dear confidant, if I am to tell you *where* my all-greatest feeling, my world-feeling, my earthly bliss was to be found, I must confess to you: it was to be found time and again, here and there, in such inseeing, in the indescribably swift, deep, timeless moments of this divine inseeing.[8]

[7] *Psychoanalysis,* p. 21.

[8] *Introduction to These Paintings* (Mandrake Press, 1929). Letter to

And such inseeing for both writers contrasts sharply with the purely mental consciousness that both saw as infallibily destructive of life and creativity. "It is easy to see why each man kills the thing he loves," Lawrence wrote, for to *know* [intellectually to know] a living thing is to kill it. You have to kill a thing to know it satisfactorily [e.g., "we murder to dissect"]. For this reason, the desirous consciousness, the SPIRIT, is a vampire." [9]

Thus, after an unsatisfactory sexual encounter with Gerald, Gudrin lies "wide awake, destroyed into perfect consciousness . . . an exhausting superconsciousness . . . She was conscious of everything—her childhood, her girlhood . . . It was as if she drew a glittering rope of knowledge out of the sea of darkness, drew and drew and drew it out . . . of the past, and there was no end to it." Birkin and Ursula, on the other hand, accomplished in their loving intuitional knowledge of each other, "smilingly . . . delighted in each other's presence, pure presence, not to be thought of, even known." [10] Similarly for Rilke, as Gabriel Marcel perceptively notes, "the mechanised world [like the world of Gerald and Gudrun] . . . becomes also the world of pure consciousness, that which burns without

---

Magda von Hattingberg, 17 February 1914, quoted by Leishman in Introduction to *New Poems,* pp. 18–19.

[9] *Studies,* p. 79. Lawrence's metaphysical terminology is frequently confusing and inconsistent, but his ideas are usually well-ordered. "Knowledge" is perhaps his most ambiguous word. He generally sees "upper" or "nerve-brain" knowledge as a bad thing, at least when it supplants "blood" knowledge. Thus to "know a living thing" purely in the "nerve-brain" sense may "kill it," but "blood" knowledge can be life-giving. The child who has "a directness of knowledge that frightens us" is nevertheless not afflicted with the killing sort of knowledge that burdened Poe. Lawrence's thoughts on the "blood/brain" duality can be schematized as follows:

Blood	vs.	Brain
Knowledge	vs.	Thought (or consciousness)
Being	vs.	Knowledge

so that they look redundant or contradictory, but in fact are not.

[10] *Women in Love,* Ch. XXIV: "Death and Love," and Ch. XXIII: "Excurse."

giving any light and gives light without any warmth," and it is only through an "Orphic" process of inseeing that the poet can "attain to the reality of things which is candour and participate with [his] very being in this imperishable innocence." [11] One must "schliefe/Tief mit den Dingen"—"sleep deeply with things"—Rilke tells us in the *Sonnets to Orpheus*, to know or *become* them, and return transformed "zum anderen Tag, aus der gemeinsamen Tiefe"—"to another day out of the common deep." Out of such "sleep with things," Rilke wrote those works perhaps most comparable to Lawrence's, the *New Poems* and the *Sonnets to Orpheus*. Out of *his* sleep or trance of attention, Lawrence wrote the best of *Birds, Beasts and Flowers*.

ii

Within Lawrence himself there was, more than in most men, a central "crucifixion" into an intellectual and an intuitional consciousness. On the one hand the writer was, as Frieda tells us, "the Englishman, Puritan and highly conscious." [12] On the other hand, he was an artist who had a special faculty for what Nietzsche called Dionysian "becoming." It was no doubt the "highly conscious" Englishman who gave rise to the "Salvator Mundi" side of the poet, the self who willfully imposed his own ideas on natural objects. It was the intuitional artist who "communed" with objects by being at one with them, and who, "instead of exploiting an egotistical pathetic fallacy, submerged [himself] completely in the object of contemplation." [13]

It would be wrong to imagine, however, despite the vehemence of Lawrence's advocacy of blood-knowledge, that he did not recognize the inevitability both of his own and of every man's crucifixion into a double consciousness. Though the

[11] Gabriel Marcel, *Homo Viator*, tr. Emma Craufurd (New York, 1962), pp. 268–269.

[12] Frieda Lawrence, p. vii. "When Lawrence first found a gentian," she recalled elsewhere, "I remember feeling as if he had a strange communion with it." (Nehls, V. 1, p. 1670)

[13] Hough, p. 7.

method of the most successful poems in *Birds, Beasts and Flowers* is chiefly based on the blood-self's intuitional response to a universe of otherness, several poems in the volume explicitly present both the necessity of the nerve-brain self, and the tragic necessity of conflict between the two selves. "Almond Blossom," for instance, is not only, like many of Lawrence's flower and fruit poems, a work about the wonder of natural process—about how out of the "iron fastness, the bitterness and death of December"

> in a great and sacred forthcoming steps forth, steps out in one stride
> A naked tree of blossom, like a bridegroom bathing in dew.

It is a poem about that consciousness of separateness which is also a knowledge of death, that consciousness which is "the last sore-heartedness,/Sore-hearted looking." The triumph of the almond-tree is that it can "come forth in blosson/From the snow-*remembering* heart" [italics mine]. For the tree as Lawrence sees it—and, in Rilke's sense, he *in*sees it—is animated by a nerve-brain knowledge of finality against which its blood-self, its "dawn-heart," must struggle, "sweating his drops of blood through the long-nighted Gethsemane," a prolonged Passion leading ultimately to the crucifixion of two selves reconciled in one and the rebirth such reconciliation portends: "The Cross sprouting its superb and fearless flowers!"

A kind of unconscious faith is what enables this tree or cross of life to vanquish fear. "His [the tree's] blood ripples with that untellable delight of once-more-vindicated faith,/And the Gethsemane blood at the iron pores unfolds, unfolds." But even as that which is "life-divine . . . life-blissful" unfolds itself, fearlessly "looking about/With such insuperable, subtly-smiling assurance,/Sword-blade born," even as it opens and submits itself to all the experience of the world—to "the snow-wind, and the sun-glare, and the dog-star baying epithalamion," even as it radiates *itself:*

> Five times wide open
> Six times wide open
> And given, and perfect,

it is

> Red at the core with the last sore-heartedness,
> Sore-hearted looking,

exacerbated (if a tree can be spoken of in such terms) by consciousness of a universe of objects unalterably other than itself, like the child Lawrence describes in *Psychoanalysis and the Unconscious* who, in "looking across the gulf" is "fixing the gulf." Yet "the coming to perfection of each single individual" —of tree (in a metaphorical sense) as well as man—"cannot take place without . . . the twofold passional circuit" of blood-knowledge and nerve-knowledge, of intuitional inseeing and intellectual realization, "a realization which includes a recognition of abysmal *otherness*." [14] In "St. Matthew," Matthew reminds his Savior, who epitomizes nerve-brain consciousness,

> That my heart which like a lark at heaven's gate singing,
>   hovers morning-bright to Thee,
> Throws still the dark blood back and forth
> In the avenues where the bat hangs sleeping, upside-down
> And to me undeniable, Jesus.

In short, "to stress any one mode, any one interchange, is to hinder all, and to cause corruption in the end." [15]

iii

Although Lawrence accepted the inevitability of the two modes of consciousness, it is obvious that he felt a strong personal preference for the intuitional blood-consciousness that

[14] Both quotations are from *Psychoanalysis*, p. 40. "From the . . . satisfaction of the objective finality," Lawrence adds, "derives the sense of fatality . . . of the isolation of the self."
[15] *Ibid.* In *Psychoanalysis* Lawrence also expresses these dualistic ideas in more complicated images of thoracic centers or *chakras*.

154

submerges the observer in the "object of contemplation," rather than separating him from it. To this attitude we may attribute not only many of his stylistic devices (such as the free verse which is itself no more than a submission to feeling, and the animation of, for example, the almond-tree), but also his frequently expressed preference for darkness rather than light, for touch rather than sight. "Sometimes I am afraid of the terrible things that are real in the darkness," Lawrence wrote to Bertrand Russell, that apostle of luminous geometry,

and of the entire unreality of these things I see. It becomes like a madness at last, to know one is all the time walking in a pale assembly of an unreal world—this house, this furniture, the sky and the earth—whilst oneself is all the while a piece of darkness pulsating in shocks, and the shocks and the darkness are real.

And "passion is not in heat" or light, he told Lady Ottoline Morrell, "but in . . . the burning darkness which quickens the whole ball of this earth from the centre." [16]

Poems in *Birds, Beasts and Flowers* like "Tropic" and "The Revolutionary," in addition to such fictions as, most notably, "The Blind Man," "The Ladybug" and parts of *Women in Love* and *The Rainbow,* deal specifically with this central darkness which, unlike the "bonfire built upon the surface," cannot be known by "sore-hearted looking" but only by touch or by intuition. Touch, indeed, is for Lawrence a form of intuition. "I believe in the unseen hosts," cried Birkin-Lawrence in *Women in Love;* but how could one *know* them? One could in a sense intuit them through touch. "Darkness and silence must fall perfectly on her," Lawrence wrote of Ursula in the same novel. "Then she could know mystically in unrevealed touch." [17]

Like Lawrence himself (for whom he is clearly a mask), and like Birkin and Ursula, blind Samson in "The Revolutionary" has a mystical knowledge of the darkness behind appear-

[16] *Letters,* pp. 330, 326.
[17] *Women in Love,* Ch. XI: "An Island," and Ch. XXIII: "Excurse."

ances through touch, as well as through hearing and through a kind of kinetic intuition. He is capable of that "profound, pre-visual discerning" which is almost impossible for people with a high degree of essentially visual, mental consciousness. It is they, the "mental" people, who are in

> Pale-face authority,
> Caryatids,
> Pillars of white bronze standing rigid, lest the skies fall,

but "What a job they've got to keep it up," the speaker exclaims, elaborating further on the conceit of the Samson story that forms and informs the poem,

> Their poor, idealist foreheads naked capitals
> To the entablature of clouded heaven.

Samson-Lawrence sets himself passionately against those "pillars of society," those mentalized, Christian-spiritual idealists who uphold "the high and super-gothic heavens" of the daytime intellect, the "heavens above, that we yearn to and aspire to."

> To keep on holding up this ideal civilisation
> Must be excrutiating: unless you stiffen into metal, when it is
>   easier to stand stock rigid than to move.

Yet rigid and numerous as are these idealistic pillars,

> They are not stronger than I am, blind Samson,
> The house sways. . . .

> Am I not blind, at the round-turning mill?
> Then why should I fear their pale faces?
> Or love the effulgence of their holy light,
> The sun of their righteousness?

Darkness, the dark sun that is ultimately the source of all energy, is stronger than light. Light, as Ursula discovered in *The Rainbow*, is no more than an interval in the infinitely unfolding darkness.[18] Blind Samson with his sexual and crea-

---

[18] See *The Rainbow*, Ch. XV: "The Bitterness of Ecstasy."

tive power is stronger—for the very reason that he is blind, Lawrence would say—than the sighted Philistines, for the blind man, like Maurice Pervin in the story, does not suffer from the limitations of seeing, but is able to devote himself to inseeing. The intuitional blood-self endures and explores in places where the nerve-brain self is shattered by its own rigidity.

"To me, the earth rolls ponderously, superbly," cries blind Samson, whose blindness enhances his flexibility, making him one with the motion of all things, "coming my way without forethought or after thought," without, that is, the twin abstractions of past and future.

> To me, men's footfalls fall with a dull, soft rumble, ominous
> and lovely . . .
> To me, men are palpable invisible nearnesses in the dark,
> . . . pitch-dark throbs of invitation.
> But you, pale-faces,
> You are painful, harsh-surfaced pillars that give off nothing
> except rigidity . . .
> You staring caryatids.

Like Hermione in *Women in Love,* these pillars of ideal society stare "out all the time on the narrow but to [them] complete world of the extant consciousness." But "in the darkness" they do not "exist. Like the moon, one half of [them is] lost to life." [19] Therefore Samson, the intuitional man, the blood-self, speaks his words of triumph:

> See if I don't move under a dark and nude, vast heaven
> When your world is in ruins, under your fallen skies,
> Caryatids, pale-faces.
> See if I am not Lord of the dark and moving hosts
> Before I die.

iv

If Lawrence, then, despite his acknowledgment of the existence of the nerve-brain self, came to believe in the creative

[19] *Women in Love,* Ch. XXII: "Woman to Woman."

superiority of a darker self, what function, if any, did the mental consciousness have in the production of his poetry? As we have seen, his free verse was largely an intuitional response to the feelings of the moment as they welled into his mind from "unknown sources," and his metaphors and images also sprang from intuitional inseeing. The answer, strangely, is that for Lawrence, in the best of *Birds, Beasts and Flowers,* as in the best of the *Look!* poems, the true job of the conscious mind was *to keep the conscious mind from imposing itself on the poems.* This will sound paradoxical, but it only apparently involves a contradiction. The job was one that had to be done in order for Lawrence's poems to become acts of *"pure* attention," acts, that is, of anti-ironic attention.

When one surrenders conscious control over the mind, in an effort to lose oneself in the response of the intuitional self, the mind as it is *fully* constituted nevertheless keeps on working. Nerve-brain consciousness does not stop merely because one is determined to yield to blood-consciousness. On the contrary, when intellectual discipline is relaxed the most that can happen is that both modes of knowing will coexist. Hugh Kenner, for instance, points out that T. S. Eliot, influenced by his studies of Bradleyan idealism, attempted in his earlier poems to reproduce the total state of consciousness, the exact way in which the mind, without the shaping control of intentionality, responded to reality.[20] In a sense, then, we might almost expect Kenner to suggest that Eliot's poems, different as they are from Lawrence's, are also perceptual processes, acts of attention. There seems initially to be the same surrender of control over the directions of the mind in the Bradleyan-Eliotian duplication of experiential reality as there is in the Lawrentian submission to intuitional response.

Eliot, however, makes little or no attempt to *focus* the consciousness out of which his poems emerge; the mind or, as

[20] Hugh Kenner, "Bradley," *The Invisible Poet: T. S. Eliot* (New York, 1959).

Kenner puts it, "the Voice" of his poems is simply "the European mind," being itself almost purposelessly. But it is for precisely this reason that Eliot's relaxation of control and the diffuse consciousness that results from such letting-go entails just the sort of irony which was for a number of reasons repellent to Lawrence. For if one forces oneself to become aware not merely of the principal thing one is doing or observing at any moment but rather of all the objects and processes, large and small, (apparently) significant and (apparently) foolish that make up the entire field of consciousness at that moment, irony is inevitable. Such deliberately expanded, self-conscious consciousness is by definition ironic. When one allows oneself to become fully aware, for instance, not only that one is at a certain moment writing ambitious metaphysical sentences but also that one is writing such sentences at a kitchen table with a ballpoint pen, one's awareness of the first —the metaphysical goal—is ironically modified by one's awareness of the second—the material circumstances.

Unlike Eliot, who almost willfully exaggerated this natural diffusion of consciousness, Lawrence made every effort to obliterate from his mind all awareness except awareness of the object that was to be the subject of his poem. The job of his mental consciousness, in his view, was not to comment on the responses of his intuitional consciousness, and then select and shape the resulting double vision into the complex texture of an ironic poem: rather, it was deliberately to suppress its own responses and thus to suppress the irony that inevitably arises when a single object is perceived by the two modes of awareness. In *Lady Chatterley's Lover,* for instance, Connie is, in one crucial scene, destroyed "by her own double consciousness":

This time the sharp ecstasy of her own passion did not overcome her . . . do what she might, her spirit seemed to look on from the top of her head, and the sort of anxiety of his penis to come to its little evacuating crisis seemed farcical. Yet, this was love,

159

this ridiculous bouncing of the buttocks, and the wilting of the poor insignificant, moist little penis. This was the divine love! [21]

Just as in the sexual act, in writing poetry of attention, in striving to become one's object, one must continually struggle against the impulse of the nerve-brain self ironically to mock or demolish the responses of the blood-self. Gudrun, in *Women in Love*, like Eliot's Prufrock, is a good example of a person unable to escape the unbridled assertiveness of the upper consciousness. Even as she lies in her lover's arms, straining, like Connie Chatterley, to surrender the glittering burden of conscious awareness, "a terrible cynicism began to gain upon her, blowing in like a wind. Everything turned to irony with her: the last flavor of everything was ironical." And after Gerald's death, though she hides "her face in Ursula's shoulder" as if overcome by grief, she "could not escape the cold devil of irony that froze her soul." [22]

It is she who is truly the daughter of that ironical and "realistic" Anna, who, while Will surrendered himself to the soaring arches of the Cathedral at Lincolnshire, seized on the ironic grotesquery of the gargoyles to prevent the loss of control with which the church mysteriously threatened her. Inevitably Gudrun is attracted to Loerke, whose "ironical, playful remarks" seem to her "like a rising above the dreariness of actuality, the monotony of contingencies." [23] Yet it is to just this rich texture of contingencies that the artist, in Lawrence's view, must submit, and his effort must be precisely *not* to rise above them. Thus the control he surrenders is not the shaping control of intentionality but the mental control of irony. Like Rilke, he focuses his mind with the meditative intensity of a medieval mystic, consciously hurling his poems like so many inkwells at the "cold devil" of nerve-brain irony who threatens the dark gods of the intuitional unconscious.

Such deliberate focusing of consciousness constituted for

[21] *Lady Chatterley's Lover,* Ch. XII.
[22] *Women in Love,* Ch. XXIX: "Continental."
[23] *Ibid.* Ch. XXX: "Snowed Up."

Lawrence, as for Rilke, what Gabriel Marcel calls "creative absorption," that creative absorption which, rather than irony, is essential to successful poetry of attention.[24] "The soul stirs," Lawrence wrote in *Etruscan Places*, "and makes an act of pure attention, and that is a discovery." [25] In its absorption, however, the soul of the poet must cultivate, as Wordsworth recommended, a "wise passiveness." The activity of consciousness is merely negative: to reduce activity. What Lawrence believed is what Marcel says "Rilke teaches us . . . that there exists a receptivity which is really creation itself under another name." [26]

Ultimately, however, such deliberately intuitive and receptive poetry is, as Lawrence was to imply in *Etruscan Places*, a species of divination, a way of divining the nature either of the self or of the other. For this reason, too, both modes of consciousness must be involved in the process of creation—the intellectual mode to focus attention and the intuitional mode to provide receptive energy, for success in divination, Lawrence wrote, depends on "the amount of *true*, sincere, religious concentration you can bring to bear on your object. An act of pure attention, if you are capable of it, will bring its own answer. And you choose that object to concentrate on which will best focus your consciousness." [27]

[24] Marcel, p. 244.
[26] Marcel, p. 264.

[25] *Etruscan Places*, p. 92.
[27] *Etruscan Places*, p. 92.

—11

The Living Cosmos:
Varieties of Otherness

i

The objects that best focused Lawrence's poetic conscious-
ness at this point in his career were the plants and animals of
Birds, Beasts and Flowers, and therefore we must try to under-
stand the precise meaning these non-human objects had for
him. As we have seen, he was particularly disillusioned with
humanity in this period, and he fled in reaction to what seemed
the innocence of animals and plants. This purity of non-
human life constituted its chief "otherness" for him. A peach
was fully itself—*en soi*—as a man could never be fully himself,
and one of the things that fascinated Lawrence about animals
was that they seemed to be creatures exclusively in the mode
of the anti-ironic blood-self. "The animal lifts its head, sniffs
and knows [only] within the dark, passionate belly," he wrote
in his study of "Crèvecoeur." "It knows at once, in dark mind-
lessness." [1] As Rilke wrote in the Eighth *Duino Elegy,* the
animal's direct and pure perception of reality appears to be
free of that nerve-brain knowledge of death which is distinc-
tively human.

> I-h-n sehen wir allein; das Freie Tier
> hat seinen Untergang stets hinter sich
> und vor sich Gott, und wenn es geht, so gehts
> in Ewigkeit, so wie die Brunnen gehen.

[1] *Studies,* p. 40.

Wir haben nie, nicht einen einzigen Tag,
den reinen Raum vor uns, in den die Blumen
unendlichen aufgehn. Immer ist es Welt
und niemals Nirgends ohne Nicht . . .

We see only death; the free animal
has its decease perpetually behind it
and God in front, and when it moves, it moves
into eternity, like running springs.
We've never, no, not for a single day,
pure space before us, such as that which flowers
endlessly open into: always world,
and never nowhere without no.[2]

Like Rilke, Lawrence is working in a tradition that goes back
at least as far as Burns, who envied the field-mouse because
"the present only toucheth thee!", and Shelley, whose distinc-
tion between himself and the skylark was based upon the fact
that "We [mankind] look before and after,/And pine for what
is not:/Our sincerest laughter/With some pain is fraught."

For Lawrence, moreover, it is precisely because of the un-
consciousness of the animal's or plant's knowledge, the purity
or singleness of its being, that it not only antedates man but
will be able to endure when man's crucifixion into double
consciousness destroys humanity entirely. "In the end," the
writer asserted in *Etruscan Places,*

that which lives lives by delicate sensitiveness. . . . It is the grass
of the field, most frail of all things, that supports all life all the
time . . . Brute force crushes many plants, yet the plants rise
again. The pyramids will not last a moment compared with a

<hr>

[2] Tr. J. B. Leishman and Stephen Spender. Rilke, influenced by his
friend Rudolf Kassner, is making something like Sartre's distinction
between the *en soi* and the *pour soi.* Later in this elegy he adds that the
animal's being is—for itself—"infinite, inapprehensible,/unintrospective,
pure." See also Randall Jarrell's "The Woman at the Washington Zoo,"
which, perhaps following Rilke, distinguishes between the woman's knowl-
edge of death and the animals' freedom from such knowledge.

daisy. And before Buddha or Jesus spoke the nightingale sang.
. . . And in the beginning was not a word, but a chirrup.[3]

In this same vein, Wallace Stevens, a more deliberately artful poet than Lawrence but one whose attitude toward life, death and incarnation was often significantly Lawrentian, wrote in "Sunday Morning" that "there is not any haunt of prophecy,/ Nor any old chimera of the grave . . . that has endured/. . . as April's green endures."

Yet though his nerve-brain self enables—even forces—man to go beyond the instinctive *being* of animals to a form of knowledge that transcends nature, man is nevertheless irrevocably part of nature. He has a blood-self which, like April's green, endures beneath the flux of mental consciousness, and through his sense of this darker self he unconsciously participates in the vast process of natural life, in that which, like the almond tree, is "life-divine, life-blissful at the core." Because of this, Lawrence's engagement with the non-human in *Birds, Beasts and Flowers,* though it began with his intuition of otherness, was ultimately twofold: first, to explore the inhuman *otherness* of animals and plants, and second, to bring to consciousness that unconscious participation in natural process which makes man *like* birds, beasts and flowers.

But because both objective otherness and the "life-divine" blood-being of all things are expressed in nature in so many ways, Lawrence attended in this volume, within the general provenance of his twofold, overall aim, to at least four different categories of "life-divine" otherness. In ascending order from the simplest to the most complex, from the visible to the invisible, these categories are, first, animals and plants treated as pure examples of living otherness, such as "Fish," "Baby Tortoise," "Bare Fig-Trees," "Peach," "Pomegranate," "Snake," "Bat," "Mosquito," and "He-Goat"; second, animals and plants that represent the otherness of the primitive world or the oth-

[3] *Etruscan Places,* p. 53.

erness of the past, such as "Sicilian Cyclamens," "Cypresses," "Men in New Mexico," "Kangaroo," and "Hummingbird"; and as a corollary of this, places or objects that somehow represent the otherness of the future, such as "The Evening Land"; third, animals, plants and objects that seem to summarize the mysterious otherness of what Lawrence called "the living cosmos," such as "Peace," "Tropic," "Southern Night," "Eagle in New Mexico," "Men in New Mexico," "Autumn at Taos"; and fourth, animals, plants, and creatures that suggest either a kind of divine otherness within ourselves, such as "Medlars and Sorb Apples," or the otherness of memories, such as "Spirits Summoned West."

These categories may, of course, seem arbitrary, for a number of the poems could certainly fit into more than one. Indeed, it is the implicit connection of all things, a kind of great chain of being, that Lawrence's book is designed to reveal. A reversal of the old hermetic motto "as above, so below" to "as below, so above" might well be his slogan (as it might be Jung's). What we know of that which is in a sense "below" our humanity, of the pure blood-being on which our being is founded, we know in glimpses, through our knowledge of the natural world of birds, beasts and flowers. What we know of the world of the past that is "below" our present life we know through the intimations of certain natural objects we necessarily know in the present. What we know of the dark cosmos whose reality seethes "below" appearances we know through knowing appearances. What we learn of the other self, which lives beneath the surface of our nerve-brain awareness, we learn through focusing on some object that can lead us "down the darker and darker stairs" to profound self knowledge.

Thus, for Lawrence, like some latter day hermeticist, every thought becomes a living creature, and every creature a thought. As for the ancient augurs of whom he wrote in *Etruscan Places,* for Lawrence "hot-blooded birds flew through the living universe as feelings and premonitions fly through the breast of a man, or as thoughts fly through the mind." [4] One may choose "that object to concentrate upon which will best focus [one's] consciousness," but in one sense, anyway, every object leads to every other, and every thought involves every other. The otherness of animals implies the otherness of man's past, which in turn suggests both the otherness of the whole, pulsating cosmos and the otherness within each man himself.

ii

Nevertheless, though each poem in *Birds, Beasts and Flowers* is importantly related to all the others and in a way participates in all four of the categories I've proposed, Lawrence's chain of being is made up of a number of separate links. The first category, then, though it implies all the others, consists of poems that deal with the otherness of birds, beasts and flowers primarily for their own sake, with that "causeless created nature of [each] individual being" which "is the same as the old mystery of the divine nature of the soul," for, says Lawrence in *Psychoanalysis and the Unconscious*, "religion was right and science was wrong. Every individual creature has a soul," and "we are forced to attribute to a starfish, or to a nettle, its own peculiar and integrated consciousness." [5]

To understand the "defiant otherness" of these plant and animal souls is, Lawrence believes, one of man's major problems, for such souls are in a sense *prior* to man's; they have a primordial purity his divided consciousness lacks. Attending to a "naked fig-tree" on his trip to Sardinia, Lawrence wrote with wonder that "a fig-tree come forth in its nudity . . . like some sensitive creature emerged from the rock . . . is a sight to behold." But ultimately its otherness, its inaccessibility, baffled

[4] *Ibid.,* p. 91.
[5] *Psychoanalysis,* p. 15. But "nothing is so detestable as the maudlin attributing of . . . human consciousness to animals," declared Birkin in *Women in Love,* Ch. XXII.

him. "Ah," he exclaimed, "if it could but answer, or if we had tree speech!" "Bare Fig-Trees," his poem on the subject, was therefore an effort to penetrate through creative intuition to what George Eliot called in *Middlemarch* "the other side of silence," or to invent a "tree-speech" so as to understand the nature of "this wicked tree,/That has kept so many secrets up its sleeve,/And has been laughing through so many ages/At man and his uncomfortablenesses." [6]

Similarly, "Mosquito" is an effort to comprehend the soul of a living creature which, though "queer" and "hateful," with an "evil little aura," is nevertheless virtually "a nothingness." "When did you start your tricks,/Monsieur?" the poet demands, aware of and yet baffled by this "streaky sorcerer" with his "length of shredded shank." "Nothing" as the mosquito is, he is yet mysteriously *something,* something both other than and like ourselves. And "Baby Tortoise" illustrates this nothing/something duality even more clearly. Though he is no more than "a tiny, fragile, half-animate bean," the little turtle must open his "eye of a dark, disturbed night," the eye of all unfolding blood-being, and "row against" a "huge vast inanimate . . . an incalculable inertia" with "all life carried on [his] shoulder," for as we learn in "Tortoise Shell," this small bird, this rudiment,/This little dome" is no less than the "pediment/Of all creation."

Animals and plants are nothing yet something, other yet the same: these are the primary paradoxes to which Lawrence addresses himself in *Birds, Beasts and Flowers,* and the dialectical process of his style is particularly suited to capturing them. In the two bat poems, for instance, he conducts a kind of seminar with himself, the reader, and even a bat, on the subject of bat-nature.

[6] *Sea and Sardinia,* p. 100. For "the other side of silence," see George Eliot, *Middlemarch,* Bk II, ch. 20. "If we had a keen vision and feeling of all ordinary human life, it would be like hearing the grass grow and the squirrel's heart beat, and we should die of that roar which lies on the other side of silence."

Look up, and you see things flying
Between the day and the night;
Swallows with spools of dark thread scwing the shadows to-
  gether,

he remarks, casually enough. Then he immediately questions
this assumption:

And you think:
"The swallows are flying so late!"

Swallows? . . .

Never swallows!
Bats!

But bats, with their eery pipings and odd "wings like bits of
umbrella," inexplicably represent all that is alien to man.
"Bats, and an uneasy creeping in one's scalp," shudders Law-
rence only half-comically. But why the shudder? How *can* one
living thing be so foreign to another? Perhaps it is precisely
the inanimate quality of the bat—its *thingness*—that makes it
seem hostile to life and thus repels a man. It is "like a glove,
a black glove thrown up at the light," its ribbed wings like
fragments of a ribbed black unbrella; ranks of bats "hang
themselves . . . upside down like rows of disgusting old rags."
  Yet the poet is willing to concede that one might have a
different view of the bat; perhaps, he suggests, his vision of
the creature's thingness is only a function of his *own* feeling
about it. "In China the bat is symbol of happiness," he
punctiliously notes, and in noting this he introduces a second
mode of otherness. Unfolding beyond the otherness of the bat
is the otherness of the Chinese, who have such different feel-
ings about the bat. Furthermore, in "Man and Bat" Lawrence
concedes that there is a "God who is maker of bats," implying
a third mode still, the otherness of a God who can produce
such disparate creatures as man and bat. "Bats," he admits in

addition, *"must* [italics mine] be bats," and indeed "the human soul," capable of knowing this, is fated to "wide-eyed responsibility/In life," responsibility—if necessary—even for the welfare of bats, for man must not deny his own "bat-winged heart," of which Lawrence spoke in "St. Matthew." Most important, he concedes, at the very end admitting the bat himself into the seminar room, that to the bat bathood is natural, and humanity, the daytime consciousness that seems so natural to us, is absolutely alien.

There he sits, the long loud one!

pipes Lawrence's bat, describing the poet in just barely translatable bat-speech,

But I am greater than he.

We are left finally with an impression of infinite rooms of selfhood mysteriously opening into each other—the bat, the poet, the Chinese, God, and so on—yet each, too, mysteriously closed against, *other* than, all the others.

Even more than the bat, the mosquito or the tortoise, however, the fish is for Lawrence a symbol of primordial nonhuman otherness. More than any of these other creatures, he has a kind of pure blind indifference to contingencies: to him, perpetually "subaqueous . . . and wave-thrilled . . . so little matters."

Whether the waters rise and cover the earth
Or whether the waters wilt in the hollow places,
All one to you,

the poet wonderingly declares, for the life of the fish is literally the life of oneness.

As the waters roll
Roll you.
The waters wash,
You wash in oneness
And never emerge.

More than any other non-human creature, the fish represents for Lawrence what Sartre calls the *en soi,* that which is totally itself without knowledge of negativity, without, in fact, what we would consider knowledge of any kind. You "Never know,/ Never grasp," Lawrence tells the fish; and knowing and grasping represent the two principal ways a being can escape itself and communicate with external reality.

Bats, mosquitoes and tortoises, after all, are creatures of the air and to some extent of the light. More, their shape—and therefore their experience—is in a way analogous to man's. They are capable of grasping, of directly communicating, of embracing. "Even snakes lie together," Lawrence recalls. But for the fish the only knowledge is the blood-knowledge of sensation, and the only embrace is the embrace of the waters.

> Your life a sluice of sensation along your sides,
> A flush at the flail of your fins, down the whorl of your tail,
> And water wetly on fire in the grates of your gills,

Lawrence writes in one of his most organically rhythmic passages. Even the fish's "fixed water-eyes" seem to be, rather than instruments of independent perception, no more than a function of the element with which this creature is at one. And

> oh, fish, that rock in water
> You lie only with the waters;
> One touch.
> No fingers, no hands and feet, no lips;
> No tender muzzles,
> No wistful bellies,
> No loins of desire,
> None.

The fish is truly

> Himself, all silvery himself
> In the element,
> No more,

and as such he represents a fundamental selfhood that consists in no more than pure appetite, "gay fear" and "joie de vivre"—*joy* of being—"all without love," and without the knowledge of otherness and finality love implies. The fish is "loveless and so lively!"—literally and figuratively *quick* and gay with a life that, though it may involve fear (for fear is unconscious, instinctive), contains no knowledge of death. He was

> Born before God was love,
> Or life knew loving.
> Beautifully beforehand with it all.

Still, Lawrence feels at first a poet's inevitable desire to humanize this completely inhuman being. He sees "a slim young pike, with smart fins/And grey-striped suit . . . Slouching along/Like a lout on an obscure pavement,"

> But watching closer
> That motionless deadly motion
> That unnatural barrel body, that long ghoul nose . . .
> I left off hailing him. . . .
>
> I didn't know his God. . . .
>
> Which is perhaps the last admission that life has to wring out of us.

The last admission and yet the first, for, as we've seen, the first step in the crucifixion that is human consciousness is the coming into nerve-brain awareness of the limits of selfhood and of the existence of otherness. To recognize that there are "other Gods/Beyond my range . . . gods beyond my God," is to recognize that there are other natures beyond one's own nature, that there is another experience—the experience of self-contained blood-being, the experience of the living creature which yet appears *en soi* as a table is *en soi*—beyond or beneath the double experience of the human being who so irrevocably exists both within and without himself.

More, for Lawrence to say that the fish "outstarts me,/And

I, a many-fingered horror of daylight to him have made him die," is not only for him (seeing his own otherness from the fish's point of view as he earlier saw it from the bat's) to tell us that he has literally made one particular fish, with "his gorping, water-horny mouth" and "horror-tilted eye" die in the course of a fishing expedition, but that he, like all men, has inevitably made the fish—the pure blood-being—*in himself* die; that he, the man, has inevitably evolved beyond the "mucous, leaping life-throb" of the fish into the crucifixion of blood-being/nerve-brain knowledge that makes man human.

Yet at the end of "Fish" Lawrence reminds us of what he considers a crucial fact:

> In the beginning
> Jesus was called the Fish . . .
> And in the end.

The nerve-brain knowledge of otherness on which Christian love is based is itself founded on that primordial singleness of being the fish represents. Furthermore, because Jesus in his divine origin and holy, self-sacrificial death symbolizes the pure, immortal soul—the soul without a doom and therefore without a knowledge of death—swimming out of and into eternity, he represents, like the fish, "the *anima,* the animate life, the very clue to the vast sea, the watery element of the first submission." [7] Original and oblivious though he is, loveless and lonely, the fish ultimately represents for Lawrence not only the foundation of man's being, but its goal—for the goal of all knowledge is ultimately being; "the final aim is not *to know* but *to be.*" Yet unlike the fish, who instinctively possesses the state of pure being, man must paradoxically attain that

---

[7] *Etruscan Places,* p. 89. In "the first Christian centuries," Lawrence added, "Jesus was the anima of the vast, moist, ever-yielding element which was the opposite . . . of the red flame the Pharaohs . . . had sought to invest themselves with." *Cf.* also H. P. Blavatsky, *Isis Unveiled* (Theosophical University Press, 1960—first published 1877), V. II, pp. 256–257, a related "occult" speculation which may have influenced Lawrence.

state through knowledge: just as throughout *Birds, Beasts and Flowers* Lawrence himself must use his mental consciousness primarily to suppress his mental consciousness, so "we [all men] *must* know, if only in order to learn not to know." [8] But the reward is worth the effort. If you can achieve such a state, Lawrence says, if you can "turn into the Fish, the Pisces of man's final consciousness . . . you'll start to swim again in the great life which is so frighteningly godly that you realize your previous presumption." [9]

In "Snake" Lawrence dealt essentially with this same matter, with the paradoxical godliness of that which is not only other than but also apparently less than man. Like the fish, the snake, as Lawrence wrote in *Fantasia of the Unconscious,* has a "consciousness [that] is *only* dynamic and non-cerebral . . . [it] has no mental life, but only an intensely vivid dynamic mind." [10] Thus, emerging from the "burning bowels of the earth" like a messenger of blood-being, it reaches Lawrence's water-trough before the poet; just as the fish was "born in front of my sunrise," the snake is a forerunner; Lawrence waits behind him "like a second-comer." Yet despite the vivid, moving and straightforward way in which the snake is presented to us as a blood-being, flickering "his tongue like a forked night on the air, so black,"

> Seeming to lick his lips,
> And [looking] around like a god, unseeing, into the air . . .
> And slowly, very slowly, as if thrice a dream
> [Proceeding] to draw his slow length curving round . . .
> Deliberately going into the blackness,

"Snake" is finally a more complex work than it at first appears, and certainly a more complex poem than "Fish."

For one thing, unlike "Fish" (which referred only in passing to the Christian associations of the fish), it depends on a richly elaborated set of classical illusions: the snake in the garden of

---

[8] *Fantasia,* pp. 105, 112.
[9] "The Proper Study," *Phoenix* (I), p. 723.   [10] *Fantasia,* p. 215.

Eden, the serpent of eternity, the phallic god. Moreover, Lawrence's way of handling these traditional images is to turn them upside down, surprising—though not necessarily disappointing—our customary expectations. The Satanic snake, he demonstrates, is not evil but good; like Blake's vision of Milton's Satan, he is "a king in exile, uncrowned in the underworld,/Now due to be crowned again." The worm of eternity, rather than transcending the earth, emerges from and withdraws into its "burning bowels." The phallic god is one of the "lords of life," though our "accursed human education" teaches us that he is dangerous, "venomous."

Most important, through his use of dialectical process in "Snake," Lawrence illuminates the crucifying conflict between the two modes of consciousness, a conflict which, though implicit in "Fish," is never really examined in that poem. On the one hand, the voices in "Snake" that say "If you were a man/You would take a stick and break him now" are the voices of the nerve-brain intelligence, anxious to protect not only the body but also the assertive daytime selfhood of the poet. The part of Lawrence, on the other hand, that instinctively likes the snake, that feels honored he has "come like a guest in quiet, to drink at my water-trough," is the intuitional blood-being, what Marcel calls the creative-receptive aspect of the self, grateful to and restored by the life-divine phallic vision.

What the poem as a whole finally makes clear, moreover, is that while we may prefer blood-being, we inevitably are both blood and nerve-brain beings. Our nerve-brain distrust of the snake is as much a part of us as our intuitive recognition of his phallic godliness. We *must* know in order not to know; we must, so long as we are human, be crucified into double consciousness. The true relationship between man and snake, then, is a relationship between a creature in whose nature knowledge of separateness, "sore-hearted looking," must coexist with the pure bliss of being, and a creature of pure, unconscious bliss. Later, in a number of the works in *Last Poems,* Lawrence would deal even more carefully with this problem of man's crucified consciousness and its implications for his moral and spiritual relationships with less agonized creatures, but of all his poems so far, "Snake," with its haunted, painfully human self-questionings:

> Was it cowardly, that I dared not kill him?
> Was it perversity, that I longed to talk to him?
> Was it humility, to feel so honoured?

and its moment of bitter revelation,

> And so, I missed my chance with one of the lords
> Of life,

is his most effective exploration of the way the often majestic otherness of natural objects impinges on the mind of man.

iii

While animals and plants are the ultimate forerunners, exemplifying with their blood-being the foundation on which man's more complicated nature is raised, Lawrence was also able to find such otherness within man himself. In a number of the poems in *Birds, Beasts and Flowers* he was reminded, through focusing his consciousness on certain animals and plants, first of the primitive, pre-human world in general, of, for instance, the "other world/Primeval-dumb, far back" in which hummingbirds "went whizzing through the slow, vast, succulent stems" and in which the kangaroo "in the silent, lost land" of Australia still has its being, and then, interestingly, of some of the *human* forerunners of modern man.[11]

The primitive human world, as Lawrence envisions it, while still *other* than the animal world, occupies a position halfway between the animal kingdom and modern human society. In Lawrence's view, primitive man, though inevitably burdened with a certain self-consciousness, is nevertheless enabled by

[11] Lawrence remarked that he had "a glimpse [of] the world before the Flood" at the Pera hera in Ceylon. (*Letters*, p. 710)

his naiveté to participate more deeply in the intuitional blood being of non-human life. "The ancients thought in images," [12] Lawrence tells us (rather than in abstractions, presumably) and "The animals and savages are isolate, each one in its own pristine self," he writes in *Studies*.[13] He even finds a significant otherness in Sardinian peasants, who, in the midst of the mechanized, self-conscious, modern world, still cling to the old, unself-conscious spontaneity of the blood-mode. "There is a gulf between oneself and them," he asserts in *Sea and Sardinia*. "They have no inkling of our crucifixion, our universal consciousness. Each of them is pivoted and limited to himself, as the wild animals are." [14] Lawrence is being hyperbolical here, and he himself was no doubt aware of it, as he must have been aware that his comparison of savages to animals was essentially metaphorical. But he was using hyperbole and metaphor to illuminate what seemed to him an important perception of human as well as non-human otherness.

This human otherness is first conveyed to Lawrence and to us, however, by a non-human object. Grapes, with their "tendrilled vines," remind him of "the lost, fern-scented world" of human pre-history, a world, like that inhabited by the hummingbird, of "creatures webbed and marshy,/And on the margin, men, soft-footed and pristine," men with the intuitive "sensitiveness . . . of a tendril which . . . reaches out . . . by an instinct more delicate than the moon's as she feels for the tides." "Before petals spread, before colour made its disturbance, before"—significantly—"eyes saw too much," before nerve-brain consciousness gained on man's blood-being, there was this natural culture of which, Lawrence thinks, "the negro might know a little." It is, the world of blind Samson, the speaker of "The Revolutionary" (which for good reasons follows "Grapes" in the collection), and in order to

[12] Letter to Frederick Carter, 18 June 1923, *Letters*, p. 745. *Cf.* Marcel, p. 247, who quotes a similar passage from Romano Guardini.
[13] *Studies*, p. 40.   [14] *Sea and Sardinia*, p. 101.

save ourselves from our overly mental "vistas democratic," our perversely sober soda fountains and tram-cars, Lawrence declares that we must

> Take the fern-seed on our lips,
> Close the eyes, and go
> Down the tendrilled avenues of wine and the otherworld

to find our lost, intuitive selves, "for we are on the brink of re-remembrance."

In "Cypresses" Lawrence tries more specifically to remember the otherness of that ancient wisdom. Yet because he is a modern man trapped in and by history, the secret of "the long-nosed, sensitive-footed, subtly-smiling Etruscans,/Who made so little noise outside the cypress groves" is irredeemably other, irrevocably mysterious to him. "Tuscan cypresses,/What is it?" he asks, but he knows from the first that no answer is possible, for the ancient secret of being at one with oneself, like the faculty of thinking in images, is gone. The Tuscan cypresses with their subtle insinuation of an ancient message are "folded in like a dark thought,/For which the language is lost," and though in disbelief the poet asks "Are our words no good?" he knows that

> tongues are dead, and words are hollow as hollow seed
>   pods,
> Having shed their sound and finished all their echoing
> Etruscan syllables,
> That had the telling.

The knowledge is a function of his modernity. He must, if only involuntarily, participate in the process of history that has obliterated the Etruscans.

"Tongues are dead, and words are hollow"—not only is the Etruscan tongue dead, the language undeciphered, a shell hollow of meaning, but in Lawrence's view all modern tongues are in a sense dead, all our words inevitably hollow because they are words of the nerve-brain mode, divorced from that blood meaning which gave imagery to ancient thought. For this reason, though the Etruscans themselves are irrevocably lost, Lawrence hopes he—and all of us—can revive or "re-remember" at least their spirit, which contains "so much of the delicate magic of life," the spirit that should inform our hollow words. "They say the fit survive," he tells us (rather sardonically, for he believed Darwinian evolution to be as much a human construction as any other story of man's history),

> But I invoke the spirits of the lost,
> Those that have not survived, the darkly lost,
> To bring their meaning back into life again.

He is determined to restore the meaning of the Etruscan *way* of seeing, if not the secret of what they actually saw. "The ancients saw, consciously, as children now see unconsciously, the everlasting wonder in things," he points out in *Etruscan Places*. Even their supposedly pornographic drawings "have the same naive wonder in them as the rest, the same archaic innocence, accepting life, knowing all about it, and *feeling the meaning* [ital. mine] which is like a stone fallen into consciousness, sending its rings ebbing out and out to the extremes." [15] What one can learn from contemplation of the ancients is specifically how to combat the assertiveness of the nerve-brain vision that increasingly threatens to devour blood-consciousness.

Yet most modern men, Lawrence notes, accept the Roman view of the Etruscans as evil, just as they accept the traditional vision of the snake as evil; the nerve-brain self ever more violently rejects blood-being, and in this rejection inheres the sickness of the modern world, for just as without man to *néantiser* the world there would be no nothingness, so without man to think evil there is no pure evil, no wrong in itself; only the thought of evil is evil.[16]

[15] *Etruscan Places*, pp. 114–115.
[16] *"Néantiser":* Cf. Sartre, Part One, Ch. 1, and Marcel, p. 166 ff.

> There is only one evil, to deny life
> As Rome denied Etruria
> And mechanical America Montezuma still.

The only real wrong is to fail to perceive the delicate selfhood of each living thing. To know good is to know there are "many worlds, not one world" and to mourn the fact that "alas, the one world [is] triumphing more and more . . . leaving a dreary sameness . . . that means at last complete sterility." [17] The otherness of "the Mediterranean morning when our world began" that Lawrence discussed in "Sicilian Cyclamens" as well as in "Cypresses," and the otherness of still extant primitive cultures—of the Stone Age peoples of the Pacific [18] and of the Sardinian peasants, of the negroes in Africa and of the American Indians—is being swallowed, Lawrence feels, by that metal, mental monster of the future represented by "mechanical America" denying "Montezuma still."

But rather than consistently rejecting this future outright, as in "The Revolutionary," Lawrence (as a corollary of his attempt to remember and comprehend the otherness of the past) tries to attend to the future's frightening otherness, for insofar as it is all a great sameness, the future symbolized by mechanical America "the evening land" will be other than the world to which he is accustomed. In fact, though this new American world seems chillingly automatic, even human contact resounding with an "iron click" and everything wrapped in "the winding-sheet of . . . self-less ideal love,/Boundless love,/Like a poison gas," Lawrence suspects that on this futuristic sunset continent there is the "deep pulsing of a strange heart,/[a] New throb, like a stirring under the false dawn that precedes the real."

Though the "blood-thirsty sun" of America, like the blood-thirsty American eagle in New Mexico, sucks up blood "leaving a nervous people"—a people entirely committed to the nerve-brain mode—the future, he believes, is "nascent," "de-

[17] *Aaron's Rod,* Ch. XIII.   [18] See *Studies,* p. 144.

monish"; and "dark, elvish,/Modern, unissued, uncanny America," despite its nerve-brain democratic modernism and fixed, mechanical will, is closer to what is aboriginal in man even than the old Mediterranean morning one can still glimpse now and then beneath the tired surface of Europe. Perhaps, Lawrence implies, the future will finally be a closing with the past, a coming full circle back to the blood-self that still lurks "among the undergrowth/Of many-stemmed machines and chimneys that smoke like pine-trees," for "in the tension of opposites all things have their being." The "futurism" of America could only exist in conjunction with—or more precisely in reaction against—some aboriginal spirit that may yet guide the future down the dark trails of the past.

iv

Not only the mysterious spirit of the past stirs beneath surface appearances in *Birds, Beasts and Flowers,* however. The radiant otherness of the natural objects on which Lawrence focused his attention in this volume suggested to the poet an enigma beyond human and animal mysteries, the vast and only apparently inanimate cosmos that was for him charged with a life of its own, a life both alien to man's understanding and profoundly connected with his being. The poems I have grouped as a third category are expressions of Lawrence's concern with this *spiritus mundi.*

In "Peace," "Tropic," and "Southern Night," Lawrence attempts through attention to geological and astronomical mysteries—the volcanic center of the earth, the relationship between earth and its satellite—symbolically to penetrate to the not-alive but powerfully living heart of being itself, the energy of which man is merely a manifestation or which, conversely (and the two ideas are not as different as they seem) is a manifestation of man's energy.[19] Thus in "Peace" he rejects the

[19] See *Fantasia,* pp. 56–57: it "still seems to me . . . the clue to the cosmos" that "instead of life being drawn from the sun, it is the emanation from life itself . . . which nourishes the sun."

apparent peace of "dead" lava on the earth's surface—"black peace congealed"—and declares paradoxically that the only real peace is to be found in the turbulent life beneath the silent crust.

> My heart will know no peace
> Till the hill bursts,

he cries, imagining the

> Brilliant, intolerable lava,
> Brilliant as a powerful burning-glass,
> Walking like a royal snake down the mountain towards the
>   sea,

and

> Naxos thousands of feet below the olive roots,
> And now the olive leaves thousands of feet below the lava
>   fire.

The olive, traditionally the plant of peace, must be drowned in lava, a kind of anagrammatical rearrangement of itself, before real peace can be achieved.

Significantly, in the process of imagining the "soul" of earth that must erupt as part of the cycle of fire and rock which maintains the planet's geological "peace," Lawrence touches on two powerful images of animal and human otherness—the "royal snake," suggesting pure blood-being, and buried Naxos, representing the Mediterranean morning of man's past. Each symbol is related to every other, each variety of otherness powerfully linked to all the rest, for "as within, so without," and "as below, so above." The fire at the heart of earth is like the dark fire at the heart of man, or like the blood-fire of the snake that holds within it something of the ancient's capacity for intuitional understanding.

In "Tropic" and "Southern Night," too, Lawrence projects the "dark burning" of man's fundamental selfhood—the blind, unconscious selfhood of all living things—into earth and moon. "Sun, dark sun," he begins in "Tropic," one of his most fluid and incantatory poems,

> Sun of black void heat,
> Sun of the torrid midday's horrific darkness:
>
> Behold my hair twisting and going black,
> Behold my eyes turn tawny yellow
> Negroid;
> See the milk of northern spume
> Coagulating and going black in my veins
> Aromatic as frankincense.

In touch with the terrifying, black heat of the cosmos, he finds himself transformed into an earlier self that can move with soft sureness in the "horrific darkness" as blind Samson did, a self with some of the knowledge men had when "God was all negroid, as now he is fair," and which, like the volcanic earth transforming him, is "as frictional, as perilous, explosive as brimstone."

Again, in "Southern Night" the burning equatorial landscape reveals a night-power that balances the transformational power of the "torrid mid-day." In this universe alive like a great but alien organism—alien, anyway, to man's northern nerve-brain self—even the moon is a "red thing . . . blood-dark," rather than a pale, lifeless satellite of earth, and the throbbing, Van Gogh-esque night in which mosquitoes bite "like memories" is folded in a "membrane of tranquil stars." Ancient augurs, Lawrence wrote, "gazed into the hot liver, that was mapped out in fields and regions like the sky of stars, but these fields and regions were those of the red, shining consciousness that runs through the whole animal creation." [20] Conversely, for Lawrence as for the augurs, the "sky of stars" is alive with the total inter-animation of a universe where mosquitoes are memories and memories mosquitoes. "Is not each soul a vivid thought in the great consciousness stream of God?" the poet rather ironically asks on behalf of St. John in

[20] *Etruscan Places*, p. 92.

"St. John." But he clearly wants us to realize that bodies are thoughts as much as souls are, for the world-soul is embodied in all things.

In such an animate universe, as in the wonder-filled cosmos of the ancients, even the sun may be charged with the power and burden of life.

> Does the sun in New Mexico sail like a fiery bird of prey in
> the sky
> Hovering?

Lawrence speculates in "Eagle in New Mexico."

> Does he shriek for blood?
> Does he fan great wings above the prairie like a hovering,
> blood-thirsty bird?

And in "Men in New Mexico" the sleep of the Indians, "a membrane of sleep, like a black blanket," representing their closeness to unconscious blood-being, becomes a function of the landscape, for though "the Indians thought the white men would awake them," even the "white men scramble asleep in the mountains" of America,

> And ride on horseback asleep forever through the desert,
> And shoot one another, amazed and mad with somnambulism,
> Thinking death will awaken something.

The *mountains* are "blanket-wrapped," therefore men are "born with a caul,/A black membrane over the face . . . And though the sun leaps like a thing unleashed in the sky," neither men nor mountains can rouse themselves from the primordial sleep of the landscape; both are "under the blanket."

"They are under the blanket," they are stifling, oblivious, asleep—but most important, men and mountains are not deadened or inanimate. On the contrary, sleep for Lawrence is a state of mysteriously deepened life; it is the state in which we approach most nearly to what we apprehend as being *en soi,* the condition of the intuitional blood–self in which one cannot separate oneself from oneself. As to Wordsworth, so to

183

Lawrence "the winds come . . . from the fields of sleep."
Thus, awake or asleep, landscape is always alive, the earth
itself, its hills, rivers, roots and rocks, always glowing with an
electric charge of life, an expression of the breath within and
without, the sun below and above. Trotting his little pony
"through the aspen trees of the canyon," Lawrence envisions
himself "trotting at ease betwixt the slopes of the golden/
Great and glistening-feathered legs of the hawk of Horus,"
and "under the pines" he goes "as under the hairy belly of a
great black bear." The desert is strewn with "an ash-grey pelt/
Of wolf all hairy and level, a wolf's wild pelt," and "the
rounded sides of the squatting Rockies" are

> Tigress brindled with aspen,
> Jaguar-splashed, puma-yellow, leopard-livid slopes of Amer-
> ica,

slopes that radiate the animal heat of "the living cosmos itself,
dazzlingly and gaspingly complex . . . divine and [to] be
contemplated only by the strongest souls." [21]

V

If it requires strength to confront the otherness of the cos-
mos, however, it requires even more courage to confront the
powerful forces of otherness within oneself. As we saw earlier,
Lawrence did achieve such a confrontation in some of the
Look! poems, a confrontation that was a direct result of the
"self-accomplishment" through love that volume recorded.
The "man who has come through," a surrogate for the poet
himself, was able to admit the three strange angels who rose
from deep recesses of his own being. But having achieved him-
self in Look! and in the two great novels contemporary with it,
Lawrence no longer felt so urgent a need to wrestle with "the
charge of fulfillment" through self-understanding.
Yet such a discovery of the otherness within himself and

[21] *Etruscan Places*, p. 85.

within all men was an inevitable byproduct of many poems in
Birds, Beasts and Flowers. Because these works deal with the
way all things are related, each necessarily involves some aspect
of the interior otherness that, polarized with the familiar sur-
face of consciousness, makes man human. Thus both "Snake"
and "Fish" explore not only the inhuman otherness of these
two creatures but also the inner human state they represent.
Matthew, writes Lawrence in "St. Matthew," "being a man,"
nightly "must resume [the] nakedness [of] a fish, sinking down
the dark reversion of night/Like a fish seeking the bottom."
In the day he is "lifted up" like a lark or "a rocket ending in
mid-heaven" in the scintillating, luminous flight of nerve-
brain consciousness. But at night his fish-, snake-, or bat-like
blood consciousness, his "bat-wingéd heart of man,/Reverséd
flame," shudders "a strange way down the bottomless pit,/To
the great depth of its reversèd zenith"—to what is apparently
the nadir yet really the zenith of the heaven within. In these
"fields of sleep," this inner landscape outer geography merely
mirrors, the human soul makes its strangest but most impor-
tant discoveries of alien-familiar selfhood.

"Medlars and Sorb Apples," one of the most moving and
successful poems in *Birds, Beasts and Flowers,* deals most spe-
cifically with this contradictory nature of selfhood. Savoring
the "delicious rottenness," the "rare, powerful, reminiscent
flavor" of these overripe fruits, Lawrence asks

> What is it?
> What is it, in the grape turning raisin,
> In the medlar, in the sorb-apple,
> Wineskins of brown morbidity,
> Autumnal excrementa,
> What is it that reminds us of white gods?

What is it, in other words, that leads us to sense a godly yet
mysterious self like a seed at the core of decay:

> Gods nude as blanched nut-kernels,
> Strangely, half-sinisterly flesh-fragrant

As if with sweat,
And drenched with mystery.

And the answer is that while *ripening* is for each living thing a process of becoming ever more purely itself, *rotting* is not, as one would expect, a kind of corollary falling away from the self but rather, to use Hopkins's word, a further "selving." Where in ripening, however, one becomes oneself by addition, through growth, through the accumulation of substance and experience, in "the stages of decay" one becomes "ever more vividly" oneself through exclusion, through a winnowing out of all that is not essentially oneself. Rotting is not putrefying but, paradoxically, purifying. "Wonderful are the hellish experiences," Lawrence tells us, evoking the "Orphic, delicate/ Dionysos of the Underworld"—the unimaginable, alien "soul" that is the seed of each individual's distinctive and forever isolated being, and which emerges only when the world's reality is sloughed off.

The sloughing-off, in keeping with the poem's Dionysiac quality, is sexual as well as deathly:

> A kiss, and a spasm of farewell, a moment's orgasm of rupture,
> Then along the damp road alone, till the next turning,
> And there a new partner, a new parting, a new unfusing into
>   twain,
> A new gasp of further isolation,
> A new intoxication of loneliness among decaying, frost-cold
>   leaves.

But for several reasons this intrusion of sexuality should not be surprising. Not only has Lawrence from the first associated sex and death in some of his best poems, such as "Love on the Farm," "Snapdragon," "A Young Wife," and "Hymn to Priapus," but he has consistently done so for a purpose: death, after all, must precede rebirth, the fruit must rot before the seed can emerge, and it is sex, Lawrence reminds us in "Tortoise Shout," one of his major statements on the subject, that makes us aware of our loneliness, our finiteness. The cry of the tortoise "in the spasm of coition," the crucifixion into sexual selfhood, is

> Worse than the cry of the new-born,
> A scream,
> A yell,
> A shout,
> A paeon,
> A death-agony,
> A birth-cry,
> A submission.

It is a "war-cry, triumph, acute-delight, death-scream reptilian," the primordial utterance of forever isolated "interiority," and it reminds Lawrence of all those cries of pain or pleasure, all those "first elements of foreign speech/On wild dark lips" which are the first expressions of the knowledge of self-limitation that must inevitably be a knowledge of death: the knowledge to which sexuality brings us. Eating the forbidden fruit, Adam and Eve bit into sex and death together; eating, they were plunged into Blake's realm of generation, where sex and death are necessary complements, for as Joseph Campbell has written

[Among many peoples] the basic myth is of a dreamlike age of the beginning, when there was neither death nor birth, which, however, terminated when a murder was committed. The body of the victim was cut up and buried. And not only did the food plants on which the community lives arise from those buried parts, but on all who ate of their fruit the organs of reproduction appeared; so that death, which had come into the world through a killing, was countered by its opposite, generation, and the self-consuming thing that is life, which lives on life, began its interminable course.[22]

Thus sex, implying death, is "the Cross,/The wheel on which our silence first is broken," evoking "the same cry from the tortoise as from Christ, the Osiris-cry of abandonment,

[22] Campbell, *The Masks of God: Oriental Mythology* (New York, 1962), p. 4.

That which is whole torn asunder,
That which is in part finding its whole again throughout the
　　universe.

If, however, Lawrence ended "Tortoise Shout" with the
"making whole," the culmination of the process of sexuality
that leads to rebirth, he is more concerned in "Medlars and
Sorb Apples" with the "tearing asunder" in which the soul
discovers with finality its own isolate and alien nature. In
orgasm after orgasm of separation, in gasp after gasp of lone-
liness, the individual falling past ripeness through the deadly
"stages of decay" becomes more and more himself. One goes

　　down the strange lanes of hell, more and more intensely
　　　alone,
　The fibres of the heart parting one after the other,

and yet, despite this anguish, one must continue "naked-
footed,"

　　ever more vividly embodied
　Like a flame blown whiter and whiter
　In a deeper and deeper darkness,
　Ever more exquisite, distilled in separation.

This purifying process is almost like the process by which
Yeats envisioned the soul—"Hades bobbin bound in mummy-
cloth"—spinning away the accretion of memories constituting
its apparent selfhood, and becoming that breathless essence it
always was beneath the random and ragged garments of mor-
tality. At last, for Lawrence as for Yeats, the soul discovers its
final, subterranean self and departs "with its own isolation,/
Strangest of all strange companions,/And best," departs like
Orpheus down "the winding, leaf-clogged, silent lanes of hell."
　　Hell here is not Dante's infernal kingdom of retribution,
but rather that underworld to which Lawrence so often turned
in thought, the blue-shadowed Hades of Orpheus and Perseph-
one, cool with the damp loneliness of underground caverns,

labyrinthine as the mind's own darkness.[23] Into this grave of nature dead leaves sink like abandoned souls in autumn, and into this frost-cold hell the soul falls like a leaf in its isolation, falls in abnegation of its worldly selfhood and in acceptance of the ultimate isolation and passivity to which all creatures must be reduced.

Lawrence uses the metaphor of drunkenness to express his sense of the nature of this final but "strange companion" that is one's own interior otherness. The soul's farewell to its upper self—its earthly consciousness—is an "Orphic farewell, and farewell, and farewell," dizzily prolonged, but this *"jamque vale"* is merely the prelude to a new and mystic consciousness:

> the *ego sum* of Dionysos,
> The *sono io* of perfect drunkenness,
> Intoxication of final loneliness,

in which, precisely because of its abandonment of nerve-brain controls, the soul is paradoxically expanded and perfected. In drunkenness, after all, intuitional knowledge gains ascendancy over the soberer "ordinary mind," and when we "take the fern-seed in our lips,/Close the eyes, and go/Down the tendrilled avenues of wine and the otherworld," we come as close as we ever can to that state of pure being Lawrence considered in some respects the ultimate, if mysterious, fulfillment. Surrendering to otherness, the self—the ego—finally triumphs; isolated, it becomes one with itself; rotting, it ripens into the wholeness of Orpheus and Dionysos. It is this wholeness, this rebirth, that is, to venture a baroque phrase, at once the promise and the premise of natural process. And this wholeness, achieved through an imaginative integration into the consciousness of unknown modes of being, is finally the object of all Lawrence's acts of attention to birds, beasts and flowers.

[23] See Moore, *Heart,* pp. 448, 508.

——PART IV

MAN ALL SCARLET

Man that is man is more than a man.
No man is man till he is more than a man.
Till the power is in him
Which is not his own.
              "Third Song of Huitzilopochtli"

For the thing that is done without the glowing as of
    god, vermilion,
were best not done at all.
        "For the Heroes Are Dipped in Scarlet"

—12
A Yearning Myth:
Man More Than Man

i

Because Lawrence's poetic career was a continual process of self-development, just as his best poems were processes of attention, he could not allow himself simply to repeat the successful performance of *Birds, Beasts and Flowers* in later verse. For one thing, he had attended as intently as possible in that volume to non-human nature. How long, after all, can a writer who believes that his business is the whole man alive turn in horror from "these little swarming selves" to the purity of animals and plants? Even though Lawrence continued to feel "there is [no] very cordial or fundamental contact between me and society, or me and other people,"[1] sooner or later he would have to reconcile himself to man, his major subject and his only audience.

Of course, the antihuman bitterness persisted. Like Kate in *The Plumed Serpent,* Lawrence still felt that "the longer I live the more loathsome the human species becomes to me."[2] "I love life, I love life so dearly, I could almost die/Of chagrin at being a man," he declared in a "pansy" written perhaps as late as 1929.[3] But in the years following the publication of *Birds, Beasts and Flowers* he was, again like Kate, nearing forty. "The

---

[1] "Autobiographical Sketch," *Assorted Articles,* p. 151.
[2] *The Plumed Serpent,* Ch. II: "Tea-Party in Tlacolula."
[3] "Life and the Human Consciousness," *CP,* p. 837.

first half of [his] life with its flowers and its love and its stations of the cross"—the era, as he saw it, of purely personal experience—was over. "Now [he] must turn over and the page was black, black and empty." [4] Lawrence must have recognized that he could not fill it merely with hate; he was a sick man who must make his peace with the world. Yet feeling as he did about man as he is, how could he return to the kind of loving, detailed consideration of humanity that had occupied him in novels like *The Rainbow* and in some of the early fictionalized poems?

Lawrence's solution to this problem was to immerse himself in an idea of man not just as he is but *as he should be,* in a "yearning myth" [5] of man as fully man when, paradoxically, "more than a man." "Man is only perfectly human/When he looks beyond humanity," he wrote in one of the late "pansies," [6] and from this image of "man all scarlet" with fully achieved being, from this concept of man as, in a sense, the myth of himself, derives much of the power of *The Plumed Serpent,* with its mass of otherwise perhaps unjustified poetry, and of *Lady Chatterley's Lover,* and of many of the *Pansies.*

Looking again at some of the misanthropic statements Lawrence makes both in his own voice and through his characters, we can see that he himself was perfectly conscious of this Carlylean distinction between man as he is and man as he should be, man all grubby and man all scarlet. [7] "How I *hate* the attitude of ordinary people to life. How I loathe ordinariness!" he wrote to Aldous Huxley after a particularly trying visit from his sister Emily. [8] But "If a man looked at me for one moment as the sun does,/I could accept men," he admitted in another "pansy." [9] And, like his creator, Ramon, the messianically inclined demi-hero of *The Plumed Serpent,* reflects that

[4] *The Plumed Serpent,* Ch. III: "Fortieth Birthday."
[5] Lawrence's phrase in *Studies* for Cooper's "Leatherstocking" novels.
[6] "Service," *CP,* p. 650.
[7] Cf. Carlyle's distinction between mechanical "profit-and-loss" thinking and "Natural Supernaturalism" in *Sartor Resartus.*
[8] *Letters,* p. 1084.   [9] *CP,* p. 840.

"mere *personal* contact, mere human contact, filled him . . . with disgust." As they are in themselves, his friends and associates repel him. "But this was because, or when, he met them on a merely human, personal plane . . . He had to meet them on another plane, where the contact was different; intangible, remote." [10] Like Lawrence, he has to meet them on a mythical plane, where they are "more than men," self-transcendent abstractions of themselves.

For Ramon, and for Lawrence, Kate must no longer be Kate Forrester-Tyler-Leslie, a particular person who has had a particular series of largely unsatisfactory husbands. She must become Malintzi, the green-gowned goddess of fertility, wife to generations of godlike men and mistress of the dreams of even more.[11] And Cipriano cannot be merely Cipriano Viedma, an impulsive and cruel Mexican general. Instead he must become the Red Huitzilopochtli, the fiery god of the phallus and of the male courage that Lawrence calls "the second strength"—a Pan figure, a column of blood. "In the shadowy world where men were visionless," thinks Kate, "and winds of fury rose up from the earth, Cipriano was still a power." And "No, thank God! I have not got a life of my own!" exclaims Ramon-Quetzalcoatl's young second wife, Teresa. "I have been able to give it to a man who is more than a man, as they say in their Quetzalcoatl language." [12]

Similarly, in *Lady Chatterley's Lover,* Mellors and Connie, redeemed through sacramental sensuality, discover their second, mythological selves in their own bodies. No longer a particular, harassed lady and her rather literary game-keeper, they become John Thomas and Lady Jane, playfully but also, Lawrence tries to show, in all seriousness, god and goddess of phallus and vulva. Ritually wreathed in flowers, they enter a purer, more scarlet realm, literally and figuratively filled with

[10] *The Plumed Serpent,* Ch. XVII: "Fourth Hymn and the Bishop."
[11] This is probably why Lawrence devotes space to what Hough (p. 130) witheringly calls "sartorial and cosmetic detail."
[12] *The Plumed Serpent,* Ch. XX: "Marriage by Quetzalcoatl," and Ch. XXV: "Teresa."

"the second strength," "the other power" of the supra-personal blood. In the end, having decided to abandon the old particular world of Wragby and Tevershall, they meet "outside the Golden Cock, in Adam Street."

In some of the poems in *Pansies* Lawrence expresses this relationship between a person's lesser and greater selves most directly.

> What's the good of a man
> unless there's the glimpse of a god in him?

he asks.

> And what's the good of a woman
> unless she's a glimpse of a goddess of some sort.

And he adds that

> When men and women, when lads and girls are not thinking,
> when they are pure, which means when they are quite clean
> from self-consciousness . . .
> you may see glimpses of the gods in them.

Thus in "For a Moment," perhaps his most successful poem on this subject, Lawrence describes a tram-conductor, a servant-girl, his wife Frieda, and his Italian publishing associate Pino Orioli caught up in those moments of godly self-transcendence that Kate, Ramon, Cipriano, Connie and Mellors experience in the novels. But of course Frieda, becoming Isis, is no longer Frieda. Pino Orioli-as-centaur is no longer Pino Orioli, the Florentine publisher of *Lady Chatterley's Lover*. And Lawrence himself, praying in the ironically titled "Conceit" for this divine translation, returns to the paradox with which he had worked in *Look!*—the paradox that in order to become fully oneself, one may have to relinquish some of one's particularity. "Now let me be myself," he asks,

> now let me be myself and flicker forth,
> now let me be myself, in the being, one of the gods.

196

For all Lawrence's early interest in self-achievement and particularity, then, for all his conviction that "there are many ways, not one way," he could only, finally, justify the ways of man to man (and to God) by effacing the personal particularity of each individual and making him a mask or vessel for a more abstract, even mythical, force. In several late works he provides the explicit rationale behind this carefully worked-out conciliatory myth. In *Etruscan Places*, for instance, he presents what he believes to be the ancient idea of "man, amid all the glowing welter, adventuring, struggling, striving for

one thing, life, vitality, more vitality: to get into himself more and more of the gleaming vitality of the cosmos . . . the active religious idea was that man, by vivid attention and subtlety and exerting all his strength, could draw more life into himself, more and more glistening vitality, till he became shining like the morning, blazing like a god. When he was all himself he painted himself vermilion like the throat of dawn, and was god's body, visibly, red and utterly vivid . . . There you have the ancient idea of kings, kings who are gods by vividness, because they have gathered into themselves core ofter core of vital potency from the universe, till they are clothed in scarlet, they are bodily a piece of the deepest fire.

For Lawrence, scarlet perfectly represents man's godhood, his intensity when he is purely himself. Earlier in *Etruscan Places* he tells us that when the American Indians "wish to figure in their sacred and portentous selves they smear their bodies all over with red . . . Man all scarlet [is] his bodily godly self." [13] Scarlet is the color of fire, the destroyer and, radiating from the sun, the creator of all life. Scarlet is also, Lawrence adds, the color of men's bodies when they go naked in the sun, which for him—as for Stevens—should be "naked among us as a savage source." Finally, scarlet is the color of blood, and therefore emblematic of what is, in Lawrence's view, the essence and sustenance of man.

[13] *Etruscan Places*, pp. 84–85, 72.

A passage from *The Plumed Serpent* vividly illustrates all these points

> As [the sun] flushed along the surface of the lake, it caught the body of Cipriano and he was red as fire, as a piece of pure fire. The Sons of the Morning! The column of blood! [Kate] looked at him in wonder, as he moved, pure red and luminous, further into the lake, unconscious. As if on fire!

Almost every word of this little scene can be readily related to Lawrence's myth of man, but the phrase "the column of blood" is central. *"The blood is one blood, we are one blood,"* the men of Quetzalcoatl seem to Kate to be saying, and it is because of this, she sees, that "blood sacrifice [was once] so potent a factor of life." For through such ritual "the blood of the individual is given back to the great blood-being, the god, the nation, the tribe." [14] Blood, readily transfused from man to man, represents, Lawrence suggests, not just the instinctive, "passional" self, but also our common humanity, the great, sacred community in which we have an existence beyond our merely personal existence as individuals. Thus Cipriano, becoming his greater self, becomes "Huitzilopochtli,/The red Huitzilopochtli,/The blood-red," with "Yellow of the Sun,/Sun in the blood," and "White of the bone,/Bone in the blood" [15]—with godly blood that contains all the heat and strength of the cosmos.

Like Emerson, Lawrence seems to believe that modern man is "the dwarf of himself" but that once "he filled nature with his overflowing currents," and nature, reciprocally, filled him.[16] He differs from Emerson, however, in hopefully affirming that mythic man still waits like a seed in "the manhood of men," like a "stirring in the blood." "[Man] no longer fills the veins

---

[14] All these quotations are from *The Plumed Serpent,* Ch. XXVI: "Kate is a Wife." Lawrence isn't endorsing "blood-sacrifice," just explaining it.

[15] *Ibid.,* "First Song of Huitzilopochtli."

[16] Ralph Waldo Emerson, *Nature,* Ch. VIII: "Prospects."

and veinlets; he is shrunk to a drop," mourns Emerson. But "I watch by the fire,/I wait behind men," asserts Huitzilopochtli, the god-man.

Waiting to be realized or revealed in the flesh is, in fact, for Lawrence one of the central characteristics of the god that is man. "The only gods on earth are men," he writes in "Hopi Snake Dance," "for Gods, like man, do not exist beforehand . . . The cosmos is a great furnace, a dragon's den, where the heroes and demi-gods, men, forge themselves into being. . . . Gods are the outcome, not the origin." [17] But if Gods are to *be* the outcome, if all the Ciprianos of the world are to become the Huitzilopochtli that is in them, if all the Lady Chatterleys are to discover their second, Lady Jane selves, they must be furnished with models of their divine potential—which is what Lawrence's myths are; and sometimes, when Lawrence is in a polemical mood (as in some of *The Plumed Serpent* poems and in many of the *Pansies*) he feels he must tell people directly what they should be.

Urgent as Lawrence thought his message, however, neither his concept of man as god nor his corollary vision of man *becoming* god is unique. The myth of man has firm roots in Whitman, Carlyle, Emerson, and others, and the belief that life is a process of becoming is a Romantic one, formulated, for instance, in Keats' vision of the world as a vale of soul-making. Furthermore, in our own century a new kind of anthropomorphism discovers in man—in the manhood of Jesus, for instance—the redemptive value formerly assigned to Christ's godhood. Yeats, Camus, Lawrence, Stevens, and Thomas are all at one time or another writers in this tradition. "Whatever flames upon the night, man's own resinous heart has fed," declares Yeats. "Man be my metaphor," Thomas commands. And "Shall our blood come to be the blood of paradise?" asks Stevens—rhetorically, for he already believes that it is so.

Yet of all these writers only Lawrence (and perhaps Stevens)

[17] *Mornings in Mexico,* pp. 150–151.

really required the myth of man as more than man, the myth of man as god, in order to be reconciled to man at all. For Camus, certainly, it is man's absurd frailty as much as his paradoxical strength, that makes him admirable. And Yeats, at least the Yeats of *The Winding Stair* and *Last Poems*, is passionately anxious to "cast out remorse" for the inadequacies of manhood. "A living man is blind and drinks his drop," he agrees, yet, paradoxically, for this reason "we are blest by everything,/Everything we look upon is blest." For Lawrence, however, the particular individual, with all his pain and his uncertainty, is always faintly contemptible, just as for Stevens life without a commitment to the imagination's capacity for a "Supreme Fiction" is always somehow impoverished. One must be "a manifestation as well as a man," [18] Lawrence punningly asserts, for "the gods are only ourselves as we are in our moments of pure manifestation." [19] Like Kate, in these late years of his life he can only really admire "dark, collective men, non-individual," and there is even a part of him that can only care about Kate when she is "gone into her greater self, her womanhood consummated in the greater womanhood." [20]

ii

The part of Lawrence that particularly needs to thinks of Kate as Malintzi, Woman, rather than Kate Leslie, a woman, seems to me specifically the part of him that is a poet. As a novelist, he must accept the existence of Kate Forrester-Tyler-Leslie with all her faintly tawdry permutations—what other choice has he?—but as a poet he finds that his imagination is moved by Kate the Woman more than woman. Despite some of his early successes in the fictionalized mode, like "Love on

[18] *The Plumed Serpent,* Ch. XX: "Marriage by Quetzalcoatl."
[19] "The Gods," *CP,* p. 673.
[20] *The Plumed Serpent,* Ch. VII: "The Plaza." Kate's (and Lawrence's) longing for the collective, the abstract, contrasts curiously with the writer's usual dislike of abstraction. Significantly, Kate later (in Ch. XXVII) expresses resentment against "all this abstraction, and *will.*"

the Farm" and "Snapdragon," Lawrence the poet was inclined to reject the qualified vision he necessarily employed in his novels. His fiction might be ironic, but for the most part his poetry was not. Rather, it attentively celebrated pure being, the thing-in-itself. Yet though such a poetic mode is well suited to the religious vision of Man as more than man, what could be more unsuitable than such a vision of "pure manifestation" to the ironies of the novel?

Having noted this, I ought to concede that a writer of Lawrence's skill always, at his best, finds ways around such difficulties. Thus, in *Lady Chatterley*, he uses the multiple ironies of the novel form to show how Connie and Mellors, with much trouble and hesitancy, *bring* their second, Adamic selves into existence. The whole book in fact is a demonstration that man can become god, or godly—and paradoxically can become so through a tender cultivation of what might be thought of as human frailty. Even so, however, it is precisely the last part of the book, where Mellors and Connie have achieved their "greater" selfhood, that disturbs most critics. To Graham Hough, for instance, the pagan romp in the rain and the ritual wreathing of the newly deified John Thomas and Lady Jane seem merely gratuitous.[21] And perhaps they are, in terms of what we would ordinarily expect from a novel. Such moments of pure manifestation are subjects Lawrence himself felt would be better treated in poetry.

Certainly his major reason for introducing verse into *The Plumed Serpent* was to enable him to deal more purely—less ironically—with the greater manhood he believed Cipriano and Ramon would achieve in becoming Huitzilopochtli and Quetzalcoatl. And, despite a widespread critical judgment that the hymns and rituals are tedious and irrelevant, the *Plumed Serpent* poems are frequently very successful when read for their own sakes. Indeed, "The Coming of Quetzalcoatl," "Quetzalcoatl Looks Down on Mexico," "What Quet-

[21] Hough, p. 161. See also Noel Annan, "Love Story," *N.Y. Review of Books*, Vol. XVII, No. 6 (Oct. 21, 1971), 12.

zalcoatl Saw in Mexico," "The Living Quetzalcoatl," "Welcome to Quetzalcoatl" and "First Song of Huitzilopochtli" express their themes more surely and arouse fewer misgivings in us than any comparable prose scenes or passages.

"The Living Quetzalcoatl," "Welcome to Quetzalcoatl" and "First Song of Huitzilopochtli" in particular make Lawrence's essentially religious points about greater manhood with a terse intensity impossible or at least implausible in "the glowing welter" of a fictionalized situation. "All things that lift in the lift of living between earth and sky know me," affirms Quetzalcoatl in his triumphant song, and using Aztec metaphors (some drawn directly from translations he found in Lewis Spence's *The Gods of Mexico*) Lawrence has him explain

> For I am Quetzalcoatl, the feathered snake.
> And I am not with you till my serpent has coiled his circle
>   of rest in your belly.
> And I, Quetzalcoatl, the eagle of the air, am brushing your
>   faces with vision.
> I am fanning your breasts with my breath,
> And building my nest of peace in your bones.
> I am Quetzalcoatl of the two Ways.

Such a verse-passage is neither tedious nor irrelevant, for Lawrence has accomplished exactly what he set out to do: in simple, apparently naive verse that has some of the visionary quality of a *Douanier* Rousseau primitive, to rewaken "the faculty of mythical consciousness which has degenerated" in the modern world "into intellectual consciousness." [22]

For this purpose the poetic image of the plumed serpent, so carefully elaborated in the poem, is exactly apt. As H. M. Daleski has written, it is man's simultaneous participation in the material and spiritual realms that makes him, in Lawrence's terms, godly or potentially godly.[23] Quetzalcoatl the

[22] Goodheart, p. 48.
[23] In *The Forked Flame* Daleski explores Lawrence's dualism extensively.

feathered snake, with plumes emblematic of air, heaven, spirit, and a serpentine body representative of the earth's hot heaviness, symbolically unites the two realms. Moreover, as "the Son of the Morning Star" he is "the flashing intermediary" [24] between night and day, darkness and light, symbolic of "the consummated self . . . born [again through] an acceptance of man's dual nature." [25]

> Midmost shines as the Morning Star midmost shines
> Between night and day, my Soul-star in one,

sings the newly risen Quetzalcoatl. The message is clear to the Indians, his subjects. "Ah Quetzalcoatl," they reply, in "Welcome to Quetzalcoatl." "Put sleep as black as beauty in the secret of my belly. Put star-oil over me./Call me a man." (Anoint me, that is, with the essence of manhood, "for man is the Morning Star/And Woman is the star of evening.") The message is clear to them because it can be made clear by Lawrence the poet. For the novelist, however, getting the message across is another matter—and it is to the difficulties of the novelist that critical readers respond.

For one thing, the verse statements of Quetzalcoatl and Huitzilopochtli exist on a transcendent plane which has almost nothing to do—that is Lawrence's point, after all—with Ramon and Cipriano themselves. Intoning "out of the depths of the sky, I came like an eagle/Out of the bowels of the earth like a snake," Ramon is obviously not speaking in *propria persona*. As Ramon Carrasco, a plantation-owning aristocrat with politico-literary pretensions, he is not himself "the inward star invisible . . . the lamp in the hand of the Unknown Mover." Yet despite Graham Hough's assertion that the *Plumed Serpent* hymns are "formally abominable" and that their "imagery is false" [26] it seems to me that in an incantatory hymn like "The Living Quetzalcoatl" Lawrence convinces us that there *may* be an "inward star invisible," a

[24] "Market Day," *Mornings in Mexico,* p. 96.   [25] Daleski, p. 221.
[26] Hough, 137.

"lamp in the hand of the Unknown Mover"—and it is not his job as an artist to prove that there *is* such a lamp. The imagery of the poems is only false when Ramon and Cipriano as they are are brought into necessarily ironic relation with the gods they should be. Then, because of the extrapolations of the novelist, the poetical credibility of the characters is tried.

In *Lady Chatterley* the juxtaposition of personal and impersonal selves is never a serious problem. By the end of the book Mellors' and Connie's old selves have been sloughed off. "John Thomas says goodnight to Lady Jane, a little droopingly, but with a hopeful heart." The fictional process has been put to good use, but fictional ironies are largely avoided. In *The Plumed Serpent,* however, gods and men—the greater and the smaller selves—coexist almost from the beginning, yet much of the time, for this reason, the relationship is not natural, inevitable. Lawrence believes that man must become god, but in *The Plumed Serpent* he imposes god on man. The god figures, unlike John Thomas and Lady Jane, are antecedent to the human, so that the humans—Cipriano, Ramon and Kate—must in every case fit themselves to the god-masks, a grimly Procrustean torture. Kate is herself rebelliously aware of this. "Malintzi!" she exclaims in horrified protest. "I am Kate Forrester, really. . . . Loathsome, really, to be called Malintzi—*I've had it put over me.*" [27] Unlike Connie, she has not generated this goddess in herself. Rather, she seems to have been brought into existence to serve the requirements of the goddess.

Because gods and humans have a simultaneous rather than a causal relationship in *The Plumed Serpent,* Lawrence is often obliged to sacrifice the human impulses of his characters, out of which he would ordinarily build his novel, to the exigencies of the gods. The two most fully rounded figures

[27] *The Plumed Serpent,* Ch. XXII: "The Living Huitzilopochtli." Kate's colloquial "I've had it put over me" embodies an effective pun. Really Kate Forrester, she has had "Malintzi" put over her, obliterating her individuality just as her successive "married names" did.

among the principals, for instance, are certainly Ramon and Kate—and it is just as certain that they are the two who would in the usual Lawrence novel be destined for each other. The requirements of the theocracy make such a mating impossible, however. Kate frequently catches herself yearning after Ramon, and even at one point discovers she is irrationally jealous of Teresa, but she is destined to be Malintzi, and therefore the bride of Huitzilopochtli-Cipriano, though "without Ramon Cipriano was just an instrument and not ultimately interesting to her." [28] Cipriano is not *as a man* of much interest to Lawrence, either, though as a god he fires the author's poetic imagination. But a symbol of pure maleness like Cipriano cannot be of real interest to a novelist, nor can a symbol of pure femaleness like Teresa. As gods, Huitzilopochtli, Quetzalcoatl, and Malintzi can exist in the poems, yet as they are presented to us in the novel their manhood is always seriously qualified—even violated—by their godhood. We can only conclude, therefore, that rather than the poems being irrelevant to the novel, it is the novel that is in a sense irrelevant to the poems.

[28] *Ibid.,* Ch. XXV: "Teresa.": "She resented being made so conscious of his physical presence, his full, male body . . ." See also Ch. XIII: ". . . perhaps Ramon is the only one [who] touches me somewhere inside," thinks Kate.

—13
Black Tears:
Man Less Than Man

i

There are places, however, where *The Plumed Serpent* as a novel is more than irrelevant to the poems. In a few cases it is actually destructive of them. I have already noted Lawrence's tendency to polemicize in *The Plumed Serpent,* and a kind of disgruntled preachiness certainly saps the strength of some of the less successful hymns. The "Third Song of Huitzilo-pochtli," for instance, which starts out splendidly with one of the writer's most direct statements of his great theme of these years:

> Man that is man is more than a man.
> No man is man till he is more than a man.
> Till the power is in him
> Which is not his own,

is marred by an almost paranoid sermon against cowards and traitors—"the liars . . . the thieves . . . the false and treacherous and mean" who are like "grey dogs creeping out, where my deer are browsing in the dusk." Not only does this quite unreasonably imply an animal hierarchy—why are grey dogs any "meaner" than deer or rabbits, eagles or snakes?—but it introduces a strain of moralizing that has much more to do with the exigencies of the novel than with the assumptions of the verse. "The Song of the Grey Dog," "The Lords of Life Are the Masters of Death," and "Huitzilopochtli Gives the

Black Blade of Death" are all similarly marred by self-righteous sermonizing, necessary in order to justify action in the story (such as the ritual execution of two peons) rather than any of the perceptions that are usually the business of this poet.

But some of the imagery of these poems does evolve out of a corollary of the idea that "man that is man is more than a man"—the perhaps inevitable notion that if man is not "more than a man" in Lawrence's sense, he is somehow *less* than a man. "Man is *not quite* a man," Lawrence tells us in "Man is More than Homo Sapiens," one of the *Pansies* poems, "unless he has his pure moments, when he is surpassing." If one believes, after all, that man should be godly, his ordinary, trivial humanity becomes more infuriating than it would be otherwise.

Looking around him and seeing godly manifestation only rarely, Lawrence grew even harsher in his judgment of man-as-he-is than he had been before. The concept of "the greater manhood" that had been developed as a bridge back to humanity for the embittered writer ended up widening the gulf. Those men who are not gods are "grey dogs" in the poems of *The Plumed Serpent,* gods turned backward, or they are "living dead, the dead that live and are not refreshed," or "such frogs, with stones in their bellies," or "cocks that can't crow . . . pigs that can't grunt . . . money vermin." And the world they inhabit, from *The Plumed Serpent* onward—through *Pansies, Nettles,* and *Lady Chatterley*—is either a great "nullus" or a huge nullifying mechanism, "a very vast machine," as Lawrence told Koteliansky in one of his letters, "that grinds the bones of the good man gladly." [1]

In *Pansies* and *Nettles,* even more than in *The Plumed Serpent,* Lawrence's angry disappointment with men for being "less" instead of "more than" men is everywhere apparent. While in *The Plumed Serpent* he tried consistently to see men in terms of their god-selves, and only intermittently focused

[1] *Letters,* p. 785.

on their failures to attain full manhood, by the time he wrote *Pansies* and *Nettles* he could no longer see the godhood he had postulated earlier except in "glimpses," in "flickers," in flashing moments continually balanced by the dehumanized nothingness that became his theme in these works.

"While people live the life," he admitted in "Two Ways of Living and Dying,"

> they are open to the restless skies, and streams flow in and
> out . . .
> and man is an iridescent fountain, rising up to flower
> for a moment godly like Baal or Krishna, or Adonis or
> Balder, or Lucifer.

But, he added—and it was a thought to which he obsessively returned in these years—

> when people are only self-conscious and self-willed
> they cannot die, their corpse still runs on,
> while nothing comes from the open heaven, from earth,
> from the sun and moon
> to them, nothing, nothing;
> only the mechanical power of self-directed energy
> drives them on and on, like machines.

"Nothing comes . . . to them, nothing, nothing." The statement appears deliberately ambiguous, for at this stage in his life Lawrence conceives of nothingness not merely as a negation of being but as a positive evil in itself, and he sees the universe as a Manichean battleground between two forces— the godly, light-life principle of the earth's inner and outer suns, and the cold, bleak principle of what he only half-jokingly called, in "Hymn to Nothingness," "the one Almighty Nullus."

It is out of a radical inability to deal with this "Nullus" as Lawrence would have them deal with it—by becoming gods, existentially, in the face of emptiness—that the people whom Lawrence characterizes in *Pansies* and *Nettles* dehumanize themselves, or so he would contend. Yet to us it may seem that his unsympathetic vision dehumanizes them as well, as it nullifies a universe that cannot be consistently godly. In "Bathing Resort," for instance, Lawrence describes people as objects with fascinated nausea:

> They are gold, they are brown, they are purplish, they glisten
> Like silk, they are flesh, sheer flesh;
> The dark ones are curiously purplish, like fresh
> Plums; the blond ones are gold, with less glisten. . . .
>
> Great thighs that lead nowhere
> Yet are fleeced with soft hair.
> Breasts that wink not
> Heads that think not . . .
> Without mystery, mute,
> Well-grown like potatoes on a lifted root.

Man all scarlet with sunburn rather than with the gleam of godhood is no more to Lawrence than a curiously interesting plum or a red-brown insentient potato, sexless (with "great thighs that lead nowhere") and "meaningless." Consequently he feels justified in asserting that "not one man in a thousand has even a soul to lose./The automat has no soul to lose/So it can't have one to save." Indeed, at this point and with these assumptions, he can go even further, ruthlessly declaring that "Humanity needs pruning . . . not, as in the late war, blasting/with unintelligent and evil destruction/but pruning, severely, intelligently and ruthlessly pruning."

Lawrence himself must have recognized that this statement was hardly humane. If he had lived he would have seen such a "pruning" effected as the "final solution" to a problem Hitler and others formulated in similar terms. Yet in a series of retorts to Christ ("But I Say Unto You: Love One Another," "Love Thy Neighbor," and "As Thyself!") he tries to show that most men are so hopelessly inhuman it is not possible to treat them humanely.

> I love my neighbor
> but
> are these things my neighbors?

he asks, in despair. His neighbors, he replies, are only those who are fully human.

> My neighbor, O my neighbor!
> Occasionally I see him, silent, a little wondering,
> with his ears pricked and his body wincing
> threading his way among the robot machine-people.

The robot metaphor is crucial. In Lawrence's view, people *make* themselves inhuman, and throughout *Pansies* and *Nettles* he shows that they do this in two related ways. First, they do it through yielding what should be their divine self-hood to the annihilating machine of modern society. Like automata, they substitute the impersonal gestures of mass culture for their own true impulses. "We are born so woolly and swaddled up in mass ideas that we hardly get a chance to make a real move of our own," Lawrence commented in one of the popular articles he wrote almost simultaneously with *Pansies*. "We just bleat foolishly out of a mass of woolly cloud, our mass-ideas." [2]

The bourgeois is beastly, then, in the poem "How Beastly the Bourgeois Is," because "like a fungus" he lives "on the remains of bygone life,/sucking his life out of the dead leaves of greater life than his own." Robot-hollow (like Eliot's hollow men), he is unable to think or feel for himself. "When is a man not a man?" Lawrence asks in "The Gentleman," a bitter conundrum that summarizes this point: "When he's a gentleman"—when he substitutes the lifeless mechanism of a social code for the human, potentially godly values that should grow from his own soul.

> Hardly ever, now, has a human face
> the baffling light or the strange still gleam of the gods
> within it, upon it,

[2] "Master in His Own House," *Assorted Articles,* p. 57.

declares the poet in "The Human Face."

> Holbein and Titian and Tintoret could never paint faces,
>   now:
> because those faces were windows to the strange horizons,
>   even Henry VIII;
> whereas faces now are only human grimaces,
> with eyes like the interiors of stuffy rooms, furnished.

And in "Children Singing In School" he describes how even children must "utter cog-wheel sounds" because "they have no song in their souls, none in their spirits."

Why is it, though, that the social machine is so much more powerful than the godliness of men, stronger even than the spontaneous humanity of children? The answer to this question suggests the second way men, in Lawrence's view, deliberately dehumanize themselves.

> Men wanted to be like gods
> so they became like machines
> and now even they're not satisfied.

It is what Lawrence as early as *Women in Love* called man's "fixed mechanical will"—his Faustian intellectual pride—that causes him to substitute his mind's dead artifice for nature's gleaming vitality, and thus to be controlled by his own desire for control.

> Man invented the machine
> and now the machine has invented man,

Lawrence writes in "Men and Machines."

> God the Father is a dynamo
> and God the Son a talking radio
> and God the Holy Ghost is gas that keeps it all going.

The religious parody here is of special interest—and may be especially confusing—in relation to the poet's ecstatic vision of man as god. But in Lawrence's scheme godliness springs not from man's *will* to godliness, not from man's idea of godliness, but rather from precisely that surrender of intellectual control which characterizes man in his moments of pure manifestation. When man consciously decides to become a god, he becomes a robot. Only when he forgets his will-to-transcendence and allows himself to be fully a man does he become, at least momentarily, a god.

"Oh Wonderful Machine!" expresses with savage irony what Lawrence felt to be the blasphemous nature of the creed of the intellect-machine, the modern religion of nothingness that has reduced man from the more than human being he might have become to the less than human creature he is.

> Oh wonderful machine, you are man's idea of godliness,
> you who feel nothing, who know nothing, who run on absolved
> from any other connection!
> Oh you godly and smooth machine, spinning on in your own Nirvana . . .
> how is it you have to be looked after by some knock-kneed wretch
> at two pounds a week?

We have trapped ourselves, Lawrence thought, trapped gods who should be free citizens of a strange and gleaming firmament in the terrible mechanism of a dehumanized society.

> A little moon, quite still, leans and sings to herself through the night,

he noted in "Listen to the Band," adding in despair

> and the music of men is like a mouse gnawing,
> gnawing in a wooden trap, trapped in.

It is not surprising that, feeling at times such hopelessness, he wrote to his sister-in-law, as his illness grew, that "I am so weak. And something inside me weeps black tears. I wish it would go away." [3]

[3] *Letters*, p. 1206.

To dehumanize people, however, as Lawrence so frequently does in *The Plumed Serpent, Pansies* and *Nettles,* is not to attend to them as they really are in themselves. It is at least in part to attend only to one's own "black tears." But after the trauma of the war years, Lawrence was never able to devote to any human being quite the attention he had expended on, say, the Brangwens in *The Rainbow* or, later, on birds, beasts and flowers. Especially in the poems, man for Lawrence, from 1923 onward, is either larger than life, a vaguely but ecstatically delineated god, or smaller than life, at times a corpse-like robot seen through veils of disappointment and despair, and at other times a cartoon-figure, a sad and funny caricature of humanity. In every case his attention is to the essence of his subjects rather than the accidents of their lives. For if one kind of essence is captured in the religious hyperboles of the hymnal or the distorting metaphors of despair, another is captured in the spare but irreverent lines of the cartoon.

Though Lawrence produced a number of seriously misanthropic poems to balance his poems on man as god, the best of his works on man less than Man are written in a comic mode. Just as "The Living Quetzalcoatl" is an attempt at a splendid fresco, so "The Noble Englishman," "Willy Wet-Leg," "The English Are So Nice," and many others, are basically quick sardonic sketches. By indirection, though parodic dialogue and neat spare characterization, they make more effectively the same points about man less than Man that such poems as "Humanity Needs Pruning" and "Oh Wonderful Machine" tried to make directly. Lawrence seems to have been at least intermittently aware that laughter—even bitter laughter—might be the best medicine for an inhuman society. "If we come back into our own," he rather magisterially told Mabel Luhan in 1924, "we'll prance in as centaurs, sensible, a bit fierce, and amused. . . . My gods, like the Great God Pan, have a bit of a natural grin on their faces." [4] And even in all the high seriousness of *The Plumed Serpent* there are moments when Kate relaxes into the kind of sardonic cartoonist's vision that is most consistently characteristic of Lawrence's work in *Pansies* and *Nettles*. "Of all the horrors," she thinks wryly at one point, "perhaps the grimalkin women, her contemporaries, were the most repellent to her. . . . Even the horrid old tomcat men of the civilized roof gutter did not fill her with such sickly dread." [5]

From grimalkin women and tomcat men it is not far to "the gentleman" of *Pansies* with his "very nice apple-of-Sodom rind" and his "lovely English voice/whooing and cooing and fading away with wonderful genteel deprecation." And from there it is only a short way to the miniature but incisive cartoon of "Willy Wet-Leg," with its sly, wry indictment of Christianity:

> I can't stand Willy wet-leg,
> can't stand him at any price.
> He's resigned, and when you hit him
> he lets you hit him twice.

"Ships in Bottles," "So There!" "In a Spanish Tram-Car," "Canvassing for the Election," "Altercation," "The English Are So Nice," "Britannia's Baby" and "The Man in the Street" all extend this cartoon method to other facets of man less than Man. No one, at this juncture, is safe from Lawrence's "centaur"-satire.

"Ships in Bottles," for instance, sketches a quick caricature of the writer's London friends, making through ironic allegory the same point he had made in the Pompadour scenes of *Women in Love*. Abstract and argumentative, Lawrence's friends are "Caught between great icebergs of doubt [and] all but crushed." Then, "Nipped upon the frozen floods of philo-

---

[4] *Ibid.*, pp. 770, 771. [5] *The Plumed Serpent*, Ch. XXVII: "Here!"

sophic despair/they lie high and dry," or "Reeling in the black end of all beliefs,/they sink."

> Yet there they are, there they are,
> little ships,
> safe in their bottles!

"So there!" "In a Spanish Tram-Car," "Intimates," and "True Love at Last" are more straightforward character-studies—character assassinations, one almost wants to say—which depend for effect on witty detail and dramatic surprise rather than on an extended analogy or conceit.

> It's no good my dear,
> my dear little girly-wirly
> with hair that was bobbed so early—
> you won't get away with it,

Lawrence begins "So There," one of several studies of the fashionably emancipated woman, then a comparatively new phenomenon. "No my darling child . . . my dearest laddie-lass, you won't get away with it," he adds, explaining in a series of ferociously shrewd observations that though "you look like the toppingest-topping fifth form Eton boy. . . . At fifty you're not going to be the Apollo Belvedere, don't imagine it." The tone of the poem is worldly, exasperated, and a bit fatigued. Its last two lines, which assimilate a wickedly appropriate English pun into the French equivalent of "She sells sea shells by the seashore," make a perfect caption for the caricature it sketches.

> Didon dina dit-on du dos d'un dodu dindon.
> Probably, as she grew older, she ate her rivals.

Another female "type," the seductive lady in the Spanish tram-car, seems to Lawrence—as if in ironic parody of his own theories of woman as goddess—to be "half Madonna, half Astarte." Yet though "Her yellow-brown eyes looked with a flare into mine;/—we could sin together! . . . The spark died out . . . swiftly."

> She can keep her sin.
> She can sin with some thick-set Spaniard.
> Sin doesn't interest me.

The poem's comic surprise inheres in the extraordinary contempt and indifference of the narrator. But, re-reading, we can see that "the wisp of modern black mantilla" and the irony of "half Madonna, half Astarte" should have given us a clue. The Spanish lady, after all, only appears to be a goddess —and a confused sort of goddess at that. Perhaps she is only wearing a goddess costume, and not really being an Astarte-Madonna in herself. Yet finally the speaker's response is unaccountably funny: "Sin doesn't interest me" is another cartoon caption, the ultimate modern put-down of the idea of Satan.

"Intimates" and "True Love at Last," both moralities on the corrupting power of self-absorption, are also both largely based on comic surprise rather than, like "So There!," on carefully selected detail. But they elaborate their little fables, more carefully than 'In a Spanish Tram-Car" does. If the caricature-poems we have considered so far can be characterized as single-frame cartoons—swift sketches of essentially static situations—these two, and a number of others like them, might be described as cartoon-strips—simplified narratives of a series of comic events. "Intimates," for instance, obviously consists of three "frames," a structure reflected in the stanza divisions: 1) "Don't you care for my love? she said bitterly." 2) "I handed her the mirror, and said: Please address these questions to the proper person . . ." and 3) "She would have broken it over my head/but she caught sight of her own reflection/and that held her spellbound for two seconds/while I fled."

Similarly, in "True Love at Last" the feelings of "the handsome and self-absorbed young man" and "the lovely and self-absorbed girl" are related in a series of simple stanzas in parallel structure. Like Lucy and Charlie Brown in a *Peanuts* strip, each has a frame to himself or herself, in which to utter sardonically worded confessions: "Her self-absorption is even as strong as mine./I must see if I can't break through and absorb her in me." "His self-absorption is even stronger than mine!/What fun, stronger than mine!/I must see if I can't absorb this Samson of self-absorption." Finally, like Lucy and Charlie Brown, the two characters are brought together to confront the irony of their situation.

> So they simply adored one another
> and in the end
> they were both nervous wrecks, because
> in self-absorption and self-interest they were equally matched.

The moral is clear and conventional: do not do unto others what others might be likely to do unto you.

But while a number of Lawrence's cartoon-poems deal with such psychological "truths"—general insights into the frailties of man less than Man—some are devoted to more specific commentary on the British national character and British politics. These poems might be compared, to press the metaphor a little further, to political cartoons. "I find that here in London they all instinctively hate me," Lawrence disingenuously informed Mabel Luhan, and it is no wonder if they did, considering his unmerciful satire of the "right little, tight little island" on which he was born.[6] "The English Are So Nice," for example, is a parodic monologue that reduces post-Victorian smugness to absurdity:

> The English are so nice
> so awfully nice
> they are the nicest people in the world.
> And what's more, they're very nice about being nice
> about your being nice as well!
> If you're not nice they soon make you feel it . . .

6 *Letters,* p. 771.

And in "Britannia's Baby," "Change of Government," "The British Workman and the Government"—to name just a few —Lawrence attacked the benevolent despots, the "aunties," of British bureaucracy, impartially and irreverently satirizing Labour, Conservative, Liberal and Communist positions.

In a few of his ideological cartoons, however, Lawrence transcends the specifically national consciousness of the Britannia series to satirize the basic moral presuppositions of modern society. "Modern Prayer," one of the best of these, seems to rise smoking from the pen of a Feiffer-cum-Swift.

> Almighty Mammon, make me rich.
> Make me rich quickly, with never a hitch
> in my fine prosperity! Kick those in the ditch
> who hinder me, Mammon, great son of a bitch!

Finally, in "The Man in the Street," Lawrentian caricature reaches absurd depths with a paranoid little drama of modern alienation.

> I met him in the street,
> I said: How do you do?—
> He said: And who are you
> when we meet?—
>
> I sadly went my way
> feeling anything but gay,
> yet once more I met a man and I had to stay—
> May I greet——?
>
> He cut me very dead,
> but then he turned and said:
> I see you're off your head
> thus to greet
> in the street
> a member of the British Public: don't you see
> the policeman on his beat?
> Well, he's there protecting *me!*—

But! said I,
but why——?

And they ran me in, to teach me why.

Though on the surface mere journalistic doggerel, these lines
suggest something like the irreverent intensity of Blake's

And priests in black gowns were walking their rounds,
And binding with briars my joys and desires.

—14

Sun in Me:
The Myth of the Self

i

"Man all scarlet," "black tears,"—some of Lawrence's
phrases suggest a quality of passionate intensity that *The
Plumed Serpent, Pansies* and *Nettles* have in common. In
these books, despite their differences in mode and method,
the writer himself is consistently a "man all scarlet" with
emotion. This rage of feeling accounts not only for the hyper-
bolic vision of Man more than man that appears in *The
Plumed Serpent* and the cartoon-vision of man less than Man
in *Pansies* and *Nettles,* but also for a return in the latter two
books to a confessional poetry Lawrence had not written since
Look!, and an increase in the kind of polemical poetry we
earlier encountered in *Birds, Beasts and Flowers.*

The open expression of emotion—of anger as well as love,
enmity as well as friendship—had always been a central tenet
of Lawrence's thought (and behavior) as many stories apoc-
ryphal and otherwise attest. "True Nirvana," he wrote to the
Buddhist, Earl Brewster, in 1921, "is a flowering tree whose
roots are passion and desire and hate and love. Your Nirvana
is a cut blossom." And "Desire and anger are from God," he
added a few years later. "Give me anything which is from
God, desire or anger or communion of saints or even hurts.
But nothing any more of the dreariness and the mechanism of
man." [1]

[1] *Letters,* p. 650, and p. 905.

To be fully—divinely—human, Lawrence thought, is to be fully and openly oneself. And such a notion arose naturally from his belief in anti-ironic commitment to feeling. He had always written confessional or semi-confessional verse out of a sense that it was good to—in Yeats' words—"lie down . . . In the foul rag and bone shop of the heart." Now he confessed himself out of a sense that it was godly to lie down there, "where all the ladders start." Even dying, "defeated and dragged down by pain/And worsted by the evil world-soul of today," he affirmed in *Last Poems* that "life is for kissing and for horrid strife."

Some of Lawrence's "pansies" in this semi-confessional mode are less nakedly personal than others. Both "There is Rain in Me" and "November by the Sea," for instance, are personal only because they are first-person accounts of inner states. They do not, however, deal with problems that are specifically Lawrence's. Rather, they explore emotions and experiences common to most men and, appropriately enough, they use traditional hermetic metaphors of correspondence—as above, so below; as without, so within—to do so. The moving "November by the Sea," which looks forward to *Last Poems* in its fiercely serene reconciliation to death, states most explicitly a Lawrentian doctrine of correspondence reminiscent of the Yoga-influenced dogmas of *Fantasia*.

> Now in November nearer comes the sun
> down the abandoned heaven.
>
> As the dark closes round him, he draws nearer
> as if for our company.
>
> At the base of the lower brain
> the sun in me declines to his winter solstice
> and darts a few gold rays
> back to the old year's sun across the sea . . .
>
> downward they race in decline
> my sun, and the great gold sun.

And "There is Rain in Me" expands the metaphor to suggest the infinite variety and passionate potential of inner landscape: "there is rain in me," the poet asserts, "there is ocean in me"—and "angry is old ocean within a man."

It is, however, when he treats his own specific life-crises—the death of desire, a problem just for some men, rather than death, a problem for all men; his own special anger rather than archetypal oceanic anger—that Lawrence at this point writes what must be considered truly confessional verse—poetry which, though it doesn't name names as Lowell's or Plath's or even Yeats' does, deliberately uses the personal as a model for the universal.[2] "Desire Goes Down into the Sea" is a good example of this poetry. Using the same metaphorical correspondences as "There is Rain in Me" and "November by the Sea," even the same symbolically setting sun, Lawrence works now with a personal theme—the theme of impotence, illness, emotional exhaustion, which pervades so much of the confessional poetry he wrote in this period.

> I have no desire any more
> towards woman or man, bird, beast or creature or thing.
>
> All day long I feel the tide rocking, rocking
> though it strikes no shore
> in me.
>
> Only mid-ocean.—

Mid-ocean? We wonder: does Lawrence mean the mid-ocean of "salty nothingness" (to which he refers in "The Sea, the Sea")? Or does he mean the old mid-ocean that is angry "within a man?" Or perhaps the two are one, for, confessing the failure of desire, Lawrence admits the kind of corrosive anger that obliterates personal relationships and leaves the sufferer alone in a "great pause" of being, alone with his own

[2] See Rosenthal's discussion of the "confessional school" in *The New Poets* (New York, 1967), pp. 15 ff.

deepest self and ultimately with the gods. "Always,/at the core of me," he writes in "Image-Making Love,"

> burns the small flame of anger, gnawing
> from trespassed contacts, from red-hot finger-bruises, on my
> inward flesh,
> from hot digging-in fingers of love,

for he has concluded that

> Nakedly to be alone, unseen,
> is better than anything else in the world,
> a relief like death.

Elsewhere Lawrence confesses, however, what leads us to believe that in "Image-Making Love" he may be simply making a virtue of necessity. "I cannot help but be alone," he notes in "Man Reaches a Point," "for desire has died in me"; and an even grimmer tone is given to a similar brief confession in the Biblical "Grasshopper Is a Burden" (to which the omission of the article from the title gives a curious tone of gasping despair):

> Desire has failed, desire has failed,
> and the critical grasshopper
> has come down on the heart in a burden of locusts
> and stripped it bare.

"Stripped it bare": all these poems are in one way or another about stripping—about declining, about setting, about burning away. Like a younger Lear, Lawrence is deliberately, openly, putting off the lendings of his life in a serious effort to discover what is permanent and fundamental in himself and the world around him, and what is merely superficial, illusory. For this reason all the confessional poems of *Pansies* and *Nettles*, both the obviously personal ones and the ones that deal with more general human situations, paradoxically make use of Lawrence's "myth of man," for each bases what Lawrence would call its "passional" structure on a distinction between a real, permanent, godly inner self, and a deceptive, transient, and comparatively worthless outer identity.

In "Image-Making Love," for instance, the poet asserts that he must preserve his "naked" soul, an angry soul like that of Huitzilopochtli, who represents the "anger of the manhood of men," from the mistaken feelings of others, which are directed toward the "simulacrum" that is the outer man.

> Always
> in the eyes of those who loved me
> I have seen at last the image of him they loved
> and took for me
> mistook for me.

> And always
> it was a simulacrum, something
> like me, and like a gibe at me.

Though it is the self usually involved in "personal" relations, the outer self is a mocking parody of the true, inner self. But the great relationships for Lawrence are not and never were "merely personal." What Birkin wants with Ursula is a "star-polarity"—the impersonal relationship of two fiery, more than human beings—and though she scoffs, it is a measure of their success as lovers that in the chapter called "Excurse" they are able to transcend a "personal" squabble and, consummating their love in the legendary darkness of Sherwood forest, enter the supra-personal mythical darkness of the Pharaohs. Kate and Cipriano, Mellors and Connie, all meet on the godly impersonal plane, even donning god-masks that denote their true selves—Malintzi and Huitzilopochtli, Lady Jane and John Thomas. But of course the relationship of Lawrence and Frieda began with just such a transcendence of ordinary personal existence.

> We have died, we have slain and been slain,
> we are not our old selves any more,

the young lover declared in *Look! We Have Come Through!*
And in the "Song of a Man Who Has Come Through" he
identified a godly otherness within himself—"Not I, not I,
but the wind that blows through me!"—a greater self fore-
shadowing the Man more than man he was to define in later
works.

It is not surprising, then, that in later poems about his own
love-relationships, not only "Image-Making Love" and the
"Desire" series, but also "Fidelity" and "Know Deeply, Know
Thyself More Deeply," two poems addressed specifically to
Frieda, Lawrence develops the same distinction. "Go deeper
than love," he advises his wife in "Know Deeply":

> the soul has greater depths;
> love is like grass but the heart is deep wild rock
> molten, yet dense and permanent.
>
> Go down to your deep old heart, woman, and lose sight of
>   yourself.
> And lose sight of me, the man whom you turbulently loved.
>
> Let us lose sight of ourselves, and break the mirrors.

Lawrence often confusingly changes terminology between one
work and another, but his meanings remain constant. What
he called the "image" or "simulacrum" in "Image-Making
Love" is here the false human "self" that must be abandoned,
and the heart is the enduring god-self (the "core" or soul of
"Image-Making Love") that is "deep, wild rock." Yet the
external self of "Know Deeply" still contains the idea of im-
ages, for instance in the line "Let us lose sight of ourselves,
and break the mirrors." The illusory outer self *is* merely an
image, and it can be known easily through the eyes. But such
knowledge, as Lawrence demonstrated in "The Revolution-
ary," is the most trivial "personal" sort, compared to the deep
impersonal knowledge of touch and intuition which, he tells
his wife, must come now that "the fierce curve of our lives is

moving again to the depths,/out of sight, in the deep dark living heart."

The references to motion, to the deep flow of time, emphasize the theme of all these confessional poems. As always in Lawrence's writing, triumph is achieved in these works through surrender. To try to stop time is to cling to the outer self "that now is shallow and withered" and "that has passed like a last summer's flower." But "the universe flows in infinite wild streams" and in surrendering to the flow one reaches one's most enduring self—the more than human self.

In what seems to me the best of the confessional *Pansies*, "After All the Tragedies Are Over," Lawrence fully works out this idea of surrender, describing it once more in terms of an inner landscape that mirrors the outer world.

> After all the tragedies are over and worn out
> and a man can no longer feel heroic about being a Hamlet—
> when love is gone, and desire is dead, and tragedy has left
>   the heart,
> then grief and pain go too, withdrawing
> from the heart and leaving strange cold stretches of sand.

Here *all* is stripped away; what earlier was the "deep wild heart" becomes nothing but a desolation of sand, and even the angry elements of the god-self—fire and ocean—are withdrawn. "The sea is lost/in the lapse of the lowest of tides." "Ah, when I have seen myself left by life, left nothing!" the poet cries, ruthlessly confessional. Yet still, he asserts, through all this nothingness, the fundamental structure of the self endures. And still the old dynamic godly connection with the cosmos survives.

> Even waste, grey foreshores, sand, and sorry far-out clay
> are sea-bed still, through their hour of bare denuding.
> It is the moon that turns the tides.
> The beaches can do nothing about it.

Ultimately, as long as the deep godly self is recognized and accepted, and as long as the godly connection remains, there is hope of renewal, revival, resurrection.

As early as *Look! We Have Come Through!* (in "New Heaven and Earth," "Manifesto," and "Spring in the World") Lawrence had presented his apocalyptic vision of a personal and suprapersonal cycle of death and rebirth. In *Pansies* and *Nettles* (as well as such works as *The Plumed Serpent* and *Lady Chatterley*) he returns once more to those apocalyptic metaphors of renewal which in *Last Poems* and in *The Man Who Died* will become part of a final series of myths of resurrection. Almost imperceptibly the "nothingness" of "After All the Tragedies" becomes the "pause" of "Basta," the "creative pause" of "Nullus." "And in these awful pauses," Lawrence declares, "the evolutionary change takes place."

> A sun will rise in me,
> I shall slowly resurrect,
> already the whiteness of false dawn is on my inner ocean.

ii

It is in the nature of the vocabulary of apocalypse to move almost inevitably from the particular to the general, from the personal to the universal. Lawrence's confessional poems certainly modulate this way into a kind of sociopolitical, polemical intensity that the poet also reached by other routes. "Nullus," for instance, though it begins with a purely personal statement —"I know I am nothing"—concludes with an exhortation to others, most of whom are assumed to suffer from the same malady.

> The tragedy is over, it has ceased to be tragic, the last pause
>   is upon us.
> Pause, brethren, pause!

And in "Dies Irae" Lawrence frankly extrapolates a universal apocalypse from his personal one.

Even the old emotions are finished,
we have worn them out.
And desire is dead.
And the end of all things is inside us . . .

Our epoch is over.

From a poem like this it is only a small step to such po-
lemical esays, sermons and exhortations as "What Have They
Done to You?" "The People," "Dark Satanic Mills," "We
Die Together," "Fight! O my Young Men" and "The Spiral
Flame." Like Lawrence's more personal confessions, these
works are all in some sense emotional effusions— "O ruddy
god in our veins, O fiery god in our genitals!" or "Ah the
people, the people!/Surely they are flesh of my flesh!" But the
emotion confessed is no longer a private feeling; here it be-
comes a public emotion, a Whitmanesque transcendence of
the smaller self in favor of a larger, more social and empathic
self—a Self.

"We Die Together" is perhaps the best example of such
empathic transcendence. The poem begins with Lawrence's
"private" feelings:

Oh, when I think of the industrial millions, when I see some
    of them,
a weight comes over me heavier than leaden linings of coffins.
and I almost cease to exist, weighed down to extinction,
and sunk into a depression that almost blots me out.

"Almost blots me out" seems like standard Lawrentian hyper-
bole, but it is an important phrase because it describes the
central movement of the poem—an extinction of the self-
aware, and self-limited, private personality in a larger con-
sciousness. "Then I say to myself," the poet continues, "Am I
also dead? is that the truth?" And the intensity of his feeling,
spilling over from the private conduit into public channels,
leads him to conclude "that with so many dead men in mills/
I too am almost dead."

And enshrouded in the vast corpse of the industrial millions
embedded in them, I look out on the sunshine of the South,
and though the pomegranate has red flowers outside the win-
dow
and oleander is hot with perfume under the afternoon sun
and I am "il Signore" and they love me here,
yet I am a mill-hand in Leeds
and the death of the Black Country is upon me
and I am wrapped in the lead of a coffin-lining, the living
death of my fellow men.

As an instance of Lawrence's poetic and philosophic evolu-
tion, what is most notable about this work is how strikingly
its conclusion differs from some of the positions Lawrence had
taken in *Women in Love* or *Birds, Beasts and Flowers*. In
those books it had been enough for the poet-novelist that "the
pomegranate has red flowers outside the window/and
oleander is hot with perfume under the afternoon sun." His
great faith seemed to have been not so much "a belief in the
blood, the flesh, as being wiser than the intellect," [3] but a
certainty that non-human nature was at every point wiser and
worthier than human nature. With *The Plumed Serpent*,
Pansies and *Nettles*, however, Lawrence seems to have felt the
necessity for returning man to a central position in the natural
scheme. If he had earlier been justifying God's—or nature's—
ways to man, he seems now to want to justify man's ways to
nature. Yet, still lingeringly misanthropic, he could only do
this by postulating a greater manhood, a manhood found in
myths, in journeys inward, and—as in "We Die Together"—
in journeys outward. A number of the poems in which he
seeks this manhood, ranging from "Quetzalcoatl Looks Down
on Mexico" to "The Gods, the Gods," "Know Deeply," "The
Spiral Flame" and "We Die Together," as well as a number
of the cartoon and polemical poems in which he laments its
absence, seem to me as intellectually forceful and distinctive as

[3] *Letters,* p. 180.

any poems he ever wrote, but whether his style was demonstrably equal to this subject matter has still to be considered before I attempt a final evaluation of the *Plumed Serpent* hymns, *Pansies* and *Nettles*.

—15
Hymns in a Man's Life: Stylistic
Elements in the *Plumed Serpent* Poems

i

Just as Lawrence's return in the poems of *The Plumed Serpent, Pansies, Nettles,* and *More Pansies* to the "problem" of man reflects his fluidity as a thinker, so his attempts at new verse forms and styles in these works mirror the restless experimentation that particularly marked his career as a poet. In *The Plumed Serpent* he returned in some pieces to the more regular metrics and conventional stanza structures of the early "Rhyming Poems," in some experimented with the incremental repetition of primitive incantations, and in others assimilated the essay-structure of *Birds, Beasts and Flowers* poems into a more formal, almost Biblical free verse. In *Pansies, Nettles* and *More Pansies* he worked with rhymed and unrhymed doggerel, with ballads, monologues and dialogues that almost parody some of the earlier fictionalized poems, and with free verse that is an extension or perhaps even (though not in a pejorative sense) a disintegration of the free verse of *Birds, Beasts and Flowers.*

The rhymed hymns of *The Plumed Serpent* are easiest to account for, especially in the light of Lawrence's later essay on "Hymns in a Man's Life." "It is almost shameful to confess," he remarked there, "that the poems which have meant most to me, like Wordsworth's 'Ode to Immortality' [sic] and Keats's Odes, and pieces of 'Macbeth' or 'As You Like It' or

'Midsummer Night's Dream,' and Goethe's lyrics . . . and Verlaine's . . . all these lovely poems woven deep into a man's consciousness, are still not woven so deep in me as the rather banal Nonconformist hymns that penetrated through and through my childhood."

He gives as an example

Each gentle dove
And sighing bough
That makes the eve
So fair to me
Has something far
Diviner now
To draw me back
To Galilee.
O Galilee, sweet Galilee,
Where Jesus loved so much to be,
O Galilee, sweet Galilee,
Come sing thy songs again to me!

And though he never directely imitated these stanzas in any of the formally structured *Plumed Serpent* hymns, we can recognize their cadences in a number of them—in, for instance,

Someone will enter between the gates,
    Now at this moment, Ay!
See the light on the man that waits.
    Shall you? Shall I?

or

Farewell, farewell, *Despedida!*
The last of my days is gone.
Tomorrow Jesus and Holy Mary
Will be bone.

In both of these, the straightforward language and the simple four-line stanza recall the didactic and enthusiastic simplicity of the Methodist hymnal.

Methodism and Mexico may appear to make for a strange mixture, and at least one of *The Plumed Serpent's* few defenders even refuses to grant the presence of what Roger Dataller calls "Eastwood in Taos." [1] The hymns in the book "resemble . . . little those that Lawrence had known and loved all his life," declares L. D. Clark. "Lawrence, with a long-developed preference for free verse, was attempting to compose not Moody and Sankey hymns for a revival of Methodism but Indian hymns as a way to pre-Columbian salvation." [2] Yet as Lawrence describes the hymns of his boyhood, their spirit is not incompatible with the spirit of Don Ramon's Aztec revival. "They live and glisten in the depths of the man's consciousness with undimmed wonder, because they have not been subjected to any criticism or analysis," he tells us. And such wonder, he adds, "is the *natural* religious sense." [3] But since it is precisely this sense of wonder Don Ramon is trying to reach with *his* hymns, it is not surprising that their versification should at times recall the Methodist hymnal. Strongly stressed, conventionally rhymed lines like

> Someone will knock when the door is shut.
> Ay! in a moment, Ay!
> Hear a voice saying: I know you not!
> Shall you? Shall I?

seem to represent an attempt on the part of the sophisticated middle-aged writer to return to the naiveté of his first religious feelings and to the unquestioningly conventional literary styles he had admired long before the inner conflicts of young man, novelist and demon had become major psychic realities.

ii

It would be hard to argue however, that the poet-in-Mexico was *not* influenced by the translations of Indian "hymns" and

[1] See Roger Dataller, "Eastwood in Taos," quoted by Harry Moore, *Heart*, p. 393.
[2] L. D. Clark, *Dark Night of the Body* (Texas, 1964), p. 90.
[3] "Hymns in a Man's Life," *Assorted Articles*, pp. 157–158.

songs published by such contemporary scholars of comparative religion as Lewis Spence and Washington Matthews. The three "Songs of Huitzilopochtli" most obviously draw some of their imagery from Spence's translations of Sahagún. We have only to compare, for instance, Spence's

> Uitzilopochtli, the warrior, no one is my equal;
> Not in vain have I put on the vestment of yellow feathers,
> For through me the sun has risen,[4]

with Lawrence's

> I am Huitzilopochtli,
> Yellow of the sun,
> Sun in the blood . . .
>
> Deeper than the roots of the mango tree
> Down in the centre of the earth
> Is the yellow, serpent-yellow shining of my sun,

or with his

> The power is in me from behind the sun,
> And from middle earth.
> I am Huitzilopochtli,

to see that Lawrence is working with the kind of sun-symbolism that is important in Spence's translation of the Song of Uitzilopochtli.[5] Again, Spence's version of another Uitzilopochtli hymn, the "Song of the Shield," has such elements as serpent symbolism and "quaking" earth or flame in common with Lawrence's hymns.[6]

[4] See Lewis Spence, *The Gods of Mexico* (New York, 1926), "Song of Uitzilopochtli." Through Uitzilopochtli, notes Spence, the time of sacrifice has arrived. But Lawrence would interpret the phrase more broadly.

[5] Such sun-symbolism also emerges in Zelia Nuttall's *Fundamental Principles of Old and New World Civilizations* (Mass., 1901), a book that interested Lawrence. See her commentary (pp. 13 and 54) on the Mexican "black sun" as representative of "the Below."

[6] Cf. Spence, p. 81: "He [is Uitzilopochtli] who gained his heroic title on the serpent mountain," an allusion to the fact that Uitzilopochtli's

Less obvious, but equally relevant, are echoes in Lawrence's Quetzalcoatl hymns of some of the other songs Spence translates. Passages from two "Songs of Cinteotl" (the maize-god) are of particular interest. The first, describing the birth of the god "In the House of Descent . . . In the place of waters and of mist,/Where the children of men are made," is echoed by the lines from "The Coming of Quetzalcoatl" that read "In the place of the west . . . in the stillness where waters are born,/Slept I, Quetzalcoatl./In the cave which is called Dark Eye . . . is the place. There the waters rise,/There the winds are born." [7]

The other "Song of Cinteotl" describes the journey of the maize-god.

> I came to the place where the roads meet,
> I the Maize-God.
> Where shall I now go?
> Which way shall I take? [8]

Not only does this foreshadow the journey-imagery and rhetorical questions of Lawrence's

> Someone will enter between the gates,
>   Now, at this moment, Ay!
> See the light on the man that waits.
>   Shall you? Shall I?

(which also, as we saw, drew upon a Methodist hymn), it suggests both the motif of the "two ways" that is important

---

mother, Coatlicue or "Serpent-Skirt," hid on Coatepec, the "serpent-mountain," when pregnant with the god, who later defeated his enemies —her other children—there. "Serpent-flame" in the "First Song of Huitzilopochtli" may refer to the infant-god's "serpent made of torches" (Spence, p. 79).

[7] Spence, p. 174. For the origin of the cave "Dark Eye" consult Nuttall, who discusses the Aztec idea that the dark and light suns are united in the astromomical "eye" of Heaven by the constellation Ursa Major.

[8] Spence, p. 175. See also Washington Matthews, "Songs of Sequence of the Navajos," *Journal of American Folklore*, 7 (1894), 185–194, for another stylistic parallel.

throughout *The Plumed Serpent* and the opening stanza of "The Living Quetzalcoatl."

Finally, the motif of the periodic migration of the gods, signifying their death and rebirth, a motif Spence shows to have been as characteristic of Aztec mythology as it is of the Christian tradition, appears in a passage Spence translates from another Mexican song, the "Hymn to Chicomecoatl" or "Seven-Snake," a maize-goddess. This hymn was evidently sung in the autumn, when the harvest was in, and it is markedly similar to Lawrence's "The Coming of Quetzalcoatl," and to other passages in "Jesus' Farewell" and "The Song of Don Ramon." [9]

iii

Despite these parallels in theme, image, and symbol between Spence's Aztec translations and the *Plumed Serpent* hymns, it is likely that the profoundest effect Spence and Washington Matthews had on Lawrence's songs was stylistic, for a number of those hymns not in the Methodist hymnal mode are deliberately primitivistic in language and structure. If a return to the enthusiastic verses that thundered through the green-walled simplicity of the ("Primitive") Methodist Chapel in Eastwood was one way of re-attaining "wonder," a revival of the incantatory thunder of the drums was another. Discussing Lawrence's Indian sources, L. D. Clark juxtaposes a Washington Matthews translation of the Navajo "Night-Chant" with Ramon's prayers to the "Bird of the Beyond" in order to point out interesting parallels of imagery and wording. What is most significant about the Matthews hymn, though, is its dependence on the sort of incremental repetition that is almost always crucially important in primitive hymn and prayer. "O Male divinity," the chant begins,

[9] Spence, p. 171: "Goddess of the seven ears, arise, awake!/For, our mother . . . Thou goest to thy home in Tlalocan." Lawrence: "My name is Jesus, I am Mary's son./I am coming home. . . ." etc.

With your moccasins of dark cloud, come to us
With your leggings of dark cloud, come to us . . .
With the dark thunder above you, come to us soaring.
With the shapen cloud at your feet, come to us soaring . . .[10]

Lawrence exploited such incremental repetition (together with a certain amount of pseudo-primitive syntactical inversion) in his most effectively "primitive" hymns, a category that would certainly have to include the three "Songs of Huitzilopochtli." Not only does the first of these begin with a series of incremental repetitions that beat like what Don Ramon calls "drums for the beating heart"—

I am Huitzilopochtli,
The Red Huitzlipolochtli,
The blood-red.

I am Huitzilopochtli,
Yellow of the sun,
Sun in the blood,

but the "Second Song of Huitzilopochtli" consists of a chorus that simply repeats the first song (with a few variations) in the third person. One of Lawrence's favorite stylistic devices had always been the technique of "continual, slightly modified repetition," but in volumes like *Look! We Have Come Through!* and *Birds, Beasts and Flowers* he had used the method more subtly and covertly than he does in these Huitzilopochtli poems. There he had been writing a poetry of disguised or partly disguised grammatical parallels; here he writes a poetry of openly drumming, incantatory repetition.

Neither Lawrence nor the Indians, however, regularly employed this "drumming" technique of incremental repetition quite so simply as it appears in the first few stanzas of the "First Song of Huitzilopochtli" and in the Navajo "Night-Chant." Though almost all the Spence translations, for in-

10 See Clark, p. 109, for a more extended quotation from the text.

stance, depend to some extent on such repetition, they do not use it as openly as the Matthews poem does. In "Song of the Earth-Goddesses" Spence (and, we may suppose, his Indian source) varies the form of essentially parallel sentences. Direct repetition is confined to an irregularly recurring refrain: "On the fields of the gods/She leans on her rattle-staff." [11] Similarly, in Lawrence's primitive hymns the drumming repetition never becomes droningly regular; rather, it is syncopated in a number of ways. Most simply, though perhaps least obviously, Lawrence varies the monotony of incremental repetition by a slight inversion of syntax which—while maintaining the regular rhythm he seeks to achieve—serves to stress a particularly important point:

> *Red* Huitzilopochtli
> Is the purifier.

> *Black* Huitzilopochtli
> Is doom.

> Huitzilopochtli *golden*
> Is the liberating fire . . .

or

> *Blue* is the deep sky and the deep water.
> *Red* is the blood and the fire.
> *Yellow* is the flame.
> The bone is *white and alive.*

Huitzilopochtli's association with "liberating fire"—the "serpent-yellow shining of [his] sun"—is something Lawrence particularly wants us to remember, hence the small but significant inversion. Again, that bone was "white and alive," that it had a sacred association with the gods, was a tenet of Aztec religion, and no doubt has something to do with the second inversion.

Less subtly, in a number of the Huitzilopochtli chants Law-

[11] See Spence, p. 180.

rence abruptly shifts the paradigm to be repeated—and along with it the rhythm of the incantation—every few stanzas. Thus

> I am Huitzilopochtli,
> White of the bone,
> Bone in the blood,

(the final variation in a series of three) becomes

> I am Huitzilopochtli
> With a blade of grass between my teeth,

which swiftly modulates to

> I watch by the fire.
> I wait behind men,

and so on.

Finally, even a few of the poems in the Methodist hymnal vein occasionally employ pseudoprimitive parallelism and random refrain in the context of more conventionally structured poems. "Welcome to Quetzalcoatl," for instance, uses a fairly regular four-line stanza reminiscent of the Methodist chapel, but the irregular, incantatory repetitions seem purely Indian, in the mode of Spence's translation of the earth-goddess' hymn.

> We are not wasted. We are not left out.
> *Quetzalcoatl has come!*
> There is nothing more to ask for.
> *Quetzalcoatl has come!* . . .
>
> Quetzalcoatl loves the shade of trees.
> Give him trees! Call back the trees!
> We are like trees, tall and rustling.
> *Quetzalcoatl is among the trees.*

Perhaps in the modulated parallels of "Give him trees! Call back the trees!/We are like trees . . . *Quetzalcoatl is among the trees*" the common purpose of the two hymn-styles appears most clearly: there is a childlike wonder in the repetitive symplicity of these lines—a wonder Lawrence remembered from his Methodist childhood and sensed in the Indian vision of Ciuacoatl, the earth-goddess, leaning on her rain-rattle—wonder and, by implication, the kind of naiveté that "breaks the stiff neck of sophistication."

iv

There are poems in *The Plumed Serpent,* however, which do not obviously depend on either Methodist or Indian hymn styles. These seem to combine the kind of free-verse essay technique Lawrence had brought to maturity in *Birds, Beasts and Flowers* with something of the incantatory moral solemnity of *Psalms, Jeremiah* and *Revelation.*[12] "Quetzalcoatl Looks Down on Mexico" and "What Quetzalcoatl Saw in Mexico" are the most notable works in this hybrid mode.

Even in these poems, which are not obviously primitive, there is an element of folk-naiveté, reminiscent of Aesop or of Kipling's *Panchatantra*-influenced fables. Lawrence seems to have been determined to preserve a consistent tone in the poetic utterances of his neo-Aztecs. Don Ramon's narration of Quetzalcoatl's return to Mexico, for instance, is as straightforward and uncluttered as any artfully transcribed legend.

> Surely, he said, this is a curious people I have found!

> So leaning forward on his cloud, he said to himself:
> I will call to them.
> *Hola! Hola! Mexicanos! Glance away a moment towards me.*
> *Just turn your eyes this way, Mexicanos!*

> They turned not at all, they glanced not one his way.

But when the god begins to sermonize the style changes, gathering polemical strength and intensity. Quetzalcoatl's angry warnings—

[12] Cf. Frank Baldanza, "D. H. Lawrence's Song of Songs," *Modern Fiction Studies,* VII (Spring, 1961), p. 113: "When [Lawrence] came to write his own set of hymns for . . . *The Plumed Serpent* . . . its Biblical prototype [was] probably the prose of Revelation."

The sun and stars and earth and the very rains are weary
Of tossing and rolling the substance of life to your lips.
They are saying to one another: Let us make an end
Of those ill-smelling tribes of men, these frogs that can't jump,

are reminiscent of some of the more choleric passages in *Birds,
Beasts and Flowers,* like the lines in "Figs" comparing "the
bursten fig" to "a prostitute, making a show of her secret."
Inevitably, though, a passage like

Tell them they must get the stones out of their bellies,
Get rid of their heaviness,
Their lumpishness,
Or I'll smother them all,

recalls the moral outrage of *Jeremiah* (4 and 5) [13] and the
apocalyptic fury of such lines as

And the stars are ready with stones to throw in the faces of
men
And the air that blows good breath in the nostrils of people
and beasts
Is ready to blow bad breath upon them, to perish them all,

reminds us of

The Lord is in his holy temple . . . Upon the wicked he shall
rain snares, fire and brimstone, and an horrible tempest. (*Psalms*
11, 4 and 6)

or of the Lord's threat to Jeremiah that

Because my people hath forgotten me . . . I will scatter them as
with an east wind, before the enemy. (*Jeremiah* 18, 15, 16 and 17).

Similarly, parts of "Quetzalcoatl Looks Down on Mexico,"
like the passage beginning *"I see dark things rushing across
the country/*Yea, Lord! Even trains and camions and auto-
mobiles," are reminiscent of Kipling's pseudo-primitive de-
scription of the "fire-carriages" of the Anglo-Indians,[14] and the

[13] Cf. *Jeremiah,* 4, 22, and 5, 21.
[14] Cf. Kipling, "The Bridge-Builders," in *The Day's Work* (New York, 1898).

bitterness of the tone recalls the social bitterness of a *Birds, Beasts and Flowers* poem like "The Evening Land." But again, the apocalyptic rhetoric of the poem's conclusion is Biblical: passages like the one that begins "Lo! I release the dragons!" obviously draw strength from the *Book of Revelation,* in which Armageddon brings darkness and agony, heat, hail, earthquakes and dragons.[15]

Despite occasional polemical interpolations, then, the hymns of *The Plumed Serpent* are in many ways the most obviously *formed,* premeditated and "objective" verses Lawrence had written since "Rhyming Poems." Because he was not uttering these verses in his own person but speaking as Don Ramon —or Quetzalcoatl or Huitzilopochtli—the poet was not trying to get at "the creative quick" of his own life, but rather, through a series of liturgical strategies, to embody the life of the universe, and to arouse a naive wonder at this life in listeners and readers. And because the hymns extol a greater world into which men can enter, an eternal though cyclically renewed world of gods and heroes, they draw heavily on traditional, highly structured religious sources—Methodist and Mexican hymns, Biblical psalms and prophecies. Thus, more than most of Lawrence's other verses, they come close to being what he called "the poetry of the beginning and the poetry of the end." They speak with "the voice of the far future . . . [and] the voice of the past." When the Greeks heard the *Iliad* and the *Odyssey,* Lawrence tells us in "Poetry of the Present," "They heard their own past calling in their hearts, as men far inland sometimes hear the sea . . . or else their own future rippled its time-beats through their blood, as they followed the painful, glamorous progress of the Ithacan. This was Homer to the Greeks . . ." And this is what Lawrence evidently hoped the myths and hymns of Quetzalcoatl would be to the Mexicans, and to his readers.

[15] Lawrence long brooded over John's *Apocalypse,* which he had known since childhood, and corresponded with Frederick Carter (author of *The Dragon of the Apocalypse*) before writing his own *Apocalypse.*

—16
Not a Wreath of Immortelles:
The Processes of *Pansies*

i

Pansies, Nettles and *More Pansies* are very different from
the hymns of *The Plumed Serpent*. Though many of them
are jeremiads of a sort—angry tirades against the nullity of
modern life, lamentations for man less than Man—it is much
harder to trace the origins or define and justify the style of
these works which, Lawrence reported, were written in a
"loose little poem form; Frieda says with joy: real doggerel—
But meant for *Pensées*, not poetry, especially not lyrical
poetry." [1]

"Especially not lyrical poetry": it is difficult to decide exactly
what Lawrence means by this phrase, but it is obviously
crucial in expressing how he, at least, felt about the style of
Pansies and *Nettles*. "Each little piece is a . . . true thought,"
he writes in his Introduction to *Pansies I* (the unexpurgated
edition), "which comes as much from the heart and the gen-
itals as from the head." But these "thoughts" do not pretend
to be "half-baked lyrics or melodies in American measure"—
unfinished rhyming poems or subtly calibrated *vers libre,* a
form that more Americans than Englishmen turned to in the
twenties. Yet they *are* verse of some kind. For, Lawrence tells
us in his Foreword to *Pansies II* (the expurgated edition), "it
has always seemed to me that real thought, a single thought,

[1] *Letters,* p. 1106.

not an argument, can only exist easily in verse, or in some poetic form." [2]

Why? Because thoughts that are "put into poetry" don't "nag at us so practically" as the didactic, "slightly bullying" prose thoughts of a Pascal or La Bruyère, and because, as he had remarked in the earlier Introduction, "It suits the modern temper better to have its state of mind made up of apparently irrelevant thoughts that scurry in different directions yet belong to the same nest." Furthermore, *pensées* in verse, unlike more logically structured prose *pensées*, can be casual, transient: "casual thoughts that are true while they are true and irrelevant when the mood and circumstance changes." Lawrence would "like them to be as fleeting as pansies, which wilt so soon, and are so fascinating with their varied faces, while they last."

Variety, transience, and a kind of organic *wholeness* ("each thought trotting down the page like an individual creature") are the three major criteria, then, that Lawrence himself set up for *Pansies* and *Nettles.* But it is not entirely clear how these criteria differ from the poet's own standards for "lyrical poetry"—for such lyric poems, for instance, as those in *Birds, Beasts and Flowers.* Certainly those works were various; certainly Lawrence strove to cast each in its own inevitable organic form; and certainly he hoped that each would somehow embody the transience of "the immediate present."

One answer is perhaps to be found in a further exploration of the pansy-*pensée* conceit, for like much Lawrentian wordplay this metaphor is not simply a casual pun. "The fairest thing in nature, a flower, still has its roots in earth and manure," the writer notes, and its scent mingles "with the blue of the morning the black of the corrosive humus." These pansy-*pensées* are not to be "merely pretty-pretty," not even to be beautiful as perhaps "lyrical poetry" should be. For "pansies, in their streaked faces, have a look of many things

[2] *CP*, pp. 417, 423. There may be other interpretations of "American measure" but I have not been able to think of any so plausible.

244

besides heartsease." Furthermore, says Lawrence, these poems are emphatically to be "a bunch of pansies, not a wreath of *immortelles*." Their transiency is not to be an embodiment of the eternal moment that Lawrence defined in "Poetry of the Present" as "the quick of all time, the quick of all the universe. . . ." It is to be the transiency of flowers that bloom and wither, for "a flower passes, and that perhaps is the best of it." [3] In other words, these rough-hewn, often corrosive and unbeautiful poems are to be truly occasional verses. Unlike the works of *Birds, Beasts and Flowers* "whose very permanency [was to be] in [their] wind-like transit," [4] these pansy-*pensées* are to be contemplated and *forgotten*. They are to be, as Frieda exclaimed, "real doggerel."

Doggerel is in several ways just the right form in which the poet could attend to his subject matter in these works. Where the verses of *Birds, Beasts and Flowers* attend to aspects of nature which, even in their "windlike transit," are eternal (for animals and plants, though mortal, are unvarying facts of reality) and where the hymns of *The Plumed Serpent* attend to the eternal possibilities of godhood, these little pansy-*pensées* attend in most cases to something very different: to the poet's own momentary thoughts and feelings, mental phenomena that make up the intellectual skin of consciousness. For Lawrence such impulses and ideas are in their nature temporary, casual, the merest "gleam on the surface of the waters," so that to embody them in anything implying permanence would be not to *attend*.

Doggerel, moreover, roughly hewn, swiftly written verse without pretensions to poetic grandeur, is a natural outgrowth of Lawrence's always anti-monumental aesthetic. It is verse written mainly to give vent—to give breath or life—to a moment's thought, and because the writer was at this point only interested in momentary structures, the content of these works might almost be said to have been determined by their form. Lawrence wondered increasingly in his later years why any-

---

[3] *Ibid.*, p. 418, 423, 424.   [4] "Poetry of the Present," *CP*, p. 183.

one should want anything—any art, any thought, any experience—that was really permanent. He admired the casual, little wooden temples of the Etruscans that were "dainty, fragile . . . evanescent as flowers," and speculated (perhaps punningly) that "We have reached the stage when we are weary of huge stone erections . . . Why has mankind such a craving to be imposed upon? . . . Give us things that are alive and flexible, which won't last too long." [5] In a late article entitled "Pictures on the Walls" he even suggested that people ought to burn or throw away their outworn pictures exactly as they would throw away dead flowers. "In every school it is taught: Never leave stale flowers in a vase. Throw them away! —So it should be taught: Never leave stale pictures on the wall. Burn them! The value of a picture lies in the aesthetic emotion it brings, exactly as if it were a flower. The aesthetic emotion dead, the picture is a piece of ugly litter." [6]

ii

Perhaps it is because of his growing preoccupation with deliberately transient art that, just as the poems of *Birds, Beasts and Flowers* owed a good deal to the critical and travel essays Lawrence was composing when he wrote them, the doggerel of *Pansies* and *Nettles* is related to slighter journalistic pieces he was publishing in the popular press in the last few years of his life. Even a glance at the table of contents of *Assorted Articles* suggests the thematic similarity between these often slangy polemics (which the writer no doubt expected would be crumpled up and used to start a fire along with the rest of the day's paper) and the pansy-*pensées* he was writing at the same time. "The Jeune Fille 'Wants to Know,' " "Sex Versus Loveliness," "Ownership," "Master in His Own House," "Cocksure Women and Hensure Men," "Is England Still a Man's Country?" "Red Trousers," "The State of Funk," "Enslaved by Civilisation," "Men Must Work and Women as

[5] *Etruscan Places,* p. 48.   [6] *Assorted Articles,* p. 181.

246

Well"—all these titles imply both the social anger and the utopian vision of a more than human society that flashes out so vividly in *Pansies* and *Nettles*. And a look at some of the poems themselves reveals that their style as well as their subject matter is journalistic. Not only are a number of the works essentially cartoons, but even what seem to be free-verse essays in the *Birds, Beasts and Flowers* manner are more editorially dogmatic than even the most polemical earlier works.[7]

"The Combative Spirit," for instance, opens as a newspaper column might, with a baldly and boldly prosaic topic sentence —"As a matter of fact, we are better than we know"—and then goes on to develop the idea through undisguised polemical argumentation. The poem's stylistic as well as thematic resemblance to such a passage as this, from "The State of Funk," is clear: "I am convinced that the majority of people today have good, generous feelings which they can never know . . . because of some fear, some repression . . . I am convinced that people want to be more decent, more good-hearted than our social system of money and grab allows them to be." [8]

But there is a significant difference, for "The State of Funk," is, after all, a prose work, while "The Combative Spirit," though prosaic, is written in verse, if only a kind of free-verse doggerel.[9] Though Lawrence was convinced that thoughts like these could be more effectively presented in verse than prose, we must wonder what the verse does for these social sermons that the prose of *Assorted Articles* could not. One way to find out is to try "prosifying" "Wages," a more successful "editorial" poem than "The Combative Spirit." Put into prose, it would read as follows:

[7] Although *cf.* "O! Americans" (*CP*, p. 774), a long polemic written before most "pansies." Lines like "Either make the Indian Bureau into a permanent office . . . /Or transfer the control to the American Institute of Ethnology . . ." are more journalistic than most of Lawrence's "articles."

[8] *Assorted Articles*, p. 99.

[9] Though such a term may seem contradictory, it seems to apply.

The wages of work is cash. The wages of cash is want more cash. The wages of want more cash is vicious competition. The wages of vicious competition is the world we live in. The work-cash-want circle is the viciousest circle that ever turned men into fiends. Earning a wage is a prison occupation and a wage-earner is a sort of gaol-bird. Earning a salary is a prison overseer's job, a gaoler instead of a gaol-bird. Living on your income is strolling grandly outside the prison in terror lest you have to go in. And since the work-prison covers almost every scrap of the living earth, you stroll up and down on a narrow beat, about the same as a prisoner taking his exercise. This is called universal freedom.

But in verse it goes like this:

> The wages of work is cash.
> The wages of cash is want more cash.
> The wages of want more cash is vicious competition.
> The wages of vicious competition is—the world we live in.
> The work-cash-want circle is the viciousest circle
> that ever turned men into fiends.
>
> Earning a wage is a prison occupation
> and a wage-earner is a sort of gaol-bird.
> Earning a salary is a prison overseer's job,
> a gaoler instead of a gaol-bird.
>
> Living on your income is strolling grandly outside the prison
> in terror lest you have to go in. And since the work-prison
>   covers
> almost every scrap of the living earth, you stroll up and down
> on a narrow beat, about the same as a prisoner taking his
>   exercise.
>
> This is called universal freedom.

The difference should be obvious. Though "Wages," like "The Combative Spirit," cannot be considered a "lyrical poem," the poetic necessity that gives it its form is undeniable, so that its prosody (the visual as well as auditory arrangement of its words) conveys a kind of logic: to write the poem out as prose is to blur the meaning. Though not Horatian in neatness and balance, in its verse-form "Wages" has the vigor and something of the inevitability of an Horatian epigram.

iii

A number of the doggerel poems in *Pansies* and *Nettles* do not, however, derive their style from the journalistic prose of *Assorted Articles*. Though deliberately rough and evanescent, they return to modes in which Lawrence had worked when he was much younger, as if the writer had at last found a suitably anti-monumental use for the awkward formalities of his rhyming style. "Fight! O My Young Men," "Nottingham's New University" and some of the "Songs I Learnt at School" (such as "Neptune's Little Affair with Freedom" and "13,000 People") are just a few examples of these slyly rhymed, often parodic verses which are all doggerel in the true sense. Though "Fight! O My Young Men," for instance, is in the hortatory, editorial vein of "The Combative Spirit," it also depends on what one critic once called the "joke of rhyme":

> Old money-worms, young money-worms,
> money-worm professors
> spinning a glamour round money, and clergymen
> lifting a bank-book to bless us.

But the joke of rhyme is even more evident in the comical parodic verses. When poor naked Neptune visits Britannia's "right little, tight little island," there instantly rises

> a great uproar
> of Freedom shrieking till her throat was sore;
> Arrest him, he's indecent, he's obscene what's more!—
>
> Policemen and the British nation
> threw themselves on him in indignation
> with handcuffs, and took him to the police-station.

The sea-god said, in consternation:
But I came at Freedom's invitation!—
So then they charged him with defamation.

Seldom had the young Lawrence used rhyme so effectively.
Again, in "13,000 People" skillfully manipulated rhyme gives
the poem a sardonic power. The 13,000 people, viewing the
poet's "obscene" paintings in a London gallery, exclaim

Oh boy! I tell you what
look at that one there, that's pretty hot!—

And they stared and they stared, the half-witted lot
at the spot where the fig-leaf was not!

and when Lawrence wonders naively

But why, I ask you? Oh tell me why?
Aren't they made quite the same, then, as you and I?

his ironic innocence is so cleverly conveyed by naive, doggerel
rhymes that we wonder if Ogden Nash or even Blake (out of
whose journals such a poem might have come) could have car-
ried the thing off better.

Not only does Lawrence return to rhyme in some of these
works, he also returns to the dialect verse of a number of the
early fictionalized poems. But, again, with a difference. The
satiric dialect of "The Little Wowser" may have been in-
cipient in the serious drama of "Whether or Not," just as the
deliberately self-conscious and provocative dialect of Mellors
was potentially present in the unself-conscious natural dialect
of his anagrammatically named predecessor, Morel, but it is
hard to imagine that the young Lawrence could have con-
ceived the ironies of

There is a little wowser
John Thomas by name,
And for every bloomin' mortal thing
That little blighter's to blame.

Only the embittered author of a book like *Lady Chatterley's Lover,* which had been banned and almost burned, only the outraged painter of those pictures at which "13,000 people" had gaped and gawked, could have had the angry energy for the slangy, exactly rhymed cartoon-journalism of

> I think of all the little brutes
>   As ever was invented,
> That little cod's the holy worst.
>   I've chucked him, I've repented.

And in some of the fictionalized "Pansies," Lawrence moves beyond the Midland dialect of "Whether or Not" into such parodies of English middle and upper-class speech as "The English Are So Nice," "The Oxford Voice," "Canvassing for the Election," and "Altercation." In the last of these a middle class voice ("Now look here,/if you were really superior,/ *really* superior,/you'd have money, and you know it") is set against a jeering lower-class dialect ("All right, guvnor! What abaht it?") with fine irony.

Perhaps the most amusing of these late dialect poems, however, is "What Ails Thee," a witty self-parody one might not have expected from the author of *Lady Chatterley's Lover,* who usually took his role as sexual and social prophet so seriously.

> What ails thee then, woman, what ails thee?
> doesn't ter know?

asks the familiar voice of Lawrence-Mellors-Morel.

> If tha canna say't, come then an' scraight it out on my bosom.

To which an equally familiar voice—that of Frieda-Ursula-Clara—replies:

> —In the first place, I don't scraight.
> And if I did, I certainly couldn't *scraight it out.*
> And if I could, the last place I should choose
> would be your shirt-front, or your manly bosom either.

No one at this point is safe from Lawrence's centaur-satire—
not even the writer himself.

iv

Besides extending the free verse essay-style of *Birds, Beasts
and Flowers* into epigrammatic or journalistic doggerel, be-
sides expanding the conventional stanzas and dialect verses of
"Rhyming Poems" into anti-conventional comedy, Lawrence's
Pansies and *Nettles* do something else—something that might
have become, if the writer had lived, even more significant for
his development as a poet. Many pansy-*pensées disintegrate*
the sonorous *vers libre* of *Birds, Beasts and Flowers* in an in-
teresting way.

A look at almost any page in *Birds, Beasts and Flowers,* fol-
lowed by a glance at a page of *Pansies,* will explain the word
disintegrate. The poems in *Birds, Beasts and Flowers* are
among the longest Lawrence ever wrote (with the exception
of "Manifesto" and "New Heaven and Earth"). "Cypresses,"
"Fish," "Snake," all have the substance and the aesthetic in-
tegrity of little essays. The "pansies," on the other hand, are
consistently the shortest poems Lawrence ever wrote. On two
sides of a typical page in *More Pansies (Complete Poems*
pp. 653–654), for instance, the editors have printed eleven
brief poems which, if they had been more carefully shaped,
might have seemed like eleven splenetic *haiku,* but which, in-
stead, could be more properly characterized as *bits:* bits and
pieces of epigrammatic doggerel.

"As for your humble," Lawrence wrote to Murry in 1925,
"he says his say in bits, and pitches it as far from him as he
can." [10] He was not necessarily referring to *Pansies,* but the
scrappiness of those poems (in both senses of the word) is cer-
tainly implicit in his statement. In 1929, he told Charles Lahr
that "I am thinking, why don't we start a little fortnightly
magazine, about 10 pages and about as big as this sheet of
paper—called the *Squib*—and just fire off squibs in it . . .

[10] *Letters,* p. 875.

let us put crackers under their chairs, and a few bent pins un-
der their bottoms." [11] Along with the letter, he sent Lahr a
sample squib—the savage little *pensée* on Thomas Earp, which
may indeed have nettled that hostile art critic, if he ever read
it. But some of the eleven epigrammatic bits referred to ear-
lier, including the "Retort to Whitman" ("And whoever
walks a mile full of false sympathy/walks to the funeral of the
whole human race") and the "Retort to Jesus" ("And who-
ever forces himself to love anybody/begets a murderer in his
own body") are obviously also the sort of squibs he meant,
crackling with the intensity of Blakeian proverbs.

Other squibs seem to be almost condensations of some of
the longer journalistic polemics. "Young Fathers," for in-
stance, follows "Wages" and "The Combative Spirit," and
with its bitter description of how

>you need only look at the modern perambulator
>to see that a child as soon as it is born,
>is put by its parents into its coffin,

it seems like a vivid little cartoon illustration of the points
made at greater length in those two poems, as well as a less
tragically intense formulation of Blake's metaphor of "the
Wedding hearse." Similarly, the hyperbolical "A Tale Told
by an Idiot," the Swiftian and cartoon-like "Modern Prayer,"
the sardonic "Wellsian Futures," and the witty "Bourgeois
and Bolshevist," are all fiery bits of journalistic doggerel de-
signed to be set off like "crackers under [the] chairs" of the
"Establishment."

A number of the briefer "pansies," however, are *not* chiefly
political or social in their concern, and it is in these that we
can see most clearly the disintegration of the *Birds, Beasts and
Flowers* style. The small group of poems about elephants,
which appears near the beginning of *Pansies,* is as good an
example as any, but "Won't it Be Strange," "The Gazelle
Calf," "Little Fish," "The White Horse," and a number of

11 *Ibid.,* p. 1181.

others also exemplify this development. Like most of the pieces in *Birds, Beasts and Flowers,* "Elephant" dealt with the otherness of nature and explored the whole of a situation at the center of which loomed the mysterious elephants, "vast-blooded beasts." The weary irony of the prince of Wales was carefully set against the mystery of the elephant's "dark mountain of blood," and the poem rose through one hundred and twenty-six lines of incantatory narrative to the Carlylean longing of its conclusion. The elephants of *Pansies,* on the other hand, are characterized in a set of four almost fragmentary sketches that seem like Imagistic doodles in comparison to "Elephant,"—for instance:

> Plod! Plod!
> And what ages of time
> The worn arches of their spine support! [12]

It is as though in the later years of his life Lawrence's illness and disillusionment made it increasingly difficult for him to focus his attention on anything—even on the non-human world he loved so well—for any length of time. Just as he saw the gods in "flickers," in "glimpses," he seems to have seen natural reality in Imagistic flashes. This is more strikingly applicable to his poetry than to his prose, but even in the longer works of prose fiction he wrote in this period—*Lady Chatterley's Lover,* for example—a stylistic change can be discerned. There is a drying up of adjectives, a tightening of structures, as if the fact that he had trouble breathing and moving had its effect on his writing. As a result of this, what we find him doing in many of the *Pansies* is more conventionally "modern" than anything he had done before in verse. The proclivity of some Imagists for the short poem dominated by a single perception no doubt had its effect on him, and a poem like "The White Horse":

[12] "Elephants Plodding." I am not including the longer, more editorial "The Elephant Is Slow to Mate" in this group.

> The youth walks up to the white horse, to put its halter on,
> and the horse looks at him in silence.
> They are so silent they are in another world,

though it has analogies in Whitman, draws its main strength from the symbolist desire to summarize the essence of a situation in a single untranslatable figure.

There is another group of short *pensées*, however, that are not primarily sociopolitical doggerel but are too explicit in their content to be identified with Imagism, though they seem to result from the same process of disintegration that produced the squibs. This group includes most of the openly confessional poems. "Can't Be Borne," "Man Reaches a Point," and "Grasshopper Is a Burden" are just a few examples of these brief outbursts, which foreshadow the prayerful subjectivity of *Last Poems*. Again, it appears that the writer cannot very long sustain even a sense of his own feelings—cannot or, more precisely, will not. Indeed, some of these poems—"Can't Be Borne," for instance—may even seem, as Horace Gregory suggests, like "short-hand notes that were to take the place of poems . . . as though [Lawrence] felt the pressure of time upon him." [13]

Yet there is another factor at work in these pieces which is as important as the poet's illness. Lawrence had always given priority to content rather than form, suggesting that form must be at best a function of content. Some of the "pansies," however, seem to have been written out of a strong belief that the content itself could *be* the form. Hence a number of the confessional "bits" begin with a simple assertion of the writer's feelings:

> I wish I knew a woman
> who was like red fire on the hearth.

> I wish people, when you sit near them,
> wouldn't think it necessary to make conversation.

[13] Gregory, p. 88.

> I am worn out
> with the effort of trying to love people.

"Desire is a living stream," wrote Lawrence in "Love Was Once a Little Boy." "If we gave free rein . . . to our living flow of desire, we shouldn't go far wrong." [14] Therefore he felt justified in writing poems some critics would consider mere self-expression. In fact he felt increasingly that such art, and not conventionally sublimated Imagism, constituted his real modernity.[15]

V

To say that Lawrence's aesthetic explains the apparently fragmentary or awkward quality of some of the poems in *Pansies* and *Nettles* is not, of course, to say that it will justify these qualities for us, or even that these qualities will prove incontrovertibly characteristic of the poems themselves. Significantly, as they appear in the books in which they belong, almost all these pansy-*pensées,* especially those that seem most like "bits," are clustered together in coherent groups. Each apparent fragment is part of a larger series that in a way constitutes a poem in itself. Thus a number of the confessional "bits" are part of what we might call a "desire" series—a sequence of variations on the theme announced in "Desire Is Dead," the first and one of the best of them.

> Desire may be dead
> and still a man can be
> a meeting place for sun and rain,
> wonder outwaiting pain
> as in a wintry tree.

"Man Reaches a Point," "Grasshopper Is a Burden," "Basta!" "Tragedy," "After All the Tragedies Are Over," "Nullus," "Dies Irae," "Dies Illa," "Stop It," "The Death of Our Era,"

[14] ". . . Love Was Once a Little Boy," in W. Y. Tindall, ed., *The Later D. H. Lawrence* (New York, 1952), p. 217.

[15] *Letters*, p. 959: "I am afraid I am more modern . . . than [these modern artists] who make art out of antipathy to life."

"The New Word," and "Sun in Me," are all important stages in this little cycle of poems in which the writer works through the crucial problem of the death of desire and by a process of "continual, slightly modified repetition," arrives at that rebirth which the man who died finds in the arms of the priestess of Isis: "A sun will rise in me."

Other important sequences include a "bourgeois" series (beginning with "How Beastly the Bourgeois Is" and continuing through four poems to "To Be Superior"), a "swan" series (beginning with "Swan" and continuing through "The Spiral Flame"), a "fidelity" series (beginning with "Fidelity" and ending with "Escape"), a "work" series (beginning with "Things Men Have Made" and ending with "O! Start a Revolution") and a "selfishness" series (beginning with "To a Certain Friend" and ending with "True Love at Last"). But there are many more.

There are, however, some interesting differences among these sequences, not only in theme and subject matter, but in the way the poet organizes his material from "bit" to "bit." The poems in the "desire" series were subtly progressive, but the "selfishness" series simply consists of a set of anecdotes about egotism, with interpolated outbursts from Lawrence, while in some sequences—the "work" one is a good example —the poet seems consciously to have ordered his writing so as to produce a logical argument, as though he had expanded one of the longer, self-subsistent polemics (like "The Combative Spirit") into a set of poems that would do the same thing. Often the titles betray this argumentative coherence as well as the "bits" themselves. In the "work" series, for instance, "Things Men Have Made" is followed by "Things Made by Iron," then by "New Houses," "New Clothes," and "Whatever Man Makes," all providing the specific points that underlie "We Are Transmitters," "All That We Have Is Life," "Let Us Be Men," and "Work." Finally, "Why?" "What Is He?" and "O! Start a Revolution" conclude the argument with exhortations to action.

Even more strikingly, there are some sequences in which one "bit" openly continues another. "Talk of Loyalty," for example, is followed by "Talk of Faith," which begins with "And"—as if continuing a discussion. In the same way, the "Retort to Jesus" follows the "Retort to Whitman." Finally, in several other sequences Lawrence's thinking makes little or no progress from poem to poem. The series on "the people," beginning with "Cry of the Masses" and ending with "The Factory Cities," is a good illustration of this. The first of the poems suggests the lifelessness of the masses—"Trot, trot, trot, corpse-body, to work"—which reappears in the second ("What Have They Done to You?") as "this jig-jig-jig/tick-tick-ticking of machines," in the third ("The People") as a vision of people going "back and forth to work . . . like fearful and corpse-like fishes," and in the fourth ("The Factory Cities") as a vision of "millions of fish in panic." By continuing theme, style and imagery from poem to poem, Lawrence has produced a kind of miniature variorum: four different ways of making a single political point.

Lawrence himself was not unconscious of the clustering or sequential technique that he used in arranging so many of his pansy-*pensées*. Though his aesthetic seemed to him to justify stylistic roughness, he also intentionally "said his say in bits" that were for the most part only apparently irrelevant to each other. His assertion in the Introduction to *Pansies I* that "it suits the modern temper better to have its state of mind made up of apparently irrelevant thoughts that scurry in different directions *yet belong to the same nest*" (italics mine), indicates how careful he was in his formulation of his own method. And what he was doing was not so different from what a number of other modern poets were doing at the same time. As M. L. Rosenthal justly remarks, "the fragmentation of the long poem is an aspect of alienation," and he notes "the interesting development of the *sequence* as the characteristic form of the [modern] long poem, including the long poem of epic pretensions." [16] In this respect, *Pansies* as a self-sufficient work, an adult's garden of *versus,* may be compared with any number of other modern sequences, ranging from Pound's deliberately fragmentary and "bitty" *Cantos* to Charles Olson's "Maximus Poems" or Ginsberg's "Kaddish."

vi

A number of critics would find a comparison of *Pansies* with the *Cantos* hard to take. Just as *The Plumed Serpent* hymns are often judged to be full of "windy emptiness," [17] so the poems of *Pansies* and *Nettles* are frequently seen as "a decline from [Lawrence's] earlier poems . . . one loud hammer, hammer, hammer of exasperation." [18] To Virginia Woolf the quality of inspired *graffiti* that marks the *Pansies* and *Nettles* doggerel made Lawrence's *pensées* "read like the sayings that small boys scribble upon stiles to make housemaids jump and titter." [19] No doubt these judgments respond in part to the deliberate roughness of the versification and to the fragmentary quality of some of the poems. But just as incantatory (and not windily empty) hymn-structures are appropriate to a vision of Man more than man, so, after all, is angrily fragmentary doggerel suitable to a vision of man less than Man. Critics who can accept the infuriated comedy of Blake's diatribe against Klopstock ("If Blake could do this when he rose up from a shite,/What might he not do if he sat down to write?") should be able to accept, too, the angry irony of Lawrence's "Modern Prayer" ("Almighty Mammon, make me rich!"). Neither work is characterized by *petulant* exasperation nor by any more roughness than is necessary to express legitimate anger.

[16] Rosenthal, *New Poets,* p. 20.   [17] Hough, p. 129.
[18] Aldington, Introduction to *More Pansies* and *Last Poems, CP,* p. 595.
[19] Virginia Woolf, "Notes on D. H. Lawrence," *The Moment and Other Essays* (New York, 1948), p. 36.

What critics object to most in Lawrence's *Pansies* and *Nettles*, though, appears to be something more fundamental than the corrosive crudeness of the doggerel. They seem really to dislike the polemical or confessional directness that gives the poems their power. Many modern readers share a certainty that "the successful action of art is never direct. When Lawrence exhorts [his audience] . . . either in his own voice or in the voice of one of his characters, the effect is strident and pathetic." [20]

Yet directly stated, hortatory verse is, after all, as old or older than Horace's "Integer vitae scelerisque purus" and as new as Blake's "Jerusalem" or Shelley's "Song to the Men of England" or, more recently, Robert Bly's "The Teeth-Mother Naked at Last." Certainly Lawrence's "Spiral Flame," one of the finest achievements in *Pansies,* like many of the other poems in that volume can be placed in this honorable tradition, but just as certainly its straightforward, hortatory passion conveys Lawrence's major concern in these years, his sense of man as he is and as he should be. "I can't bear art that you can walk round and admire," he wrote to Carlo Linati in 1925. "A book should be either a bandit or a rebel or a man in a crowd. . . . I hate the actor-and-audience business. An author should be in among the crowd kicking their shins or cheering on to some mischief or merriment. Whoever reads me will be in the thick of the scrimmage, and if he doesn't like it . . . let him read somebody else." [21] In the scarlet fury of his "Spiral Flame" ("O pillars of flame by night, O my young men"), as in so many other "pansies," Lawrence literally and figuratively joins the crowd of young men who have been deprived of their humanity by the "nullus" of modern society, but who he believes will be redeemed by the apocalyptically spiraling flame of history.

Yet like the other successful "pansies" and the best of the *Plumed Serpent* hymns, the "Spiral Flame" unites, in carefully worked out imagery, the hopeful but disillusioned poet's

[20] Goodheart, p. 42.   [21] *Letters*, p. 827.

concept of the gods ("O ruddy god in our veins, O fiery god in our genitals!"), of Man as he is when he is more than man, with his hatred for the ungodly ("the upholstered dead in deep armchairs"), man as he is when he is less than Man. Such a poem transcends what may seem to be its occasional (and probably deliberate) awkwardness. Its lack of careful "melodies in American measure," its prophetic spontaneity or apparent spontaneity:

And the same flame that fills us with life, it will dance
    and burn the house down,
all the fittings and elaborate furnishings,

becomes in the end a hallmark of its anti-ironic sincerity. Such sincerity may be merely a rhetorical strategy or it may not, but the question seems irrelevant here. What matters is that Lawrence's passionate effort of attention to his own ideas is effective. Directly hortatory, openly combative though this art may be, it works, even though it is not superbly successful "lyrical poetry" of the kind we encounter in *Birds, Beasts and Flowers* and *Last Poems*. We are sometimes moved, sometimes delighted; and certainly, when we apply Lawrence's words to our own lives—to the feelings of our own young men —we are instructed.

—PART V

THE BLUE BURNING

Oh leave off saying I want you to be savages.
Tell me, is the gentian savage, at the top of its coarse
    stem?
Oh what in you can answer to this blueness?

                              "Flowers and Men" [1]

In this world—the one in which we must live—the
strange gods of D. H. Lawrence appear to be less
strange than those of Mr. Eliot.

                                  Wright Morris [2]

[1] *More Pansies, CP,* p. 684.
[2] Wright Morris, "Lawrence and the Immediate Present," *A D. H. Lawrence Miscellany,* p. 8.

—17
Kosmokrator and *Kosmodynamos:*
Lawrence's God

i

Lawrence's *Last Poems* and some of his later "pansies" have a good deal in common.[3] Both sets of poems tend to be comparatively brief, often confessional utterances, as the *Birds, Beasts and Flowers* pieces had not been. Both tend to be metrically ragged (though the *Last Poems* are in general smoother), eschewing "melodies in American measure" for forms more organically related to content. Both include sequences of variations on a theme. Finally, both share a theological preoccupation with the divine and a moral preoccupation with the problem of evil.

It is in their approach to these last two concerns, however, that the collections differ most radically, for where in *Pansies* and *Nettles* (and in the *Plumed Serpent* hymns) Lawrence was commenting on the divine possibilities in man and in the human community, he deals in *Last Poems,* perhaps because of a change in his own life, with the divine in nature and with, as a corollary, the divinity of death. Where in *Pansies, Nettles* and the *Plumed Serpent* hymns he had confronted the problem of social evil, of the less than divine in man, he deals in *Last Poems,* because the "downward curve" of his own life forced him to, with the problem of evil in the universe, of the anti-divine in nature. In *The Plumed Serpent,*

---

[3] Aldington noted in his 1932 Introduction that "the whole of Lawrence's posthumous poetry was contained in two . . . notebooks found

Pansies and *Nettles* he spoke often of the gods. But in *Last Poems* he speaks more frequently and more directly of God. In *The Plumed Serpent, Pansies* and *Nettles* he inveighed against a variety of human evils. But in *Last Poems* he sermonizes against Evil.

When he wrote *Pansies* and *Nettles,* even when he wrote *The Plumed Serpent,* Lawrence was already a sick man, and many of the distinctive characteristics of these works—their attempt to come to terms with humanity, their occasionally almost breathless brevity, the bitterness of their "black tears" —can be traced to the poet's illness. But when Lawrence wrote his "last poems" he seems to have known with inner certainty that he was dying, though he admitted this only reluctantly in conversations and letters to friends. "Europe is slowly killing me, I feel" is what he told Mabel Luhan, and "This winter makes me know I shall just die if I linger on like this in Europe"[4] is the qualified statement he made to Dorothy Brett. Despite his plans for trips back to New Mexico or visits with the Brewsters, the part of him that wrote poems —especially the ruthlessly honest demon of his youth—was already attempting, as Graham Hough puts it, "to absorb the

---

among his papers after his death." But because Ms. A (which became *Last Poems*) contained works which seemed "more pondered and *soignés*" than those in Ms. B *(More Pansies)*, he concluded not only that the two mss. represent "two different books, one a continuation of *Pansies,* the other a new series" but that "the two books must . . . have been in progress simultaneously." (Thus "A" and "B" are meant to indicate significance rather than chronology.) Precisely because Ms. B contains "prefigurations" of Ms. A, however, I think it possible that it may have been at least partly completed before B was begun, in which case some of the "later" poems in *More Pansies* can be regarded as transitional works bridging the gap between the slangy doggerel of *Pansies* and the more serious music of *Last Poems.* Certainly "pansies" like "The Gods! The Gods!" and "There are No Gods" seem to foreshadow such last poems as "Middle of the World" and "Maximus." But since many of them are quite as "pondered and *soignés*" as *Last Poems,* it is hard to think them unsuccessful drafts of poems being simultaneously reworked in Ms. A.

4 *Letters,* pp. 1230, 1231.

fact of death into the mode of consciousness that [was] . . . his own." Hence *Last Poems* may be seen as a sort of "initiation ritual," an effort "to fit the mind for an utterly unknown experience." [5] And if *The Plumed Serpent, Pansies* and *Nettles* took as paradigms hymn and polemic, editorial and caricature, *Last Poems* model themselves on prayer and sermon. They are in a real sense *religious* poetry, incantatory, meditative, worshipful verse belonging to a tradition in which we should also place many of the poems of Donne and most of the poems of George Herbert, Whitman's "Whispers of Heavenly Death" and, more recently, T. S. Eliot's "Ash Wednesday."

"I do think that man is related to the universe in some 'religious' way, even prior to his relation to his fellow men. And I do think that the only way of true relationship between men is to meet in some common belief," Lawrence wrote to Trigant Burrow in 1917. "There is a *principle* in the universe, towards which man turns religiously—a *life* of the universe itself. And the hero is he who touches and transmits the life of the universe." [6] Of course, he had felt this all along. *The Rainbow* and *Look! We Have Come Through!*, with their vividly Biblical overtones, had been first steps toward identifying that life-principle as it manifests itself in the human community. *Women in Love* had gone even further in relating it to the sexual mystery, and *The Plumed Serpent* had dealt with the common belief where men must meet in order to become godly heroes. In *Last Poems*, however, what is expressed in the communal hymns of *The Plumed Serpent* and in the social *pensées* of *Pansies, Nettles* and *More Pansies*, stripped of its public aspects, becomes more purely religious. At the same time, certain characteristics of the *Plumed Serpent* poems and *Pansies*—the devotion, the thoughtfulness— are retained and combined, so that Lawrence now addresses himself to the religious principle of things in prayers and sermons that are newly private utterances, pensive hymns.

[5] Hough, pp. 211, 214.   [6] *Letters*, pp. 993–994.

Typically, Lawrence's poetry in these final months of his life was much influenced by prose he was writing at about the same time. Just as the *Birds, Beasts and Flowers* verses were closely related to travel and literary essays he was composing in the early twenties, and *Pansies* and *Nettles* were marked by the journalistic wit of *Assorted Articles,* so the religious concern of *Last Poems* is shaped by the distinctively Lawrentian theology of *The Man Who Died, Etruscan Places,* "The Risen Lord" and *Apocalypse.* Yet though readers of Lawrence have always seen that he is in some essential way a religious writer, it has still to be established exactly *how* he is religious, especially in these late works. T. S. Eliot, after all, accused Lawrence of worshipping "strange gods" and seems to have felt that the author of "The Ship of Death" and "Bavarian Gentians" was doomed to such heresy from the start: "Nothing could have been much drearier (so far as one can judge from his own account)," wrote Eliot in a famous passage of acrimony, "than the vague hymn-singing pietism which seems to have consoled the miseries of Lawrence's mother, and which does not seem to have provided her with any firm principles by which to scrutinize the conduct of her sons." [7] And certainly Lawrence himself repudiated Christianity and even, at times, God in the conventional monotheistic sense.

At the same time it is clear that, as Hough notes, he was "haunted by Christianity," haunted even, as in *The Plumed Serpent,* by the "hymn-singing pietism" of his Methodist boyhood. "Unlike Yeats," Hough very acutely observes, "who seems never to have had any particular orientation to Christianity, Lawrence . . . had always to confute it or to get it out of the way." [8] Perhaps more importantly, he has to redefine it—as in *The Man Who Died,* "The Risen Lord" and *Apocalypse.* As early as 1913, such a process of redefinition begins in his letters.[9] But in the major Christian—or post-

[7] Eliot, *After Strange Gods* (London, 1934), p. 39.
[8] Hough, p. 56.
[9] Cf. letter to Hopkin, 18 December 1813, *Letters,* p. 255: "I am always

Christian—works of his last years, as well as in *Last Poems,* this process comes to a climax. Lawrence's Christ—the radiant *Kosmokrator* of *Apocalypse,* the newly sensual messiah of *The Man Who Died,* and the triumphantly regenerated "Risen Lord"—rises from a "oneness" with death, the painful renunciation of traditional Christianity, to a new oneness with life. He rises to "live the great life of the flesh and the soul together, as peonies or foxes do, in their lesser way." More specifically, he rises in the context not of the "new" Judeo-Christian dogma but in the way of the old gods of the pre-Christian Mediterranean, for Lawrence is determined wholly to assimilate his Christ into a pagan structure of beliefs. "In the countries of the Mediterranean," he tells us in "The Risen Lord," "Easter has always been the greatest of the holy days . . . In Sicily the women take into Church the saucers of growing corn, the green blades rising tender and slim like green light, in little pools, filling round the altar. It is Adonis. It is the re-born year. It is Christ risen. It is the Risen Lord." [10] And in *The Man Who Died* he goes further, mating his risen prophet with the priestess of Isis, who sees him as the reborn Osiris for whom she has been searching.

Finally, in *Apocalypse,* he attempts to show that "the Jesus of John's vision" is not the Jesus of popular religion today. "There is nothing humble or suffering here . . . [he is] *Kosmokrator* and even *Kosmodynamos,* the great Ruler of the Cosmos, and the Power of the Cosmos. . . . He is Lord of the Underworld . . . Hermes, the guide of souls through the death-world, over the hellish stream . . . master of the future, and the god of the present. He gives the vision of what was, and is, and shall be. . . . [He is] the Jesus of the very first communities, and . . . of the early Catholic Church . . ." In creating such a figure, Lawrence notes, John of Patmos revealed that "he knew a good deal about the pagan value of

expecting when I go to Tellaro . . . to meet Jesus gossiping with his disciples as he goes along above the sea."
[10] "The Risen Lord," *Assorted Articles,* pp. 113, 110.

symbols," and that both he himself, as prophet or seer, and Christ, as Risen Lord of the cosmos, were essentially pagan figures out of the old Mediterranean world when men lived in a state of "intricately developed . . . sense-awareness and sense-knowledge" that can only be expressed in mythic images and symbols.[11]

In Lawrence's last years this old Mediterranean world, its geography, its mythology, its very light and shade, became the vital cradle of thought, a shrine to which he brought all his religious imaginings. He had located the gods in America too, and some of his definitions of Apache ideas point toward the pagan-Christian redefinitions of *Apocalypse*.[12] But, dying, he found the electric air of America, "the continent of the afterwards," [13] too harsh and alien. He was, he seems to have discovered, intransigently European, and he had to come home to his origins, home to the eternal freshness of the Mediterranean, which still seemed "young as Odysseus, in the morning," to the "cult-lore" of the Greeks and the Egyptians, the Etruscans and the Chaldeans, and to the *Kosmokrator,* the Living God whose shadow still seemed to live on that sea.[14]

ii

Because place was so crucial to Lawrence, the "initial ritual" that is *Last Poems* begins not, as one might expect, with open invocation or formal meditation, but with a series of delicate observations that set the scene for what is to come. The place is the Mediterranean, the time is always. The Greeks, the Argonauts, the Minoans still cross and recross the sea, still "[kindle] little fires upon the shores." The old ways of thinking are still implicit in the sun and the water, simply waiting to be revived.

[11] *Apocalypse,* pp. 38–40, 59, 76.
[12] Cf. "Indians and Entertainment," *Mornings,* pp. 117–118.
[13] "A Little Moonshine with Lemon." *Ibid.,* p. 186. Also *cf.* "The Evening Land," *Birds, Beasts and Flowers.*
[14] *Letters,* p. 1205. *Apocalypse,* pp. 75–76: "Cult-lore was the wisdom of the old races. We now have culture."

> This sea will never die, neither will it ever grow old,
> nor cease to be blue, nor in the dawn
> cease to lift up its hills
> and let the slim black ship of Dionysos come sailing in
> with grape-vines up the mast, and dolphins leaping,

Lawrence declares in "Middle of the World," the best of these first poems. And he continues

> What do I care if the smoking ships
> of the P & O and the Orient Lines and all the other stinkers
> cross like clock-work the Minoan distance!
> They only cross, the distance never changes.

Modern man, with all the smoke and the stink of his "clock-work" inventions, can never alter "the Minoan distance," the mystery at the heart of things, fittingly associated with the lost civilization of Crete.[15] Indeed, his diminished consciousness cannot begin to comprehend such distances. Only with the old sense-awareness of the cosmos and of the sun and the moon, "the great travellers" who rule it,[16] can Lawrence

> now that the moon who gives men glistening bodies
> is in her exaltation . . .
> see descending from the ships at dawn
> slim naked men from Cnossos, smiling the archaic smile
> of those that will without fail come back again.

And in this state of awareness he knows that

> the Minoan Gods, and the Gods of Tiryns
> are . . . softly laughing and chatting, as ever,
> and Dionysos, young, and a stranger
> leans listening on the gate, in all respect.

It is a landscape of expectancy in which Lawrence finds himself. Dionysos, the dying and rising god of vitality, of joy

[15] Prof. Spyridon Marinatos is conducting excavations on Santorini, just north of Crete, which support the idea that "Atlantis" was located here and at Knossos. (Cf. *SF Sunday Examiner & Chronicle*, 3 January, 1971, Section A, p. 29.)

[16] *The Rainbow*, Ch. VI: "Anna Victrix."

and self-surrender, is "at the gate," waiting to be admitted, like the three strange angels of *Look! We Have Come Through!* He is still a stranger, but he will not be one for long, not for the poet himself and not, the poet hopes, for the modern culture to which he must impart his "cult-lore." For sitting on his terrace by the Mediterranean—literally the "middle of the world" as the title of this poem emphasizes— and ruled by the moon, who is "great lady of the nearest/ heavenly mansion, and last . . ." Lawrence feels he is waiting by the *umbilicus mundi,* the *omphalos* or sacred place where he can at last encounter the final mysteries of life and death, the mysteries of *Kosmokrator* and *Kosmodynamos.*

"Middle of the World" is followed by "For the Heroes Are Dipped in Scarlet," a digression from the theme of *Kosmokrator* but a natural outcome of the concerns of the first three poems; for, imagining that the men of the old world move before him and feeling that they are godly, heroic, Lawrence wishes once again to explore the nature of their heroism. Hence "For the Heroes Are Dipped in Scarlet" is one of his most careful explorations of the idea that "the hero is he who touches and transmits the life of the universe."

> For the thing that is done without the glowing as of god, vermilion,
> were best not done at all,

he asserts here, as he had in *The Plumed Serpent.* But such "glowing" can only be achieved by living "breast to breast" with the life of the cosmos. The "great lie of ideals" that "Plato told" leads unfailingly to the ironic, nerve-brain consciousness that precludes heroic blood-commitment. And the men of the old world, instinctively aware of this, "slimly went like fishes, and didn't care." At one with life, like the "loveless and . . . lively" fish of *Birds, Beasts and Flowers,* or like the regenerated Jesus of "The Risen Lord," they had "long hair like Samson," the impassioned blind hero of "The Revolutionary," and, most important,

They knew it was no use knowing
their own nothingness:
for they were not nothing.

Absorbed in blood being ("their faces scarlet . . . the
loveliest . . . red all over, rippling vermilion"), the old
heroes seem not to have been tormented by the need of mod-
ern post-Platonic men to scrutinize, and thus negate, their
destiny. *Kosmodynamos* spoke in them—in the sexual vitality
of which their long hair and beards are emblematic, their
dancing exuberance, and the driven purity with which, "clean
as arrows they sped at the mark/when the bow-cord twanged."
They were arrows or instruments in the hand of God—who-
ever or whatever He might be.

What might He be? *Who* might He be? "Demiurge" re-
turns to a direct consideration of this theological problem.

They say that reality exists only in the spirit,
that corporal existence is a kind of death,
that pure being is bodiless,
that the idea of the form precedes the form substantial,

Lawrence begins, recapitulating in greater detail Plato's "great
lie of ideals."

But what nonsense it is!
As if any Mind could have imagined a lobster
dozing in the under-deeps, then reaching out a savage and
    iron claw!

Reality is unimaginably various, unimaginably *itself*. There
is a teleology, but it is not deliberate or premeditated.

Even the mind of God can only imagine
those things that have become themselves,

Lawrence asserts, taking his stand against Plato.

"Demiurge" is the first of a series of sermons or meditations
on the nature of God which progresses through "The Work
of Creation," "Red Geranium and Godly Mignonette," "Bodi-

less God," "The Body of God," "The Rainbow" and "Maximus" to a brilliant conclusion in the pagan, Mediterranean imagery of "The Man of Tyre" and a climactic exemplum in "Whales Weep Not!" All these poems are in a real sense metaphysical, but some are more openly didactic than others. "The Work of Creation," for instance, picks up the thread of Lawrence's argument where it left off in "Demiurge" and weaves it into a more precise statement about the nature of the Living God.

> God is a great urge, wonderful, mysterious, magnificent,
> but he knows nothing before-hand.
> His urge takes shape in flesh, and lo!
> it is creation! God looks himself on it in wonder, for the first
>   time.

Kosmokrator, in other words, is subservient to *Kosmodynamos*. He manifests himself not in being, not in static pre-planned order, but in becoming, in the energetic flow and struggle that underlies being.[17] Significantly, Lawrence uses a metaphor of art to explain this idea more fully. God "knows nothing beforehand" as an artist

> knows that his work was never in his mind,
> he could never have *thought* it before it happened.
> A strange ache possessed him, and he entered the struggle,
> and out of the struggle with his material, in the spell of the
>   urge,
> his work took place, it came to pass, it stood up and saluted
>   his mind.

But just as such an artist is specifically the Romantic action-poet of Lawrence's earlier vision in "The Poetry of the Present," so the God whose analog he is is Romantically immanent and dynamic, and not, like Stephen Dedalus's Aristotelian

---

[17] Whether deliberately or not, Lawrence was recapitulating a crucial "pagan" idea. Henri Frankfort in *Ancient Egyptian Religion* (New York, 1948) quotes from a hymn in which the sun-god is "a divine youth, the heir of eternity,/Who begot [him]self and bore [him]self."

artist-God, "refined out of existence, indifferent, paring his fingernails." God's work, moreover—"the work of creation," which suggests both that which is created and the job of creation itself—is, as Carlyle, one of Lawrence's major philosophical predecessors, declared, "the mirror wherein [He] first sees [His] true lineaments." [18] The world of *Last Poems* is still the world of *Birds, Beasts and Flowers,* a universe of self-realizing processes whose products are simply points on a continuum that is never ending or whose end is unknown.

In "Red Geranium and Godly Mignonette," one of the most successful of this set of Romantic sermons, Lawrence illustrates the crucial idea expressed in "The Work of Creation." "Imagine that any mind ever *thought* a red geranium!" he rather comically proposes. But no, he adds, one can't imagine

> the Most High, during the coal age, cudgelling his mighty
> brains . . .
> to think out . . .
> "Now there shall be tum-diddly-um, and tum-tiddly-um,
> hey presto! scarlet geranium!"

Again, reality is too real, too idiosyncratically embodied, to be planned. What one can imagine, Lawrence tells us, is

> among the mud and the mastodons
> god sighing and yearning with tremendous creative yearning
> in that dark green mess
> oh, for some other beauty, some other beauty
> that blossomed at last, red geranium, and mignonette.

Paradoxically, then, this *Kosmodynamic* god the poem defines is a Darwinian creator, an artist of trial and error—even though Lawrence is famous for having told Aldous Huxley that his "solar plexus" couldn't believe in evolution.[19]

But perhaps its wit as much as its thought distinguishes

[18] *Sartor Resartus,* Book II, Ch. VII: "The Everlasting No."
[19] See Aldous Huxley, Introduction to *The Letters of D. H. Lawrence* (London, 1932), reprinted in *Letters,* p. 1252.

"Red Geranium and Godly Mignonette," preserving, as Alvarez points out, "the seriousness from sentimentality and overstatement, as [the poem's] seriousness keeps the wit from flippancy." [20] This finely honed philosophical wit, moreover, differentiates the poem from many of the *Birds, Beasts and Flowers* works that also dealt with natural process. For where in the earlier volume Lawrence had at his best (and often wittily) attended to natural objects in themselves, in *Last Poems* he uses them instrumentally, as means toward an end: the knowledge of God. As such, they are incorporated into the larger argumentative structure of the sermon sequence which, in its sustained attention to *Kosmodynamos* itself, transcends each individual manifestation of God's cosmocreative power.

"Bodiless God," following "Red Geranium and Godly Mignonette," is another attempt to formulate the nature of deity, while "The Body of God," its companion-piece, is an illustration of its main point. Like "Red Geranium," "Bodiless God" is exuberantly witty. But it is also exuberantly logical, a witty syllogism that presents Lawrence's overall argument in miniature. "Everything that has beauty has a body, and is a body," Lawrence tells us. God "is supposed to be mighty and glorious," hence he too must have a body, for the notion of an insubstantial God is logically contradictory. Though this sort of Thomistic proof is not what we immediately associate with Lawrence, the prophet of instinctual blood-being, he is using it, we should remember, to praise incarnation, and he had employed a similar technique in the clever parodic arguments of *Pansies* and *Nettles* as well as in Tom Brangwen's comic but serious disquisition on angels in the "Wedding at the Marsh" chapter of *The Rainbow*.[21] In all these works Lawrence reveals his "working intelligence," the mind in process that

[20] Alvarez, *Stewards*, p. 158.

[21] "*If* we've got to be Angels," says Tom Brangwen, "and if there is no such thing as a man nor a woman amongst them, then it seems to me as a married couple makes one Angel. . . . For . . . an Angel can't be *less* than a human being. And if it was only the soul of a man *minus* the man, then it would be less than a human being."

marks so much of his writing.[22] He reveals his belief that though

> Thought is not a trick, or an exercise, or a set of dodges,
> Thought is man in his wholeness wholly attending,

intellect should be exercised in behalf of wholeness.

But if in his best poems Lawrence had always striven wholly to attend, in this sermon-series he is attending in particular to the wholeness of things, the *Kosmodynamic* God who informs them. In "The Body of God," he enumerates some specific manifestations of this God with the uninhibited verbal wit that is characteristic of his later writings. "God," he asserts, is "the great urge . . . towards incarnation." He "becomes at last a clove carnation . . . and . . . at last Helen, or Ninon: any lovely and generous woman . . . any clear and fearless man."

> There is no god
> apart from poppies and the flying fish,
> men singing songs, and women brushing their hair in the sun.
> The lovely things are god that has come to pass, like Jesus
> came.
> The rest, the undiscoverable, is the demi-urge.

The last two lines (though ungrammatical) contain two of Lawrence's most engaging puns. Like his works, God "has come to pass"—that is, to be, and in being to pass away, as the dying and rising Jesus of *The Man Who Died* came to pass and then, newly and delightedly mortal, to pass away. Inevitably this idea recalls Stevens' "The tomb in Palestine

> Is not the porch of spirits lingering,
> It is the grave of Jesus where he lay,

for Lawrence's resurrected Jesus is now wholly human. Like Stevens' god, he does not exist "apart," or in the clouds. For this reason, "the rest, the undiscoverable," that which has not yet come to pass—to mortality—is "the demi-urge," both the

22 Alvarez, *loc. cit.*

277

"Demiurge" or maker of the poem of that name, and the half-realized urge of God which will only be when it has achieved incarnation.

But Lawrence is not saying pantheistically that God is simply men, trees, rivers, raindrops, and (as he suggests in the next poem) rainbows. Rather, he is saying, as in "Bodiless God," something like what modern philosophy says of man: God is that which both "is a body and has a body." He is both the incarnation and the urge toward incarnation, the product and the process, for, like Yeats, Lawrence wonders how we can tell the dancer from the dance.

> God is older than the sun and moon,
> and the eye cannot behold him
> nor voice describe him,

he affirms in "Maximus." "But a naked man, a stranger . . . is the God Hermes, sitting by my hearth." God is the urge, the *Kosmodynamos,* but he incarnates himself in a host of fleshly messengers. He is, for Lawrence, a paradox—urge and incarnation, dancer and dance.

All these speculations come to a conclusion in "The Man of Tyre," with its joyously sensual Mediterranean images. I quote the poem in its entirety.

> The man of Tyre went down to the sea
> pondering, for he was a Greek, that God is one and all alone
>   and ever more shall be so.
> And a woman who had been washing clothes in the pool of
>   rock
>   where a stream came down to the gravel of the sea and sank
>   in,
>   who had spread white washing on the gravel banked above the
>   bay,
>   who had lain her shift on the shore, on the shingle slope,
>   who had waded to the pale green sea of evening, out to a
>   shoal,
>   pouring sea-water over herself

now turned, and came slowly back, with her back to the
    evening sky.

Oh lovely, lovely with the dark hair piled up, as she went
    deeper, deeper down the channel, then rose shallower,
    shallower,
with the full thighs slowly lifting of the wader wading shore-
    wards
and the shoulders pallid with light from the silent sky behind
both breasts dim and mysterious, with the glamorous kind-
    ness of twilight between them
and the dim blotch of black maidenhair like an indicator,
giving a message to the man—

So in the cane-brake he clasped his hands in delight
that could only be god-given, and murmured:
Lo! God is one god! But here in the twilight
godly and lovely comes Aphrodite out of the sea
towards me!

Resonant as the poem is, it barely needs explication. The
image of the woman washing herself, even the pale green of
the "sea of evening" behind her, goes back as far as *Look! We
Have Come Through!*, to the amorous-religious ecstasy of
"Gloire de Dijon" and "River Roses." But here her "dim
blotch of black maidenhair . . . giving a message to the man"
is even more specifically one of God's manifestations, for
Aphrodite, like Hermes, is a holy messenger, and the sexual
mystery she embodies is the central mystery of the divine urge
toward incarnation. Lawrence had written of it in "Tortoise
Shout" years earlier, written of

Sex, which breaks us into voice, sets us calling across the
    deeps, calling, calling for the complement . . .
Torn, to become whole again, after long seeking for what is
    lost,
The same cry from the tortoise as from Christ, the Osiris-cry
    of abandonment,
That which is whole torn asunder,

That which is in part, finding its whole again throughout the
universe.

And now in "The Man of Tyre" and the poems leading up to
it he proclaims that the entire process—the halving, healing
and making whole to which the sexual mystery is crucial—is
godly; that it, together with its productions and reproduc-
tions, *is* the cosmocreative demiurge.

iii

Having at least partially established the dual nature of
Kosmokrator-Kosmodynamos, Lawrence turns in the next two
poems, but especially in "Whales Weep Not!," to a closer con-
sideration of the specific natural forms in which his God is
embodied. He is still writing sermons directly inspired by the
pagan Mediterranean, but where he had in other poems fo-
cused his attention on the gods who cross and recross that sea
and the God who made it, in these two pieces he concentrates
on the sea itself and the godly life it contains.

> They say the sea is loveless, that in the sea
> love cannot live, but only bare, salt splinters
> of loveless life,

he begins in "They Say the Sea is Loveless." They? It was, of
course, he himself who wrote in *Birds, Beasts and Flowers* of
the alien fish who seemed to him to be "loveless . . . and so
lively." But now he qualifies that statement. "The sea," he
declares in "Whales Weep Not!," "contains/the hottest blood
of all, and the wildest, the most urgent"—the "loving" mam-
malian blood of whales.

It is hard to read this poem without thinking of *Jonah* and
Moby Dick. Pinto and Roberts speculate that the imagery of
the work "is almost certainly based on memories of . . .
Moby Dick, a book for which Lawrence had an unbounded
admiration," and they refer readers to a passage from *Studies*
in which Lawrence quotes Melville's description of "the love-
making of these amazing monsters."

Far beneath this wonderous world upon the surface, another and still stranger world met our eyes, as we gazed over the side . . . Some of the subtlest secrets of the seas seemed divulged to us in this enchanted pond. We saw young Leviathan amours in the deep. And thus, though surrounded by circle upon circle of consternation and affrights, did these inscrutable creatures at the centre freely and fearlessly indulge in all peaceful concernments; yea, serenely revelled in dalliance and delight.

But another passage of Melville's from which Lawrence also quotes may have had an effect upon the poem too.

A gentle joyousness—a mighty mildness of repose in swiftness, invested the gliding whale. Not the white bull Jupiter swimming away with ravished Europa clinging to his graceful horns; his lovely, leering eyes sideways intent upon the maid; with smooth bewitching fleetness, rippling straight for the nuptial bower in Crete; not Jove, not that great majesty Supreme! did surpass the glorified White Whale as he so divinely swam.[23]

What is most significant about these lines which so much interested Lawrence is their religious character. Unlike the "great fish" of *Jonah,* whose stomach was the "belly of hell," [24] Melville's whales, though elsewhere even demonic, here disport themselves as Lawrence's do, godlike in the heavenly "waters of the beginning and the end." Because Lawrence, with Carlyle, advocated a kind of "Natural Supernaturalism," the copulation of his whales is like the divine sexual conflagration of Swedenborgian angels.

> And over the bridge of the whale's strong phallus, linking the
>   wonder of whales,
> the burning archangels under the sea keep passing, back and
>   forth,
> keep passing, archangels of bliss
> from him to her, from her to him, great Cherubim

[23] See Herman Melville, *Moby Dick,* Ch. LXXXVII, "The Grand Armada," and Ch. CXXXII, "The Chase—First Day." Also *cf.* "Herman Melville's *Moby Dick,*" in *Studies.*
[24] *Jonah,* 2, 2.

that wait on whales in mid-ocean, suspended in the waves of
the sea,
great heaven of whales in the waters.

And because Lawrence's religion fuses elements of Christianity and paganism into a new synthesis, his "great heaven of whales" includes not only the standard Christian paraphernalia—cherubim, seraphim, archangels—but also, like Melville's, suggests a deity of ancient Greece:

and Aphrodite is the wife of whales
most happy, happy she! . . .
and Venus among the fishes skips and is a she-dolphin . . .
dense with happy blood, dark rainbow bliss in the sea.

Though it is perhaps the happiness of the whales that makes them most godly, the poet insists that this bliss is not the joy of consciousness. Rather, it is the bliss of pure blood-being, a happiness hardly aware of itself. Moby Dick, said Lawrence in *Studies*, "is our deepest blood-nature." Thus, like the heroes dipped in scarlet who "slimly went like fishes, and didn't care," and who "knew it was no use knowing/their own nothingness," Lawrence's whales act and love in a sea "where God is also love, but without words"—without the nerve-brain consciousness that torments so many men. Urging and blowing, rocking and reeling, circling and sporting "on the surface of the ceaseless flood," they are creatures of pure *Kosmodynamos,* and their love is active rather than contemplative, the love that *moves* the world. And the flood in which they have their being is the very flood of unconscious urgent life that drowned Tom Brangwen in *The Rainbow,* a flood in which man cannot live (as *Noah* tells us) but which ultimately implies a promise to man, God's rainbow covenant. For this reason Lawrence ends the poem by describing Venus as "the female tunny-fish, round and happy among the males/and dense with happy blood, dark rainbow bliss in the sea." If *Kosmodynamos* has flung us onto the shore, cooled our blood and tempered our "drunk delight," at least we can imagine "the hottest blood of all, and the wildest, the most urgent," and, imagining, admit into our minds those urges of our own (and specifically our own sexual urges) which incarnate the demiurge.

"Whales Weep Not!," with its ecstatic specificity, is certainly the climactic poem in this series of verses that attend to the process and products of *Kosmodynamos*. The tidal power of its rhythms is generated by the kind of incantatory repetition we have noted throughout Lawrence's free verse:

> And they rock, and they rock, through the sensual ageless ages
> on the depths of the seven seas,
> and through the salt they reel with drunk delight,
> and in the tropics tremble they with love
> and roll with massive, strong desire, like gods,

and also by inversions ("they reel" followed by "tremble they") like those in some of the *Plumed Serpent* hymns. But because it is considerably shorter than many of Lawrence's earlier "Unrhymed Poems," (though a little longer than most "pansies") "Whales Weep Not!" has a surging intensity that depends also on a skillful use of conventional rhythm. The meter at which it hints is heavily stressed, rocking with animal verve. Like the whales themselves, such lines as

> And over the bridge of the whales' strong phallus, linking the wonder of whales . . .

or

> And enormous mother whales lie dreaming suckling their whale-tender young

seem to dream and reel with drunk delight, as if themselves embodying the divine *joi de vivre* of the sea.

But that joy of pure animal being is no longer entirely accessible to man. "Whales Weep Not!" is the climactic poem of the *Kosmodynamos* series not only because it is in many respects the best—the most specific, the most charged with life-rhythms—but because it goes the furthest in itself becoming

Kosmodynamic. As if he realized that he could go no further, Lawrence turned abruptly in the next few poems to the problems that arise from the fact that man, unlike whales and dolphins, not only is a body but has a body—to the problems that confront the spirit as it struggles, not always willingly, to separate itself from the flesh. Turning from the sea to the sky, from whales and poppies and flying fish to moon and sun and planets, he did not abandon his quest for God, but he did focus on an aspect of God—the spiritual, the insubstantial— which he had not yet clearly defined. "Invocation to the Moon," the first real prayer in this collection of sermons and prayers, provides an entrance into the enigmatic realms through which the poet felt he must now journey.

—18

The Longest Journey:
Lawrence's Ship of Death

i

The motif of the journey, as well as a concern with the spiritual aspect of God, is a theme that not only informs the "Invocation" but also links it with the next two apparently dissimilar poems.

> Now I am at your gate, you beauty, you lady of all nakedness!
> Now I must enter your mansion, and beg your gift
> Moon, O Moon, great lady of the heavenly few,

Lawrence declares in the second stanza of "Invocation." Again, in "Butterfly" he watches the "white speck" of an insect "in a strange level fluttering . . . go out to sea-ward," and in "Bavarian Gentians" he foresees that he must "guide myself with the blue forked torch of this flower/down the darker and darker stairs." All three journeys are spiritual quests, graphic extensions of his earlier explorations of the divine, but the first, the trip to the "silvery house" of the moon, is perhaps the most obscure.

Lawrence's obsession with the moon, which goes back at least as far as *Sons and Lovers, The Rainbow,* and the "Moony" chapter of *Women in Love,* has long interested readers. Some of the writer's friends reported to biographers that he himself was "moon-mad," a lunatic in the strict sense of the word.[1] And certainly in his novels the moon is often a

---

1 See Aldington, Introduction to *Women in Love.*

·disquieting influence, a "great, white watching" in the night, "Cybele . . . the accursed Syria Dea," as Birkin calls her.[2] But though in "Invocation" she is still a female, she is no longer the fearful, corruscating demoness of the earlier work. On the contrary, she is now a "glistening garmentless beauty," the

> greatest of ladies
> crownless and jewelless and garmentless
> because naked [she is] more wonderful than anything we can
>   stroke.

Her power and her beauty reside in the very remote and radiant spirituality that the younger writer saw as deadly. She is, or appears, insubstantial—impalpable, unstrokable—the opposite of the violently embodied whales. Hence she is the "lady of all nakedness," the lady of the soul's nakedness when it is divorced from the body and, paradoxically, the lady of the body's nakedness. And the boon the poet begs of her is a spiritual gift, because she is the "great lady of the heavenly few."

Why this should be so, however, would still be obscure if we could not turn first to a passage in *Fantasia of the Unconscious,* where Lawrence explains his sun and moon symbolism, and then to an even more illuminating passage in *Apocalypse.* The sun, he tells us in *Fantasia,* "is the great sympathetic centre of our inanimate universe . . . To the sun fly the vibrations or the molecules in the great sympathy-mode of death, and in the sun they are renewed." And just "as the sun is the great fiery vivifying pole of the inanimate universe, the moon is the other pole, cold and keen and vivifying." Furthermore, he adds, "the moon is born from the death of individuals," while "all things, in their oneing, their unification into the pure, universal oneness, evaporate and fly . . . towards the sun." Finally, he concludes,

[2] *The Rainbow,* Ch. XI: "First Love." *Women in Love,* Ch. XIX: "Moony."

There are two sheer dynamic principles in our universe, the sun-principle and the moon-principle. And these principles are known to us in immediate contact as fire and water. The sun is not fire. But the principle of fire is the sun-principle. . . . And there is another absolute and visible principle, the principle of water. The moon is not water. But it is the soul of water, the invisible clue to all the waters.[3]

Then in *Apocalypse* he tells us even more specifically that

the sun, like a lion, loves the bright red blood of life, and can give it an infinite enrichment if we know how to receive it . . . and the cool, bright, ever-varying moon . . . is she who would caress our nerves, smooth them with the silky hand of her glowing, soothe them into serenity again with her cool presence. For the moon is the mistress and mother of our watery bodies, the pale body of our nervous consciousness and our moist flesh. Oh, the moon could soothe us and heal us like a cool great Artemis between her arms.[4]

The moon, in other words, represents that in man—and in God, and in things—which is not, like the whales, of the "hot blood," but of the cool spirit, and hence she is associated with nerve-brain consciousness. More—and here is one of those Lawrentian paradoxes that are often difficult to resolve—because of her connection with individuality, with separateness and with water, the moon, despite her remoteness and spirituality, is polarized to man's "white flesh," for just as it is our fiery blood that brings us together, it is our "watery flesh," as well as our "nervous" egos, that keeps us apart. "The blood is one blood," Kate hears the men of Quetzalcoatl chanting.[5] In pure blood-being men are one, like whales and dolphins and elephants. But in the flesh, as in the mind, men can never be one: they must always be inalterably separate and "other" to each other.

If, however, the sun controls the blood-being Lawrence sees as integral to the divine health and "rainbow bliss" of life,

---

[3] *Fantasia,* pp. 183–184, 187–188. [4] *Apocalypse,* pp. 43–44.
[5] *The Plumed Serpent,* Ch. XXVI: "Kate is a Wife."

287

why, seeking regeneration, does the dying poet address the moon? Because the joy of pure animal being—the "happy blood" of whales for instance—is not only, in Lawrence's view, inaccessible to man, but also inappropriate to man.[6] Every man must have a self, a separated ego and a separated body, through which blood can flow. A *whole* man is a well-head for wonder, wrote the poet in the "Song of a Man Who Has Come Through," and not merely the wonder—the blood—that bubbles into him out of the unknown. Hence Lawrence asks the moon to "let me come past the silver bells of your flowers" and "into your house, garmentless lady of the last great gift" so that she can

> give me back my lost limbs
> and my lost white fearless breast
> and set me again on moon-remembering feet
> a healed, whole man, O Moon!

To those who do not revere her properly (like Birkin in "Moony") the moon is an "angry Artemis . . . Angry she stares down on us and whips us with nervous whips,"[7] and the "bitter night" of that goddess is the night Lawrence portrayed in the early novels. But just as "there is an eternal vital correspondence between our blood and the sun," so "there is an eternal vital correspondence between our nerves and the moon," a correspondence Lawrence himself, now frail and sick, no longer wishes to deny, for

> Now I must enter your mansion, and beg your gift
> Moon, O Moon, great lady of the heavenly few.

[6] It is inaccessible to modern man: the "heroes dipped in scarlet" seem to have made a separate peace with the problem. But that Lawrence feels man *cannot* have a pure blood-being like animals is made clear by a passage in *The Plumed Serpent* (Ch. IX): Juana's family, un-formed "primitives," are "like animals, yet not at all like animals. For animals are complete in their isolation and their insouciance. . . . But with the family there was always a kind of bleeding of incompleteness."

[7] *Apocalypse,* p. 44.

The journey Lawrence imagines himself taking in this poem is a trip into the sky, like the journey taken by Jesus in *The Plumed Serpent*. As he ascends, he tells us that

> Far and forgotten is the Villa of Venus the glowing
> and behind me now in the gulfs of space lies the golden
> house of the sun,
> and six have given me gifts, and kissed me god-speed,
> kisses of four great lords, beautiful, as they held me to their
> bosoms in farewell,
> and kiss of the far-off lingering lady who looks over the dis-
> tant fence of the twilight,
> and one warm kind kiss of the lion with golden paws.

These are the "heavenly few" in whose company the poet, attempting to live "breast to breast with the cosmos," has traveled. The six are the "four great lords" of *Apocalypse*—Mars, Saturn, Jupiter and Mercury—plus Venus, here characterized as a "far-off lingering lady," and the sun, "the lion with golden paws." Together with the moon, towards whose house he is traveling, they make up "the seven planets (including sun and moon) who are the seven Rulers from the heavens over earth and over us." [8] But Venus, the sexual goddess, and the four planets who control men's earthly natures, and the bloody, leonine sun are forgotten now, because the poet, journeying towards death and rebirth, is concentrated purely on his individual fate, his impending separation and lonely renewal.

As prayer, then, the "Invocation to the Moon" involves an act of ablution, a Yeatsian consuming away of the past and the heart, and, equally, a desire for absolution. "Give me back my lost limbs/and my lost white fearless breast," Lawrence asks—but he has not yet received them. He is still fearful, still at the threshold of the mystery. His moving plea:

> Lady, lady of the last house down the long, long street of the
> stars,

8 *Ibid.*, p. 91. See Chs. 17–21, for Lawrence on numerology.

289

    be good to me now, as I beg you, as you've always been good
        to men
    who begged of you and gave you homage
    and watched for your glistening feet down the garden path,

is one he may or may not expect to be answered, and it is cast
in deliberately fanciful language.

It is significant that, though Lawrence consciously incor-
porates into the work a number of the old pagan images he
discussed with admiration in *Apocalypse,* he expresses them
not in the sonorous vocabulary of myth and revelation, but in
the more artificial, almost whimsical style of fairy tale and
fable. The moon, for instance, is not a goddess, a "horned
Astarte," but a "great lady . . . crownless and jewelless and
garmentless." Her place in the sky is a "heavenly mansion"
and the poet-speaker at her gate is not so much the naked soul
approaching the heavenly city as a prince (or a pauper) come
hat in hand to the "long, long street of the stars" to beg a
special boon. Occasionally this "fabulous" tone even lapses
into cuteness or vulgarity, as fairy tales may: the "Villa of
Venus the glowing" and the "silver bells of your flowers, and
the cockleshells" seem needlessly coy and cloying. But perhaps
such lapses are inevitable, for what the fairy tale tone suggests
is Lawrence's own attitude toward his prayer. He does not
speak here with the certain vision of achieved faith, but with
the basically skeptical and artificial inventiveness of what
Coleridge called *fancy,* because he is still seeking to embody
an experience that he has not yet, to use Coleridge's other
term, really *imagined.*

ii

In "Butterfly" Lawrence abandons altogether the journey
upward. Not he himself but the butterfly is now the traveler,
and its trip is to be a horizontal one: with "a strange level
fluttering" it "goes out to sea-ward." The butterfly is a tradi-
tional metaphor for the soul (it lives in the air, hence it is

ethereal, spiritual, and so on), and the poet is here no doubt using it to symbolize his own soul as well as souls in general. But his use of such an *objective* correlative is certainly noteworthy, coming as it does after the direct, confessional and prayerful "I" of "Invocation to the Moon." It is as though for a moment he has removed himself and some of his fancies from consideration. His treatment of the problem of death and separation will now be less ambitious and more "realistic."

> Butterfly, the wind blows seaward, strong beyond the garden wall!
> Butterfly, why do you settle on my shoe, and sip the dirt on my shoe,
> lifting your veined wings, lifting them? Big white butterfly!

None of the great ancient images of *Apocalypse* or "Invocation" appear in these lines, nor do the poet's words imply the system of religious allusions that structured "Whales Weep Not!" Rather, the religious emotion is temporarily restrained, the opening of the poem rooted in objective, precisely observed detail.

Yet the poem as a whole is not entirely "objective." David Cavitch remarks on the flatness of the style, a quality he speculates Lawrence may have learned from the naive Etruscan wall paintings he admired.[9] But this flatness or naiveté goes back as well to the resonant simplicity of the Imagist style that influenced a number of the writer's early poems, such as "A White Blossom," "Baby Running Barefoot" or, later, "The White Horse." For the wind "polished with snow," the warm garden with its red geraniums, the big, uncertain white butterfly ("will you go, will you go?"), are images whose connotations transcend their carefully described natural setting.

The warm garden with red geraniums, for instance, is the embodied world of natural process, the world in which a

[9] David Cavitch, *D. H. Lawrence and the New World* (Oxford, 1969), p. 210.

Kosmodynamic god "sighing and yearning with tremendous creative yearning, in that dark green mess,/oh, for some other beauty, some other beauty" finally produces himself as "red geranium, and mignonette." It is the warm-blooded world of whales and dolphins from which the dying soul must, willingly or not, separate himself.

> Will you climb on your big soft wings, black-dotted
> as up an invisible rainbow, an arch
> till the wind slides you sheer from the arch-crest,

Lawrence asks, and his mention of the rainbow recalls the mysterious paradox of God, whose nature was defined earlier by analogy with that phenomenon.

> Even the rainbow has a body
> made of the drizzling rain
> and is an architecture of glistening atoms
> built up, built up
> yet you can't lay your hand on it,
> nay, nor even your mind.

Yet how much more mysterious (even oxymoronic) is an *"invisible* rainbow." Unlike the real "dark rainbow bliss" of the dolphin Venus, the obvious joy of blood-being, it represents the spiritual covenant the poet has not yet been able to find. For this reason, despite their use (for the first time in the poem) of the religious word "soul," and despite a brief lapse into the fancy of "Invocation" with the adjective "crystalline," the last lines of the poem are as restrained, as accepting of what seems for the moment an inevitable mystery, as were the first.

> Farewell, farewell, lost soul!
> You have melted in the crystalline distance,
> it is enough! I saw you vanish into air.

"Into air, into thin air." Perhaps there *is* no answer, Lawrence seems to speculate at this point. Perhaps the "invisible rainbow" can never be further defined. His conclusion recalls (besides Prospero) Stevens'

> And whence they came and whither they shall go
> The dew upon their feet shall manifest.

From earth, from "sipping the dirt on my shoe," into "air, into thin air."

Unlike Stevens, however, Lawrence could never entirely rest content with what Wordsworth called "the burthen of the mystery." While Stevens (and Wordsworth) could accept the intransigence of the wall that separates the dead from the living, Lawrence sought to journey beyond it. Thus, although "Butterfly" is uncharacteristically restrained, it is an integral link in the series "Invocation"—"Butterfly"—"Bavarian Gentians," the first real "death" series in this book of confrontations with death. The movement of the series is, first, upward in "Invocation" (in a search for "my lost white fearless breast"), next outward in "Butterfly" (in the butterfly-soul's flight of death), and finally downward and inward in "Bavarian Gentians" (toward the actual experience of death and regeneration). Significantly, white and blue are the predominant colors of the group: white of the moon, white of the poet's "lost limbs," white of the butterfly—and then blue, the dark blue burning of the gentians. Whiteness suggests the silvery pallor of the isolated soul, deprived of the blood-heat of the body and existing in the moon's mode of pure individuality. "Each soul [departs] with its own isolation," Lawrence wrote in "Medlars and Sorb Apples," "strangest of all strange companions,/And best." And it departs,

> Like a flame blown whiter and whiter
> In a deeper and deeper darkness,

in the "blue-smoking" death-darkness of the "Bavarian Gentians," "Pluto's dark-blue daze."

Its reference to Pluto, rather than its use of "blue darkness," makes "Bavarian Gentians" most clearly a poem about death. Indeed, while both "Invocation" and "Butterfly" dealt indirectly with death, "Bavarian Gentians" is the first poem in the series, even the first poem in the volume, to deal with it overtly (though still not explicitly). Lawrence never uses the word "death" in this piece, as he does later in a number of poems, and he never refers to his own sickness, as he also does in other, later poems, but he is plainly enacting a ritual of entrance into that final realm of what Ursula, in *Women in Love,* calls "pure inhuman otherness."

I deliberately revive the concept of "otherness" because for Lawrence death is not only a necessary condition for self-knowledge (as we saw in "Medlars and Sorb Apples," where through a kind of death the poet imagined the self finally encountering and assimilating its own otherness), it is also an expression of the absolute and divine otherness of God. Ursula looks forward to "the pure inhuman otherness of death. Whatever life might be," she thinks, it cannot "take away death, the inhuman transcendent death." More, for her (and for Lawrence), the particular reward of death is that "To know is human, and in death we do not know, we are not human. And the joy of this compensates for all the bitterness of knowledge and the sordidness of our humanity. In death we shall not be human, and we shall not know. The promise of this is our heritage, we look forward like heirs to their majority." [10] That death entails the particular inhumanity of "not knowing" does not, in other words, mean it is *sub*human. On the contrary, death signifies our "majority" because only through death can human beings participate in that inhuman purity of being which is divine. For only in death, to return to the Sartre analogy, does the *pour soi* finally and irrevocably become *en soi.* In Sartre's system "I only cease to make myself

[10] *Women in Love,* Ch. XV: "Sunday Evening."

nothing (*me néantir*) when I become a corpse," notes Gabriel Marcel,[11] and Hazel Barnes comments that "at the moment of death one becomes only his past and hence an in-itself," [12] an enigmatic object, a hieroglyphic archetype of otherness.

Yet where Sartre, whose emphasis is primarily ethical and metaphysical, fails to follow out the mystical implications of the *pour soi* becoming *en soi,* Lawrence, whose attentive concern is always radically mystical and prophetic, occupies himself with little else. Not content with merely classifying death as the ultimate otherness, "the great dark sky of death" as the sheltering blackness of pure, incomprehensible not-knowing—pure objecthood—he attempts imaginatively to penetrate beyond that dark barrier, to experience, in the tradition of much religious poetry, the soul's union with the divine. "One must go where the unfaltering spirit goes [he had written in *Women in Love*]. There must be no baulking the issue because of fear. No baulking the issue, no listening to the lesser voices. If the deepest desire be now to go on into the unknown of death, shall one forfeit the deepest truth for one more shallow?" [13]

Where *does* the "unfaltering spirit" go? We saw in "Whales Weep Not!" and other poems that because of man's inescapable crucifixion into a blood-being and a nerve-brain self a living man could never entirely participate in the rainbow bliss of whales—or of snakes or fish. The tacitly admitted but unspoken problem of "Invocation" and "Butterfly" was, therefore, the question of the spirit's ultimate destination when it separates itself from the body, and of the role the spiritual plays in that which is "life-blissful, life-divine." In "Invocation" Lawrence toyed, but uncertainly, with the notion of a supreme and healing silveriness, an undefined but purely spiritual renewal, and in "Butterfly" he temporarily

[11] Marcel, p. 177.
[12] Hazel Barnes, Translator's Introduction to *Being and Nothingness,* p. xxxvi.
[13] *Women in Love,* Ch. XV: "Sunday Evening."

abandoned the search. In "Bavarian Gentians," however, as in much of his other work, he begins with the idea that death, as he had written years earlier in "Snapdragon," is "better than not to be."

Death is better than not-being and, indeed, by no stretch of the imagination identical with not-being, for insofar as death is not-knowing, insofar as the dead man is *en soi,* he has a paradoxical *fullness* of being the living can never have. Thus when Birkin, looking at the frozen body of Gerald, contemplates with horror "the cold, mute, material face" [14]—the face of a subject who has, terrifyingly, become an object—he nevertheless remembers a dead face that was more beautiful, the face of one who was able to "yield to the mystery." And thus in "Bavarian Gentians" we encounter the idea of death as a kind of final knowledge—the knowledge that is not knowledge, that goes *beyond* knowledge, like the peace that passeth understanding. Himself on the verge of death, lying weak and sick in "September: my birthday month that I like so much," [15] Lawrence attempted at last the difficult task of reconciling in symbol and metaphor the blood-self and the nerve-brain self, the flesh and the spirit.

The Bavarian gentians, then, emblems of that richly shadowed underworld the poet also described in "Medlars and Sorb Apples," are not merely "big and dark, only dark/darkening the daytime, torchlike with the smoking blueness of Pluto's gloom," they are also, paradoxically, "torches of darkness," torches of not-knowing, the only lamps that can guide the wayfaring soul on its "longest journey" into "the dark of death, which is the blue burning of the one fire." [16] And death itself, the "sightless realm" into which the soul like lost Persephone penetrates, is that blind, interior world "where darkness is awake upon the dark," the primordial world out of which tree, flower and fruit, snake and tortoise, fish and bat and man himself emerge and re-emerge like vi-

[14] *Ibid.,* Ch. XXXI: "Exeunt." [15] *Letters,* p. 774.
[16] *Etruscan Places,* pp. 85–86.

sions or like flying fishes perpetually transcending and re-entering the waters of pure being. Death is "a darkness invisible enfolded in the deeper dark"—a kingdom where the paradoxes of being yet not-knowing proliferate like "torches of darkness."

Yet it is here "the lost bride and her groom" lie in the long embrace that ultimately generates all being—"the one fire." Persephone, the flowerlike daughter of Demeter, the earth goddess, is the go-between, the embodiment of *Kosmodynamos* and of the cycle of seasons that oscillates irrevocably between life and death. Like Matthew who, "being a man" is "a traveller back and forth"; like Quetzalcoatl, the morning star, whose plumes bespeak the transcendence of heaven and whose reptilian tail represents the immanence of earth; like Christ himself, whose human/inhuman selfhood symbolizes "the first submission" of knowledge to being,[17] Persephone stands at the crossroads of two truths—the truth of life and the truth of death, the truth of the spirit and the truth of the flesh—and through her Lawrence is able to show that the two truths are, as in "Medlars and Sorb-Apples," ultimately one. There, in the incomprehensible marriage with darkness, life begins again.

> Give me a flower on a tall stem, and three dark flames,
> for I will go to the wedding and be wedding guest
> at the marriage of the *living* dark,[18]

Lawrence wrote in another version of the poem. And so we have come full circle, for death, which seems at first like the only form of absolute otherness, is finally a new wedding to life. The spirit must rejoin the body, for, like God who both has a body and is a body, the spirit not only has a body but, the poet finds, *is* a body.

[17] *Birds, Beasts and Flowers,* "St. Matthew," "Fish."
[18] This is the conclusion of the "other" version of "Bavarian Gentians." For the full text, see *CP,* pp. 955–956. For a discussion of the different versions of the work, see *CP,* p. 1036.

Put baldly—as the spirit *is* a body—such a notion sounds like nonsense, and certainly if we apply to it the criteria that govern ordinary language and ordinary logic, it *is* nonsense. But in "Bavarian Gentians," more than in any of his other works, perhaps even more than in the later "Ship of Death," Lawrence was trying to fit his mind to an experience that is by definition "unimaginable," [19] and the tools he used were therefore those instruments of impossibility, paradox and oxymoron. Like Milton, who strained to explore the mind-confounding nature of Satan's "darkness visible," or Keats, who strove to capture the sweetness of "unheard melodies," he sought to characterize an indescribable kingdom as "the sightless realm where darkness is awake upon the dark." But unlike Keats and Milton, who set paradox and oxymoron into a larger argumentative structure, Lawrence concerned himself in "Bavarian Gentians" with little else. At the center of his field of vision (or, more properly, his field of intuition) was a phenomenological paradox: the impossible experience itself. And in the unfolding of this experience his old technique of "continual slightly modified repetition" was perhaps more useful than it had ever been before. For though there is a clearly defined wall between life and death, the possible and the impossible, one cannot approach or pass such a wall abruptly. The passage from possible to impossible must be a gradual shift, a slow alteration of perceptions.

Hence Lawrence's gentians transform themselves gradually, like flowers in a dream, from ordinary "Bavarian gentians, big and dark, only dark/darkening the day-time," to flowers that are "torch-like . . . ribbed and torchlike, with [a] blaze of darkness," to "black lamps from the halls of Dis." The words "only dark" in line three are significantly ambiguous: are the flowers in the beginning the *"only* dark" that "darkens the day-time," or are they at first *merely* dark, and later magically dark? In either case, the phrase sets off a crucial change in the

[19] Hough, p. 214.

298

poem, for eventually all the daytime is darkened (by the poet's imagination of death) and darkened magically.

The double nature of the gentians (torches/flowers) having been established in stanza two, stanza three introduces the final transformation, as the poet imagines himself penetrating their kingdom, the "sightless realm" of Pluto, and, in a kind of imaginative trance, witnesses the transformation of Persephone to "a voice/or a darkness invisible." Like Keats, who in the "Ode to a Nightingale" passed from daytime to the enchanted but deadly depths of the forest-night through the mediating symbol of the nightingale, Lawrence has experienced, through the mediating symbol of what at first seemed to be ordinary dark blue flowers, the central metamorphic power of nature—the slowly dissolving shadow-line between life and death.

Unlike Keats, however, whose entrance into the heart of natural process, the "embalmed darkness" of the "fast-fading violets" and the "coming musk-rose," is increasingly marked by equivocation and ambivalence, Lawrence commits himself wholly to his mystical, mysterious experience, and his repetitions are therefore useful in another way. For, like a shaman, he must induce in himself, through sensuous incantation, the certainties of the creative trance. His repetitions of "burning dark blue, giving off darkness, blue darkness" and "lead me, lead the way," are necessary preliminaries to his conviction that Persephone *does* go "just now, from the frosted September" to her "sightless kingdom" and to his certainty of the splendour of these living/dead torches of darkness.

iv

As one might expect, however, such certainty is intermittent even for Lawrence. Although in the next three poems he elaborates some of the paradoxes of "Bavarian Gentians," he begins also, gradually, to move from sonorous sureness to a more anxious concern with the separated self, the self that has fallen from God. "Lucifer," for instance, begins "Angels are bright still, though the brightest fell," and despite a momentary thought that the ostensibly evil fallen angel may still be like "a ruby in the invisible dark, glowing/with his own annunciation," Lawrence's speculations about the relationship between the individual soul and its God lead him inevitably to wonder, in "The Hands of God," "Did Lucifer fall through knowledge?" and to comment "Oh then pity him, pity that plunge."

In "Silence" the silence of fusion with God is described as the "great bride of all creation." As in religious tradition, the union with the divine is a wedding, "the marriage of the living dark" in one version of "Bavarian Gentians" and here the great bridal of Silence and the soul in "the sacred silence of gates. . . . The silence of passing through doors. . . . The great hush of going from this into that." The silence to which the soul must be wedded is, moreover, the silence of cosmic joy, the paradoxical silence of "the laugh of God . . . the last great thunderous laugh." Aside from the numerology of the "seven great laughs of God," drawn from *Apocalypse,* the imagery is Carlylean. The Victorian prophet praised just such silence in "Characteristics" and elsewhere, and described such laughter as the great laugh of Teufelsdrökh in *Sartor Resartus.* But what is now distinctively Lawrentian is the potentially anxious concentration on the moment of death: "the suspension of wholeness . . . the moment of division within the whole." This division that precedes the quasi-sexual and renewing union of the soul and God must, Lawrence thought, be approached with due reverence. We are, as in "Tortoise Shout," "torn to become most whole again," but at any moment during the process of halving and healing a soul may fall away from God into the depths of "disintegrative" self-consciousness, the "abyss of immortality."

The next four poems deal with this crucial falling sickness, and it is a subject to which the poet will return again later in the collection, when he explores further the nature and cause of evil. But he states his position at the outset, in "The Hands of God."

It is a fearful thing to fall into the hands of the living God.
But it is a much more fearful thing to fall out of them.

And by the end of the poem his comment becomes a prayer:

Save me from that, O God!
Let me never know myself apart from the living God!

His description in between, in stanzas three and four, of the "slow, corruptive levels of disintegrative knowledge/when the self has fallen from the hands of God/and sinks, seething and sinking, corrupt," recalls the "cold dissolution . . . [the] snow abstract annihilation" he had discussed in *Women in Love*.[20] But there, though a religious system of some sort was always implicit, God was never openly identified with the "creative mystery." Now, however, "all that matters," declares Lawrence in "Pax," is to be "at one with the living God,/to be a creature in the house of the God of Life." And the chief paradox with which he works is the apparently strange and puzzling idea that "through knowledge and will . . . man can break away, and fall from the hands of God [into] . . . the abyss of the immortality/of those that have fallen from God."

How can a fall from the God of Life be a fall into immortality? Though the question seems difficult, an answer is not hard to find, considering how much Lawrentian theology is revealed in poems like "Bavarian Gentians" and in earlier aesthetic statements. The God of Life is, after all, the God of death too, for in "Bavarian Gentians" the two apparently contradictory states were shown to be aspects of the same truth, different stages in the same process. And the Living God manifests himself in "the blue burning of the one fire"—the flame of death that is also, in its scarlet burning, "the cosmic

[20] *Women in Love,* Ch. XIX: "Moony."

vitality," the fire of life.[21] The frozen state of immortality, then, is the state of those who have rejected divine process, choosing instead the "artifice of eternity."

My reference to Yeats is deliberate, for at every point in this matter Lawrence sets himself against Yeats—the Yeats of *The Tower*, at least—and it is easiest to understand his ideas when comparing them to the central tenets of "Sailing to Byzantium." What for Yeats are virtues—knowledge ("of what is past or passing or to come") and immortality—are for Lawrence emblems of failure, and the human feature Yeats praises, the assertiveness of the soul that can "clap its hands and sing and louder sing/For every tatter in its mortal dress," is for Lawrence, the main flaw in our humanity.

> Only man can fall from God,
> Only man.

he declares in "Only Man," the final poem of this series.

> No animal, no beast nor creeping thing,
> no cobra nor hyaena nor scorpion nor hideous white ant
> can slip entirely through the fingers of the hands of god
> into the abyss of self-knowledge,
> knowledge of the self-apart-from-god.

To reiterate Sartre one last time, only man, because he is *pour soi* rather than *en soi*, can fall into the terrible isolation of godlessness, an isolation in which he mechanically exists (but does not live) forever.

v

The next twenty-five poems, most of them brief, pansy-like utterances, are concerned specifically with exploring two modes of being: mechanical existence on the one hand, and godly life on the other. One of the best-known of these works, "Death Is not Evil, Evil Is Mechanical," summarizes and explains the ideas of the series.

[21] *Etruscan Places*, p. 86.

Only the human being, absolved from kissing and strife
goes on and on and on, without wandering
fixed upon the hub of the ego
going, yet never wandering, fixed, yet in motion,
the kind of hell that is real, grey and awful
sinless and stainless going round and round
the kind of hell grey Dante never saw
but of which he had a bit inside him.

Here is the hell of immortality, the abyss into which the mechanical will (fixed like a wheel upon "the hub of the ego") plummets us. To it Lawrence opposes the paradoxical "living wholeness" of mortality.

Know thyself, and that thou art mortal . . .
a thing of kisses and strife
a lit-up shaft of rain
a calling column of blood
a rose tree bronzey with thorns
a mixture of yea and nay
a rainbow of love and hate
a wind that blows back and forth
a creature of beautiful peace, like a river
and a creature of conflict, like a cataract.

One must yield to the paradoxical processes of being, as in "Bavarian Gentians," rather than attempting to resolve them scientifically.

Moreover, what we perceive to be true—what we know through sense and imaginative vision to be true—*is* true: the phenomenal world, with all its radiant images and inconsistencies. "When Anaxagoras says: even the snow is black," Lawrence writes in "Anaxagoras,"

he is taken by the scientists very seriously
because he is enunciating a "principle," a "law"
that all things are mixed, and therefore the purest white snow
has in it an element of blackness.

That they call science, and reality.
I call it mental conceit and mystification
and nonsense, for pure snow is white to us
white and white and only white
with a lovely bloom of whiteness upon white
in which the soul delights and the senses
have an experience of bliss.[22]

The truth is not ironic, judicious, a "gray" attempt at reconciling opposites. It is one absolute truth one moment followed by another absolute truth the next.

And life is for delight, and for bliss
and dread, and the dark rolling ominousness of doom.
Then the bright dawning of delight again
from off the sheer white snow, or the poised moon.

And in "Kissing and Horrid Strife" Lawrence elaborates this idea, clothing his perceptions of ultimate reality in the ancient images that have a power and a glory lacking in mechanical science.

Life is for kissing and for horrid strife.
Life is for the angels and the sunderers.
Life is for the daimons and the demons,
those that put honey on our lips, and those that put salt.

The sunderers, also described in the impressive "Walk Warily," are the two "little ones," mysterious twins whose nature and origin Lawrence discusses extensively in *Apocalypse*. He traces their evolution through the Greek Dioskouri, Kastor and Polydeukes, but finds their mystical duality most convincingly embodied in the Kabiri, "whose cult [it is said] is still alive in Mohammedan countries.

[22] Marjorie Grene makes this phenomenological point in an essay on the work of Adolf Portmann. She notes that Galileo's "primary" qualities become "inauthentic" for Portmann, while what for Galileo is "secondary" because dependent on individual perception, becomes "authentic" for him. M. Grene, *Commentary*, "Portmann's Thought," XL, v (November 1965), 33.

They were the two secret little ones, the homunculi, and the "rivals." They were also connected with thunders, and with two round black thunder-stones. . . . As thunderers they were sunderers, sundering cloud, air and water. And always they have this aspect of rivals, dividers, separators, for good as well as for ill: balancers. . . . It is they who hold things asunder to make a space, a gateway. In this way, they are rainmakers: they open the gates in the sky: perhaps as thunder-stones. In the same way they are the secret lords of sex, for it was early recognised that sex is a holding of two things asunder, that birth may come through between them . . . they give the two alternate forms of elemental consciousness, our day-consciousness and our night-consciousness. . . . A creature of dual and jealous consciousness is man, and the twins witness jealously to the duality.[23]

These passages show the importance Lawrence attaches to the "horrid strife," as well as to the natural balance, that the Kabiri represent. His resolution of the basic problems of life and death is consistently and radically dualistic, and one of his chief aims in *Last Poems* is to find appropriate images for this dualism. The oxymoronic "torches of darkness," the marriages of Persephone and Pluto, of the soul and Silence, the salt that is born of the "eternal opposition/between the two great ones, Fire and the Wet," in addition to the Sunderers themselves, are all such images. So are the traditional Christian opposites of hell and heaven, God and Satan.

> When Satan fell, he only fell
> because the Lord Almighty rose a bit too high,
> a bit beyond himself,

Lawrence asserts in "When Satan Fell." And hell and heaven, he concludes, "are the scales of the balance of life,/which swing against each other.

Another important image of cosmic duality, hinted at in "Bavarian Gentians" and "Silence" and later explored in the "Ship of Death," is the image of doors. The poet tells us in "Doors" that

23 *Apocalypse*, pp. 128–130.

Life has its palace of blue day aloft
and its halls of the great dark below . . .
There is a double sacredness of doors.
Some you may sing through, and all men hear,
but others, the dark doors, oh hush! hush!
let nobody be about! slip in! go all unseen.
But evil, evil is another thing! in another place!

The "other place" he continues, in "Evil Is Homeless" (for
the three poems, "When Satan Fell," "Doors," and "Evil Is
Homeless," are a true series, each picking up where the last
left off, like the "desire" series in *Pansies*) is in a sense no
place, the no man's land of the isolated willful soul, where

men . . . sit in machines
among spinning wheels, in an apotheosis of wheels,
sit in the grey mist of movement which moves not
and going which goes not
and doing which does not
and being which is not.

Like Anaxagoras, such men are cut off from the phenomenal
world by the pointless mechanism of the intellect (for which
the wheel is an apt Lawrentian metaphor) and they are there-
fore "absolved from the sun and the earth and the moon" as
well as "from strife and kisses." Their lives and minds turn
solipsistically in upon themselves, and their senses—the doors
of their being—atrophy. But, Lawrence had written in "The
Four," one of his wittiest metaphysical statements,

To our senses, the elements are four
and have ever been, and will ever be . . .
the four Great Ones, the Four Roots, the First Four
of Fire and the Wet, Earth and the wide Air of the world.

To find the other many elements, you must go to the labora-
tory
and hunt them down.
But the four we have always with us, they are our world.
Or rather, they have us with them.

When we are *in* our senses, in our right minds, we are in the great cosmos of the ancients,[24] which, if we can only yield ourselves, will carry us inevitably onward in the "wonder-journey" of life and death. "Oh, do not tell me the heavens as well are a wheel," Lawrence declares in "The Wandering Cosmos." "For every revolution of the earth around the sun/ is a footstep onwards, onwards, we know not whither . . . but going." The statement revives his earlier concern with *Kosmo-dynamos,* for the cosmic energy—the energy of God—is that force which impels men, and all living things, and the sun, and the moon, the "great travellers" of *The Rainbow,* on their endless journey "from this into that," through the doors from life into death, down the stairs of the earth, up the street of the stars, and out onto the sea of oblivion.

vi

In the famous and sonorous series of verses entitled "The Ship of Death" the journey motif is most fully and convincingly elaborated. Here for the first time Lawrence becomes absolutely explicit about his own death and the death that every man is dying during every moment of his life. The first section, with its ellipses and its air of Rilkean *einsehen,* is certainly the most portentous.

> Now it is autumn and the falling fruit
> and the long journey towards oblivion.
>
> The apples falling like great drops of dew
> to bruise themselves an exit from themselves.
>
> And it is time to go, to bid farewell
> to one's own self, and find an exit
> from the fallen self.

[24] Cf. also *Apocalypse,* pp. 167–168: "With Empedocles in the fifth century the Four Elements . . . established themselves in the imagination of men forever . . . [as] the four elements of our experience."

The death of the apples sets the tone and states the theme of the whole work. When the apple falls, the seed, the germinal new self, destroys the ripe fruit like a death-bullet. And the old apples, no more now than "great drops of dew," lapse back into the ground. So the pure new self, the soul of each man, must "find an exit/from the fallen self."

Yet despite the serene commitment to natural process that the apple metaphor implies, Lawrence concedes in part two that the death-journey is painful, even for the most faithful man. The autumn frost is "grim," and apples fall "thick, almost thunderous, on the hardened earth," recalling the terror of "the thunderers, the sunderers," and "death is on the air like a smell of ashes!" Ashes, like dew, dissolve or disintegrate to nothingness, but unlike dew, which we associate with morning-freshness, with beginnings, they are the endings of life, all that is left to the self when the life-flame has burned itself out.

> And in the bruised body, the frightened soul
> finds itself shrinking, wincing from the cold
> that blows upon it through the orifices.

It is not easy to "bid farewell."

In part three Lawrence explores one of the alternatives that may occur to the frightened soul: suicide. The suicide controls fate by choosing the time of his own death. Lawrence describes such action with an allusion from *Hamlet* ("And can a man his own quietus make/with a bare bodkin?"), a reference which, though he later built it into an important pun, is a little too knowingly clever to be entirely successful. Still, Hamlet's speech is philosophically appropriate, for, like Hamlet, Lawrence sees death as "an undiscovered country" into which the shivering soul must travel. And, like Hamlet, in facing death he rejects the alternative of suicide—"for how could murder, even self-murder/ever a quietus make?" Murder, perhaps especially self-murder, is an act of will which, like the scientism of Anaxagoras, hurls one into the isolating "abyss of immortality." "O let us talk of quiet that we know," Lawrence pleads in section four, "the deep and lovely quiet/ of a strong heart at peace!" The only quietus available to man is the true quietus of "Pax" or of "Silence," rather than the artificial quietus of suicide. Again, one must yield oneself— quietly, peacefully, silently—to the inevitable process of one's life, the process of dying.

In parts four through eight Lawrence describes the death-journey itself more specifically than ever before. His ship metaphor is a traditional one, drawn from Egyptian and Etruscan sources, and probably from Shelley and Tennyson as well.[25] But through a delicate and precise elaboration of details he makes it quite his own. The soul, he tells us, in preparation for its longest journey, must build

> A little ship, with oars and food
> and little dishes, and all accoutrements
> fitting and ready.

And what might seem like sentimental allegory in his subsequent description of "the fragile soul/in the fragile ship of courage, the ark of faith" is tempered by the homely specificity of the boat's "store of food and little cooking pans/and change of clothes." Yet these details function allegorically too, for the spirit, as we have seen throughout *Last Poems*, re-

---

[25] The Egyptian symbolism of the "ship of death" was known to Lawrence, though I am not sure what sources he used. Readers may refer to Frankfort's *Ancient Egyptian Religion* for information about Egyptian ideas which parallel Lawrence's. Among other relevant passages in E. A. Wallis Budge's translation of "The Papyrus of Ani," *The Egyptian Book of the Dead* (Dover reprint—New York, 1967), the following are noteworthy: "May I see Horus as guardian of the rudder . . . may I grasp the bows of the *sektet* boat and the stern of the *atet* boat. . . . may there be placed for me offerings of food in my presence . . . may be made for me a seat in the boat (on) the day of the going forth of the god . . ." (pp. 3, 4, 5) and "Behold, thou shalt make an image of the dead man whom thou wilt make perfect in strength . . . in the boat; and thou shalt make it to travel in the divine boat of Ra." (p. 328) For calling my attention to these and other pre-Christian analogs with Lawrence's death-ship, I am indebted to Miss Margrett Atkinson.

quires nourishment on its journey, the sustenance of prayer and belief, and when it puts off the body, the clothing of the old life (as Yeats and Carlyle also saw), it must have another garment, another self, for the new life.

Even so, when the soul sails out onto the sea of oblivion, everything disappears.

> There is no port, there is nowhere to go
> only the deepening blackness darkening still
> blacker upon the soundless, ungurgling flood
> darkness at one with darkness, up and down
> and sideways utterly dark, so there is no direction any more,
> and the little ship is there; yet she is gone.
> She is not seen, for there is nothing to see her by.
> She is gone! gone! and yet
> somewhere she is there.
> Nowhere!

"The deepening blackness darkening still," a subtle paradox (for how can black be blacker than black?), is reminiscent of the "darker and darker stairs, where blue is darkened on blueness" down which the poet imagined himself descending into Pluto's kingdom. Yet though the little ship for a moment disappears into this profound and impossible darkness, though it is "gone!" somewhere that is nowhere, it never vanishes into the *grey* nothingness of mechanistic evil—"the grey mist of movement which moves not." Such evil, said Lawrence in "Evil is Homeless," "shows neither light nor dark,/and has no home, no home anywhere." The little ship of the journeying soul experiences, emphatically, first dark, then darker darkness, then light again. Though in the moment of oblivion there is an illusion of ending, of stopping ("It is the end, it is oblivion") the journey never really stops.

In parts nine and ten Lawrence describes what was for him by now an article of faith, the mystical rebirth of the soul.

> And . . . out of eternity, a thread
> separates itself on the blackness,

a horizontal thread
that fumes a little with pallor upon the dark.

Literally, it is the line of dawn on a far horizon; figuratively, it is the thread of life which, because life is an endless journey "onwards, we know not whither," can never really snap. "A flush of rose"—the faintest rekindling of the "scarlet flame" of life—"and the whole thing starts again."

> The flood subsides, and the body like a worn sea-shell
> emerges strange and lovely.
> And the little ship wings home, faltering and lapsing
> on the pink flood,
> and the frail soul steps out, into her house again
> filling the heart with peace.

A number of critics have puzzled over the exact intention of these lines. Was Lawrence proposing a kind of oriental or Pythagorean metempsychosis, or was he suggesting something like the Christian concept of resurrection? But while he was no doubt influenced by both these theologies (and, too, by the kind of theosophical thinking that he incorporated into *The Plumed Serpent*),[26] he had always vehemently rejected the dogmatic structure of any creed. He never particularized his beliefs beyond a faith in the majesty of a *Kosmodynamic* God whose processes he saw working themselves out everywhere, in apples and peaches and pomegranates and, by analogy, in men. He felt that in the economy of nature nothing is ever wasted or cast aside, but believed that to attempt an intellectual definition of what can only be known intuitively, through symbol and metaphor, would be an arrogant effort to comprehend "the incomprehensible."

Lawrence's own ship of death, then, was finally an "ark of

[26] See Frankfort, p. 106, for the Egyptian (and Lawrentian) relationship between the dead soul and the journeying sun: "Thou (dead soul) risest and settest, thou goest down with Ra . . . thou risest up with Isis, ascending with the morning bark of the sun."

faith," [27] an ark unencumbered with the particulars of Christian or Buddhist or pre-Socratic dogma, but impelled toward oblivion by a "fragile courage" to let being take its own course. And specifically the ship of faith that he built for himself in these last months of his life was made up of the *Last Poems* themselves, poems which, in imaginatively drawing nearer and nearer to the mystery of death, and in exploring the experience of oblivion that is to come, prepare the poet to endure the experience itself—what he knows will be its ashen bitterness as well as what he believes will be its "cruel dawn of coming back to life." What is finally most impressive about "The Ship of Death" is not the wit with which Lawrence elaborates a traditional metaphor, not the skill of the incantatory free verse (whose meter comes closer to traditional iambic pentameter than that of most of his later poetry) but the sense of personal religious urgency it communicates.

> Have you built your ship of death, O have you?
> O build your ship of death, for you will need it . . .
> death is on the air like a smell of ashes!
> Ah! can't you smell it?
>
> Oh build your ship of death, your little ark
> and furnish it with food, with little cakes, and wine
> for the dark flight down oblivion. . . .
>
> We are dying, we are dying, we are all of us dying,
> and nothing will stay the death-flood rising within us,
> and soon it will rise on the world, on the outside world. . . .

[27] The parallels with Noah's ark are clear. James M. Pryse in *The Apocalypse Unsealed* (Los Angeles, 1910), a book Lawrence knew, asserted that "The word *kibotos,* properly meaning a wooden box . . . is applied in the New Testament to the ark in the temple . . . and also to the Noachian ark. The constellation Arca, the celestial Ship . . . was also called kibotos and 'Noah's Ark'. . . . The ark is a symbol of the womb, the place of birth . . . [and of] *spiritual rebirth,* the emergence into immortality." (pp. 153–154)

It is not really the imagery of the voyage nor the traditional symbol of sacramental cakes and wine that affects us in such passages as these, but the prophetic exhortation the dying poet addresses to the reader and to all men, the oldest reminder that can be given to any man: "To everything there is a season, a time to sow and a time to reap." "Dust thou art and unto dust thou shalt return."

vii

To say, however, that Lawrence is preparing himself (and us) to endure death, is not to say that death appeared to him a wholly painful or cruel experience. He concluded that the process of halving and healing could be frightening, the journey into oblivion sad, but he felt, too, that oblivion brings health at last. "Sing the song of death, O sing it!" he exclaims in "Song of Death," one of a series of short pieces that are essentially explanatory addenda to "The Ship of Death" itself,

> for without the song of death, the song of life
> becomes pointless and silly.

And this is just a colloquial Lawrentian formulation of what Stevens says in "Sunday Morning" or Whitman in "Whispers of Heavenly Death" and other poems. Sleep, which men have always named "Death's second self," promises this healing oblivion, Lawrence writes in "Sleep" and "Sleep and Waking."

> Did you sleep well?
> Ah yes, the sleep of God!
> The world is created afresh.

Therefore he reasons, like Donne addressing death, that if

> From rest and sleepe, which but thy pictures bee,
> Much pleasure, then from thee, much more must flow.

Furthermore, because death is a sleep it is a *forgetting,* and again, while forgetting is difficult, it is healing and necessary.

"Very still and sunny here," Lawrence wrote to Laurence Pollinger in September 1929, the "slow, sad" month in which "Bavarian Gentians" is set. *"Olvidar—vergessen—oublier—dimenticare*—forget—So difficult to forget."[28] Yet one must, ultimately, lose one's memories, for in losing them one sloughs off the old self, makes room for the new.

> To be able to forget is to be able to yield
> to God who dwells in deep oblivion.
> Only in sheer oblivion are we with God.
> For when we know in full, we have left off knowing,

he explains in "Forget." Only when we have lost our memories—indeed, lost our minds—do we pass into the state of final knowledge that is beyond nerve-brain knowledge, the state into which the poet mystically enters in "Bavarian Gentians" and "The Ship of Death."

The beautiful and simple poem "Shadows" is Lawrence's last and most moving attempt to explore the oblivion, the forgetfulness, the not-knowing that is death's (and God's) final gift. Here at last he speaks in his own person and speaks directly of his own illness, as if his persistent attention to cosmos and *Kosmodynamos* throughout *Last Poems* has given him the courage—the ark of faith—with which to confront not only the destiny of all men but his own fate in particular.[29]

> And if tonight my soul may find her peace
> in sleep, and sink in good oblivion,
> and in the morning wake like a new-opened flower
> then I have been dipped again in God, and new-created.
> And if, as weeks go round, in the dark of the moon
> my spirit darkens and goes out, and soft, strange gloom
> pervades my movements and my thoughts and words

[28] *Letters*, p. 1203.

[29] In another version of "The Ship of Death" Lawrence speaks more directly than in the poem usually published. Compare the first person "I sing of autumn and the falling fruit" (*CP*, p. 956) with "Now it is autumn and the falling fruit," etc.

then I shall know that I am walking still
with God, we are close together now the moon's in shadow.

The gravely religious tone here is absolutely authentic,
though it lacks the rather ostentatious dogmatic structure of,
for instance, Eliot's

End of the endless
Journey to no end
Conclusion of all that
Is inconclusible
Speech without word and
Word of no speech
Grace to the Mother
For the Garden
Where all love ends.

Indeed, as a religious poet Lawrence is strangely reminiscent
not only of such obvious forebears as the Romantics Keats,
Whitman, Rilke and Stevens, but of the seventeenth-century
Anglican George Herbert. Like Herbert, he speaks in his best
religious verses ("Shadows," for example, and "The Ship of
Death" and "Phoenix") with a quiet assurance, a faith that
does not need to rely on the doctrinaire and even morbid
melodrama that sometimes seems to characterize the writings
of Eliot and even those of Donne. The serenity and directness
of "Shadows" parallels, for instance, the calm conclusion of
Herbert's "Even-Song."

I muse which shows more love,
The day or night; that is the gale, this th' harbour;
That is the walk, and this the arbour;
Or that the garden, this the grove.

My God, thou art all love:
Not one poore minute 'scapes thy breast,
But brings a favour from above;
And in this love, more than in bed, I rest.

And the faith that is expressed in lines like these from
"Shadows"—

> And if, in the changing phases of man's life
> I fall in sickness and in misery
> my wrists seem broken and my heart seems dead
> and strength is gone, and my life
> is only the leavings of a life . . .
>
> then I must know that still
> I am in the hands [of] the unknown God,
> he is breaking me down to his own oblivion
> to send me forth on a new morning, a new man,

is not so different, after all, from Herbert's.

Oddly enough, it is not so different from Eliot's either, despite the latter's conviction that Lawrence wrote about strange gods. In "Ash Wednesday," for instance, Eliot had not only prayed "to God to have mercy upon us," but also prayed

> that I may forget
> These matters that with myself I too much discuss
> Too much explain . . .

and had asked God to

> Teach us to care and not to care.
> Teach us to sit still.

This is essentially what Lawrence has been asking too, in poems like "The Ship of Death," "Pax," and "Shadows." Yet, perhaps even more surprisingly, it seems to me that in the end Lawrence's words carry more conviction than Eliot's, though Eliot's poems are often considerably smoother. Like Wright Morris, I believe that "in this world—the one in which we must live—the strange gods of D. H. Lawrence appear to be less strange than those of Mr. Eliot."

I do not introduce the author of "Ash Wednesday" and the *Four Quartets* so as to attack his religious poetry, but in order to make a specific point about Lawrence's work in *Last Poems*. The best of these poems succeed, as Eliot's do not, precisely because throughout the collection Lawrence has worked to make his religion *plausible* to us. His long and careful exploration of the nature of God; his examination of the relationship between body and soul, blood and nerve; his attention to the mysterious experience of death—all these endeavors bear fruit in our willingness to accept the calm and simple faith of "Shadows." Eliot, working, as R. P. Blackmur approvingly points out, in a structure of Christian orthodoxy he assumes we will accept, never explains who his God is, or why he believes in Him.[30] Yet, "in this world in which we must live," such an explanation is just what a religious poet must offer, and just what Lawrence's *Last Poems,* taken all together, constitute.[31] Indeed, even where Lawrence uses fairly conventional religious metaphors, as in "The Ship of Death," "Phoenix," or "Lord's Prayer," he does so with an explanatory specificity, a concreteness—and hence a plausibility—that makes the dogmatic orthodoxy of lines from "Ash Wednesday" like "Sovegna vos," or "Lord I am not worthy" seem shallow and even pretentious, because it has no fundamental reality for most of us.

But then "one of the great virtues of Lawrence," as Father Tiverton notes, "was his sense of the ISness rather than the OUGHTness of religion,"—that is, his attention to reality.[32] As a religious poet, Lawrence rarely lost sight of the ontology he defines in "Lord's Prayer," the relationship between God—

For thine is the kingdom,
the power and the glory.

Hallowed be thy name, then,
thou who art nameless,

and himself—

[30] R. P. Blackmur, *Form and Value,* pp. 264–267.

[31] See Alvarez, *Beyond All This Fiddle* (London, 1968), p. 7: "T. S. Eliot was the only major modern artist whose Christian orthodoxy deeply influenced his work, and it now seems that this is precisely the element that gets in the way of contemporary readers."

[32] Father Tiverton (Martin Jarret-Kerr), *D. H. Lawrence and Human Existence* (New York, 1951), p. 144.

I, a naked man, calling,
calling to thee for my mana,
my kingdom, my power, and my glory.

And surely our sense of the plausibility of poems like "The
Man of Tyre," "Whales Weep Not!," "Bavarian Gentians,"
"The Ship of Death" and "Shadows"—poems in which atten-
tion becomes meditation, meditation becomes prayer, prayer
renewal—justifies his life-long aesthetic faith that "an act of
pure attention, if you are capable of it, will bring its own
answer." [33]

[33] *Etruscan Places,* p. 92.

Index

Bly, Robert, 260
"Bodiless God," 273-274, 276-278
"Body of God, The," 274, 276, 277-278
Bottomley, Gordon, 33
Boulton, James, 26n, 52n, 112n
"Bourgeois and Bolshevist," 253
Bradley, F. H., 158
Brett, Dorothy, 266
Brewster, Earl, 123, 220, 266
"Bride, The," 62, 65-69
Bridges, Robert, 81n
"Britannia's Baby," 214, 218
"British Workman and the Government, The," 218
Brooke, Rupert, 33, 57
"Brother and Sister," 62-63, 64
Browning, Robert, 28, 56
"Bunny," 51
Burnet, John, 120n, 136
Burns, Robert, 42, 163
Burrow, Trigant, 267
Burrows, Louise, 26n, 28, 52n, 60
"But I Say Unto You: Love One Another," 209
"Butterfly," 285, 290-294, 295

Campbell, Gordon, 100-101, 122
Campbell, Joseph, 187
"Campions," 21-22
Camus, Albert, 199-200
"Can't Be Borne," 255
"Canvassing for the Election," 214, 251
Carlyle, Thomas, 28, 125, 194, 199, 254, 275, 281, 300, 310
Carswell, Catherine, 85, 112n, 124
Carter, Frederick, 176, 242n
Cavitch, David, 291
Cezanne, Paul, 150
Chambers, Jessie ("E. T.," "Emily," "'Miriam"), 28, 36, 54n, 60
"Change of Government," 218
"Cherry Robbers," 20, 49-52, 59, 111
"Children Singing in School," 211
Christianity, see Jesus Christ
Clark, L. D., 233, 236
"Cocksure Women and Hensure Men," 246
Coleridge, S. T., 12, 16, 28, 80, 128, 290

Collected Poems 1928, 25n, 34, 36n, 88, 104n
Collings, Ernest, 6n, 100, 101
"Combative Spirit, The," 247-248, 253, 257
"Coming of Quetzalcoatl, The," 201, 235, 236
"Conceit," 196
Confessional poetry, Lawrence's, 60-69, 94-97, 220-230, 255-256, 265; see also "Mother poems"
Consciousness, Lawrence's theory of, see Blood-Self and Nerve-Brain Self
Corke, Helen, 30
Crosby, Harry, 1, 4, 7, 10
"Cruelty and Love," 56, 57; see also "Love on the Farm"
"Cry of the Masses," 258
"Cypresses," 134, 165, 177-179, 252

Dahlberg, Edward, 2n
Daleski, H. M., 1n, 80n, 202, 203n
Dante Alighieri, 73, 98, 100, 111-113, 188
"Dark Satanic Mills," 228
Darwin, Charles, 178, 275
Dataller, Roger, 233
Daughter-in-Law, The, 40
Davies, W. H., 33
"Death is not Evil, Evil is Mechanical," 302-303
"Death of our Era, The," 256
De la Mare, Walter, 33, 34
"Demiurge," 273-275, 278
"Desire Goes Down into the Sea," 222
"Desire Is Dead," 256
Dialect poems, 39-42, 44, 85, 250-251; see also Fictionalized poems
"Dies Illa," 256
"Dies Irae," 227-228, 256
"Discord in Childhood," 46-48, 49, 50
Donne, John, 267, 313, 315
"Doors," 305-307
"Dreams Old and Nascent," 25-27, 29

"Eagle in New Mexico," 165, 183
Earp, Thomas, 253
"Edgar Allan Poe," 135n
Egyptian Book of the Dead, The, 309n
"Elegy," 73

ACTS OF ATTENTION

Designed by R. E. Rosenbaum.
Composed by Vail-Ballou Press, Inc.,
in 11 point linotype Baskerville, 2 points leaded,
with display lines in monotype Deepdene.
Printed letterpress from type by Vail-Ballou Press
on Warren's 1854 text, 60 pound basis,
with the Cornell University Press watermark.
Bound by Vail-Ballou Press
in Interlaken book cloth
and stamped in All Purpose foil.

Library of Congress Cataloging in Publication Data
(For library cataloging purposes only)

Gilbert, Sandra M
   Acts of attention.

   Includes bibliographies.
   1. Lawrence, David Herbert, 1885-1930.
I. Title.
PR6023.A93Z6293   821'.9'12   72-4386
ISBN 0-8014-0731-1